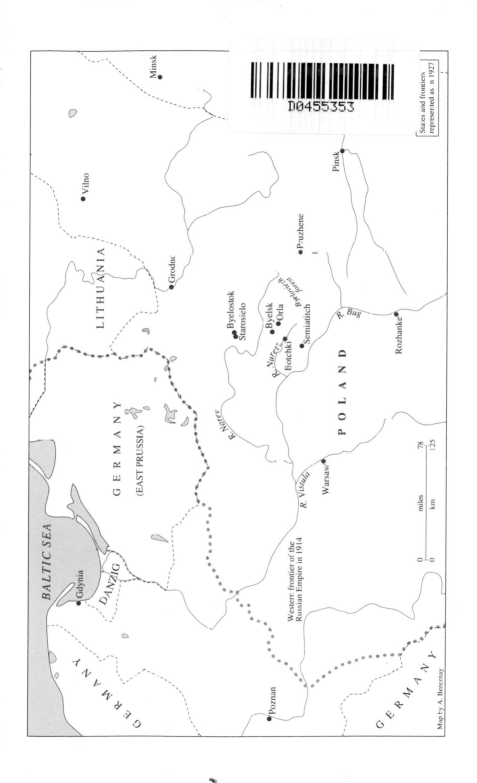

BALTIC SEA

Minsk

Vilno

LITHUANIA

Grodno

GERMANY
(EAST PRUSSIA)

Gdynia

DANZIG

GERMANY

Poznan

Pinsk

Pruzhene

Byelostok
Starosielo

Byelsk
Orla

Semiatitch

Botchki

R. Narew

R. Nuretz

Białowiez Forest

R. Bug

Rozhanke

POLAND

Warsaw

R. Vistula

Western frontier of the
Russian Empire in 1914

GERMANY

miles    0          78
km       0          125

Map by A. Bereznay

States and frontiers
represented as in 1927

D0455353

# BOTCHKI

# BOTCHKI

*When Doomsday Was Still Tomorrow*

*David Zagier*

George Braziller
New York

First published in the United States of America in 2001
by George Braziller, Inc.

Originally published in Great Britain
in 2000 by Peter Halban Publishers Ltd

© 2000 by The Estate of David Zagier

All illustrations courtesy of the Estate of David Zagier except for
the line drawing of the wooden house of prayer, which is from
*Synagogues and Jewish Communities in the Bialystok Region*
by Tomasz Wisniewski (Bialystok, 1992).

All rights reserved

No part of this publication may be reproduced in any form or by any
means without prior permission in writing from the publisher.

For information, please address the publisher:
George Braziller, Inc.
171 Madison Avenue
New York, NY 10016

Library of Congress Cataloging-in-Publication Data:
Zagier, David, d. 1998.
Botchki: when doomsday was still tomorrow / David Zagier.
p.   cm.
ISBN 0-8076-1496-3
1. Zagier, David, d. 1998 – Childhood and youth.
2. Jews – Poland – Baszki – Biography.
3. Jews – Poland – Baszki – Social life and customs.
4. Baszki (Poland) – Biography. I. Title.
DS135.P63 Z349 2001
943.8′4 – dc21
[B]   2001035276

Typeset by Computape (Pickering) Ltd, North Yorkshire, UK
Printed and bound in the United States of America

First edition

# Contents

# *Preface*

I wrote the first draft of *Botchki* on the eve of World War II when I was working in London as a foreign correspondent. It is the story of my childhood and my shtetl, and in the shadow of the destruction that was facing Europe it was a story I wanted to have written down. My mood at the time is reflected in the original preface, with which the Prologue of the present book begins.

The War made further work on the manuscript, let alone publication, impossible. I emigrated to America, was drafted, and entered American counter-intelligence (the OSS, later the CIA) to put my knowledge of Eastern Europe to use in the fight against the Germans.

Two sequels to the war rendered the resumption of work on the book and, indeed, of much of my productive life, impossible: the Holocaust – in 1947 I learned, from the only person who had escaped from the deportation caravan, that my parents and younger brother had died in Treblinka – and my indictment and dismissal (despite complete clearance on all charges) by the CIA, in which I had by that time reached an important position, during the McCarthy terror, after a year-long investigation and infamous trial.

In 1989, fifty years after the first version of *Botchki* was written, it had become safe even for a former intelligence officer and ex-Polish citizen to visit his country of birth, and I ventured for a last look at my village. I expected to find only the ashes and graveyards of my Jewish Botchki, but the ashes had been built over by our Gentile heirs and the tombstones used for the repair of farm buildings. It was like watching Botchki die a second death. And it was then that fifty years of recoil from touching the manuscript turned into a compulsion to put up the memorial promised in the original preface.

That I succeeded in the endeavour at all at the age of nearly ninety is due to the encouragement and assistance of several people: Donnali Fifield for her patient work in assisting me through the first painful weeks of the re-editing; Jenya Weinreb, who typed a new manuscript, coped with endless changes and made many valuable suggestions; and my wife and most especially my son without whose selfless initiative and inspired collaboration the book conceived so long ago could still not have come to its belated birth.

Something must be said about the many foreign words and expressions which figure in the book. The childhood it describes was subjected to a mixture of seven languages – Russian, Byelorussian, Polish, Yiddish, Hebrew, Aramaic and German – and to have put everything into English would, I felt, have destroyed some of the texture. But since few of my readers will have this particular combination of idioms in their linguistic background, some explanations are needed. To avoid a cumbersome glossary, I have italicised and defined unfamiliar foreign terms on their first appearance, and sometimes re-italicised and re-defined them if they recurred much later in the text. Some words, of course, appear so frequently that the reader will become familiar with them and need no further help – *Zeide* (Grandfather), *chaver* (pal), *shochet* (kosher butcher), *mamzer* (bastard), *arbeh kanfess* (ritual inner garment of pious Jews), *Ochrana* (Polish secret police), and many others. In any case, this is not a scholarly work and, in choosing when to translate, I have aimed at clarity rather than consistency.

A related issue was the transcription into Latin characters of Yiddish, Hebrew, and Russian words. Words and names ending in a schwa (weak *e* sound), for example, have generally been transliterated with *eh* – Gemoreh, shiveh, Gruneh – except where the word is already familiar in its English ending of *ah* – Torah, bar mitzvah, Hannah. The guttural sound of German "ach" or Scottish "loch" has been written as *ch* rather than *kh* – chaver, Chassid, cheder, shadchan – and the English *ch* sound of "church" by *tch* – natchalstvo, Semiatitch, Botchki. The sound t*s* has been rendered *tz* rather than the Germanic *z* – koortz, shvartz, hartz – and the sound of *ay* as in day by *ei* rather than *ey* – Zeide, sheitl, Feigl. Here, too, I have not striven for complete consistency and in this, as, I fear, in so many other respects, the reader will have to be understanding.

David Zagier
MONTREUX, SWITZERLAND
*August 1997*


My father died in April 1998, three months after his 90th birthday and only a few weeks too early to learn that *Botchki* had been accepted for publication. In his name I would like to thank my sister, Vega Zagier Roberts, whose efforts led to the publication and whose Epilogue speaks of her love for her father, Eva Hoffman, whose enthusiasm for the book encouraged us and who established the contact with Peter Halban Publishers, and Martine Halban, who invested endless hours and whose skilful and sensitive editing of the text have greatly improved its readability.

Don Zagier
BONN, GERMANY
*December 1999*

# Prologue

*It is August 1939, under the gathering clouds of Armageddon. My South African newspaper employers have closed their Paris office and I am back in London. I room just behind Fleet Street, as close to potential jobs as can be, and indeed I am assured of an assignment the minute war breaks out. In this state of anxious abeyance I dream the days away. I think of 1915 – I was seven – all of us Botchki refugees were trapped between the Cossack cavalry and the Kaiser's artillery in the Byeloviezh Wilderness town of Pruzhene. My older brother Chaim found me tottering about in a daze under the bellies of horses, weirdly calm. The parents whispered about an hallucination.*

*The world I know may be coming to an end, and my village, the Botchki I know, may be erased; nor will I, the I that I know, survive. In what little time may remain before the evil is upon us I must salvage what I can of our memory – Botchki's and mine.*

Without moving once, I had lived under four different flags by the time I was twelve: czarist Russian, imperial German, Bolshevik and Polish. Botchki was a shtetl of motionless Wandering Jews and goyim, non-Jews.

I am a Jew whose origins look more confusing than they are – a Russian Jew, a Polish one, and a Byelorussian. Above all I am a Lithuanian Jew – a *Litvisher Yid* and a *misnaged*; as against a *Polisher* one and a *Chassid* – and an Ashkenazi Jew rather than a Sephardi.

The one unJewish feature about me is the light grey colour of my eyes, but whether I got this from a twelfth-century Crusader, a fourteenth-century Black Death rioter, or a seventeenth-century Cossack, no one can tell. So numerous were the offspring of ravished Jewish women that the rabbis in their wisdom long ago ruled that every child of a Jewish mother is a Jew.

Without using aliases I am known by a variety of names. To a landsman in the Diaspora my Christian name, I mean my given name, is Dovid. To a landsman in the land of Israel, it is Daavid – the Sephardi way. To a Pole, it is Dawid. It is the same with the surname: in Botchki it has always been Zhager, *zh* as the *s* in usual; in Russian the *zh* looks like a pair of embroidered *k*s back to back; in Polish and Lithuanian they use a *z* with an accent on top; but that accent mark being unknown to them, the French call me Zazhiay, the Germans Tzageer, the English Zaggir, and the Americans Zeyger.

My age has not escaped unscathed, either. My father had written down my date of birth on the inside cover of his *sidder*, but the prayer book was burned with our house in 1915, and the register at the *magistrat* had its entries washed almost clean by the handpump of the village fire-brigade in the same fire. The disappearance of any reliable record of my coming into the world was not noticed until the approach of my bar mitzvah. The parents then figure that since the year of my birth was a leap year, it had to have been 5668 of the Creation or 1908 of the goyish calendar. They did recall that it was in the Hebrew month of Adar, but not which day, nor in which of the two Adars of such a full year – Adar I or Adar II.

The proper date for my first laying of *tefillin*, which would mark my bar mitzvah, had to be resolved by a *shylleh*, a problem taken to the rabbi, who ruled for the earliest day in Adar I, because a boy's entry into the fold may not be delayed beyond his thirteenth birthday but no harm can come from its taking place earlier.

Six years later, in 1927, the question of my birth date became critical. To emigrate, a young man had to furnish a birth certificate proving that he was below the military age of eighteen. In my case, I had to be born in 1910 and to prove it. Through the intermediary of a rare good goy and a petition wrapped in a dollar bill, I got born on 15 January 1910.

\*　　\*　　\*

The vital statistics of Botchki were similarly defective. The township never really knew what country to call its own, and no one knows how old it is or how it got its name.

Many hundreds of years ago, tradition has it, a woodman hacked out a clearing in the primeval forest along a swampy branch of the Nuretz, a tributary of the Bug that flows into the Vistula. Perhaps he was a Jadwingian tribesman, a Byelorussian or a Lithuanian – the movement of the peoples in our region of Podlasie being as foggy as our marshes – but he was not a Pole or a Russian. This father of all Botchkivites, some of us believed, was a maker of barrels, a *botchkar*. Others held that the name came from *bociany*, the storks so abundant in our neck of the woods.

The early Botchkivites were pagans, and their offspring worshipped the gods of the river and the lilac groves. Even in my childhood, old people told of having seen traces of a temple of Piorun, the Thunderer, in a dark grove atop the man-made hillock; and most believed the place haunted and avoided it at night and in stormy weather.

Villages such as Botchki did not then belong anywhere, for the simple reason that Byelorussia had never thought of itself as a country. This came only in 1280, when vast Byelorussian lands were absorbed into Lithuania in a rather striking manner.

On their return home, the Germans of the defeated Third Crusade transformed themselves into the Order of the Teutonic Knights, dedicated to the glory of God and fatherland. Preferring to tackle the nearby pagans of fertile Slav and Baltic lands rather than the warlike ones of the distant and arid Holy Land, these early forerunners of the German *Drang Nach Osten* wiped out many of the Baltic tribes, including the ancient Prussians and most of the Lithuanians. Only the people of the innermost Lithuanian forest vastness rose to defeat the invader and opened the way to the huge area of Byelorussia, thus turning their insignificant, pagan Grand Duchy into a great power. The Lithuanians made up for their lack of numbers by merging with the Byelorussians who outnumbered them and, in an inspired gesture, adopting Byelorussian as the official language of the land. This welded the two races so closely together that they shared a common history for centuries. From having no country to call their own, Podlasie villages like Botchki now had two motherlands in one. A third one, Poland, would join them before long.

The initial defeat of the Teutonic Knights brought no lasting relief to Lithuania, Byelorussia, or nearby Poland. Faced by many enemies – Tatar and Mongolian hordes, Muscovy and the resurging Teutonic Knights – Poland and Lithuania needed each other's support. Their chance came when the Polish parliament, the *Sejm*, became deadlocked and elected the eleven-year-old Princess Jadwiga as "king" (the Constitution did not provide for a queen). In exchange for her hand and the crown of Poland, Grand Duke Jagiello of Lithuania offered to join his country to Poland and have his pagan subjects converted by the Polish clergy. The Poles accepted and it was this union which finally crushed the Teutonic Knights, in the historical Battle of Tannenberg in 1410.

For more than a century, Poland and Lithuania formed an empire of two equal partners, each with its own sejm, its own laws and its own language. By 1568, the Poles, grown more powerful and overbearing, drastically changed the conditions of the alliance, depriving Lithuania of its voice in the selection of the joint monarch and obliging it to adopt Polish as its language. The common people of the Byelorussian, Lithuanian and Jewish communities, however, held on to their own languages.

For the outside world, Botchki now belonged to the Polish kingdom, for that was what the Union had become, but for the Botchkivites nothing had changed. The Jews, in particular, still felt themselves to be Lithuanian Jews.

When Poland was partitioned among the Russians, Austrians and Prussians in the late eighteenth and early nineteenth centuries, the czar took what had once been greater, historical Lithuania and divided it into six *gubernia*s or regions. Botchki became a township of Grodno gubernia.

From 1815 to 1915 Botchki was Russian by fiat, Lithuanian and Byelorussian by tradition and folk ways, Polish to the Poles, and an amalgam of all four to the Jews.

Botchki now had four countries to belong to, yet none to call its own.

The early history of Jewish Botchki, the shtetl, is mostly oral – legends, traditions, communal memory. Only one of the *pinkassim*, the parish annals of the Jewish community – an eighteenth-century and virtually illegible one – survives, and most of the Gentile records, too, were destroyed by marauders and by the frequent fires.

The earliest definite record of Jewish settlement on the Nuretz could be read on the sixteenth-century tombstones of the old Jewish cemetery behind the two synagogues. A peasant's plough unearthed traces of an even earlier burial ground, but its tombstones were indecipherable.

We can tie the appearance of the Jews in Botchki, as elsewhere in Poland and Lithuania, to the period of the Crusades. The Crusaders, reluctant to put off the destruction of the infidel until their arrival in the Holy Land, set torch and sword to the prosperous Jewish communities along the Rhine that had enjoyed tolerance and security since Roman times.

When the first wave of persecuted Jews reached the Slav lands, they were offered haven, freedom of worship, and trade privileges. The best-known instance was the opening of Poland by Casimir the Great in the wake of the Black Death of 1348, when the Germans accused the Jews of poisoning the wells. The charge that they used Christian blood in their Passover unleavened bread, their matzah, a charge which originated in England in the twelfth century and has never fully disappeared, as witnessed by the Blood Libel of Byelsk-Podlaski, Botchki's own county seat, in 1564, and by the infamous Bayliss Trial* in 1913 – also drove many Jews eastward.

The persecution most deeply embedded in our communal memory, however, was the Cossack Scourge of 1648, the Great Calamity. Begodan Chmielnicki, the ataman who led a Zaporozhe Cossack rebellion against his Polish-Lithuanian overlords, directed his most savage fury against the Jews, who had no defenders. A Russian historian of the uprising tells of the Cossacks flaying their victims alive, splitting, roasting or scalding them to death, eviscerating them on the Scrolls of the Torah trailed in the mud, and picking off their children on the tips of their pikes.

---

* The Bayliss Trial took place in Kiev in 1913. Menachem Bayliss was accused of draining Christian children of their blood to use it for baking matzah.

For Botchki, the memory of the Great Calamity was linked to a local hollow, the Gai, where in my childhood pious Jews would still stop to marvel at a rushing stream with no apparent source or outlet. It was called Reb Yankev Schorr's Shproong – Rabbi Schorr's leap, or spring – and was said to have sprung up when the pikemen of Chmielnicki – *yimmach shemoh*, annihilation to his name – pursued the holy man. The stream arose between them and saved this "shepherd of his people".

Even when I was a child, the Cossacks of the czar's cavalry still carried their pikes along with their carbines and still speared our children during "approved" pogroms. As late as the Russian retreat from the Byeloviezh Wilderness in 1915, we all narrowly escaped such a pogrom. The mention of the word Cossack never lost its terror for us.

The Jews in the towns and villages of our region always felt vulnerable, especially after Lithuania was subordinated by Poland. Jews were excluded from the royal towns of Byelsk-Podlaski and Bransk – our county's administrative and judicial seats respectively – but not from our township, which stood on land granted by King Sigismund I to the Sapieha princes. These princes ruled their lands as they pleased, mostly with tolerance, while the kings were often forced to yield to the pressures of a sejm dominated by the anti-Semitic gentry. As the Polish power in the Union grew, the gentry, of preponderantly "old-Polish" orientation, sought to extend the privilege *de non tolerandis Judaeis*, by banning even the "king's own" Jews – mostly court agents and tax collectors – from the royal towns. This exclusion of Jews from the royal towns continued until the partitions, even as late as 1792, three years into the French Revolution.

At the end of its period of "privilege", Bransk had twenty Jews while Botchki had more than a thousand. Except on Mondays, when the Jewish merchants, craftsmen and artisans of Botchki were permitted to trade in Bransk, covering the marketplace with their stalls and providing services without which the town could not function, commerce was non-existent in Bransk.

Upon taking possession of the historical lands of old Lithuania, the czar ended the exclusion of Jews from the royal towns, at the same time keeping them out of all of Russia proper and confining them to the Pale of Settlement, consisting of Poland, Lithuania,

Ukraine and adjacent non-Russian lands. In inverse measure as the exclusion of Jews had brought economic ruin to the royal towns and growth to the others, its abolition transferred most of our economic advantages to our neighbour. By the time I was born, there were more Jews in Bransk than in Botchki.

A traveller would have had trouble trying to find Botchki in early days, so dense and impenetrable were the forests surrounding it.

Generations of peasants have since thinned out the primeval wilderness of Byeloviezh. In place of woods sprang up villages surrounded by fields of rye, flax, wheat or potato, interspersed with the mansions and parks of Polish noblemen. Still, the Byeloviezh forest itself remained almost as forbidding as it must have been a thousand years ago, spreading for hundreds of square miles – secret, deep, impenetrable, virgin – the terror of lost wayfarers and the delight of hunters through the centuries. Wolf, bear and the last of Europe's bison still roamed among oak, birch and pine. The forest was no place to lose one's way, we were warned as children.

By more urban standards, Botchki was a mere village, but in the Podlasie region its four hundred families, four houses of worship, and three cemeteries justified its claim to township.

To the outsider, Botchki, surrounded by green and gold fields in summer and blanketed by dazzling snow against a dark wall of forest in winter, would probably have appeared charming, but slow-paced like its meandering little river and, perhaps, slow-witted. But to us on the inside, Botchki was the centre of the world, intense in its joys and sorrows, loves and hates, insights and prejudices, a microscopic universe whose denizens whirled, re-pelled and exploded, not in a random way but by God's will. To us, it was the outside that was colder, less loving, less hating, less joyous and less sorrowful – in a word, slow-paced and, be it said, maybe a bit slow-witted.

# I

# *Introducing Two Carters*

In those days – the days of Czar Nicholas II (1894–1917) – people travelled from Botchki to civilisation with one of the two Hershes: Hersh-Leib or Hersh-Loaf. Hersh-Loaf was also known as Hersh-the-Post.

The two Hershes were carters by the mercy of God and the licence of *natchalstvo*, the czarist authority; both conveyed goods and passengers to and from the nearest railway station, Byelsk. For the licence each Hersh paid three roubles a year to the exchequer and a gallon of brandy to the authority whenever the authority was thirsty, which was often.

When setting out from Botchki, the traveller had no choice as to his conveyance. After leaving home in the early morning, he trudged along ankle-deep in the dust of summer, or knee-deep in the snow of winter, to the tollgate where both carters were stationed. Weighed down by baskets, bags, cartons and leave-taking relatives and acquaintances, he knew that he would get to the railway in due course, but by which Hersh he could not say. Once in sight of the tollgate he had to halt in his tracks and wait for the two Hershes to leap from their perches and claim him. Whoever touched passenger or luggage first had the fare in accordance with the Talmudic principle of *hasakah*, that possession is nine-tenths of the law. On the rare occasion of a dead heat, the traditional ruling "let them divide" being difficult to apply, a short battle would ensue, which Hersh-Leib invariably won.

The two Hershes were not related. In fact, they had little in common beside their name and calling; in everything else they resembled each other as little as did their conveyances. Hersh-

Leib's vehicle, which was primitive but comfortable, consisted of a shallow wicker-trough well padded with golden rye-straw. In winter travellers embedded themselves in its depths, whereas in summer they sat aloft chewing a straw and admiring the wonders of Nature. Hersh-Loaf's vehicle was conceived on more ambitious lines. Imagine a wooden cage-like contraption divided into compartments and shielded from the elements by a medley of jute sacking, strips of canvas, and odd bits of leather and linoleum. Its nickname was Noah's Ark.

The chassis of each vehicle changed with the seasons. A week or two before Easter, when the snows were thawing in this forest-locked region of Podlasie, trough and ark alike were taken off their sledges and placed on four wheels for the summer. Early in October, the process was reversed. Never were these vehicles known to have been set on floats, though often enough, during the spring and autumn floods, the roads disappeared under water.

Apart from the comfort of his wicker-trough, Hersh-Leib had many other advantages over Hersh-Loaf. Hersh-Leib was a powerful red-bearded giant, two yards round the waist and father to four sets of twins, three male and one female. His six sons, known in the township, even among the Gentiles, by the biblical term of *bonim* or sons, could put the fear of God into a rowdy batch of conscripts, while his two lanky, sun-freckled daughters handled a cartful of manure or a spirited horse with the ease of a goy. Hersh-Leib's spouse, the Hersh-Leibiche, a tiny grey-haired Jewess, never contributed to the race other than in twins. Every set consisted of a red-haired and a black-haired partner, and each pair was alluded to by the name of the red-haired, aggressive twin. Thus the eldest bonim were referred to as "the Michaels", one boy was called "the Ginger Michael", the other "the Black Michael"; the daughters were "the Champes" – "the Ginger Champe" and "the Black Champe".

Hersh-Leib had other commendable attributes. He was the scion of a long line of horse thieves and recklessly courageous when roused. This, together with his fecundity, secured for him the respectful title *reb*, though his religious learning never extended beyond a laborious reading of the Psalms. Even behind his back, he was just Hersh-Leib, and not called by any nickname.

Botchki's nicknames merit a volume to themselves. Take Noske

Quack-Quack, Yosl Red Cock, Itshke Bugs' Funeral, and Sniff-Bottom. They were four good Botchkivites – a country peddler, a horse dealer, a roofer, and a boot mender. Noske became Quack-Quack when he went to live by the duck pond; Yosl was reputed to have set "the red cock" – fire – to two barns whose owners had cheated him in a deal; Itshke the roofer had so many bedbugs in his house that they were said to be lining up for a funeral; and Haikl, the bootmender, acquired his nickname from sniffing the posteriors of hens, brought him in payment, to see whether they were with egg. This Sniff-Bottom was of such humble station that his nickname alone sufficed, and, like others in the town, he even referred to himself by his sobriquet: *Shmek-toches*.

As for Hersh-Loaf, his name came from an incident involving his wife – a tall, dry Jewess from Semiatitch. Now Semiatitchers were not popular in Byelorussian Botchki, because their town lies almost on the border of the Polish Mazur province, and Botchki waited for a good opportunity to show disapproval. It presented itself barely a week after the wedding. One day Hersh set out for a trip to Byelsk and left his hamper of bread and herring behind. By the time his bride noticed the omission, the Ark was passing the windmill at the other end of town; but knowing it was bound to stop at the tollgate to pick up passengers, she gave chase. Along the main street she ran, skirts gathered up in one hand, hamper in the other, shouting at the top of her Semiatitcher-accented voice:

"Hersh, the loaf! Hersh, you forgot the loaf!"

And Hersh-Loaf and Hersh-Loafiche it remained ever after.

Hersh-Loaf was an undistinguished-looking man and no better versed in religion than his competitor. He had, moreover, a knotted beard in which folks said he stored his horse's fodder. Even Providence showed him displeasure, for he had no children; yet it did bless him in another way to show that "the Lord giveth aid to the humble and foresaketh not the poor". Hersh-Loaf received the blessing of God at the hands of the authorities. As the links between Botchki and the world beyond the forests grew, the villagers could no longer rely on chance visits to Byelsk to fetch their mail, and it became clear that a regular service was years overdue. The authorities – their mills, like God's, grinding slowly yet surely – eventually decided to institute a town postal service. When the sum of twelve roubles per annum was duly voted from the municipal funds to pay for fetching the mail from Byelsk, Hersh-Loaf was entrusted with the task. At a stroke Hersh-Loaf became Hersh-the-Post, and Noah's Ark became the Mail Van.

# 2

# West Rarely Met East

Unlike the distant deserts and lonely islands, Botchki was rarely visited by anyone more civilised than an East Prussian horse dealer, and then only on the great annual market day of St John. Western explorers gave Botchki a wide berth and never came nearer than the river Bug, which is a good twenty-five miles west.

Once a foreign firm of boot-polish manufacturers had, in a spirit of foolhardy enterprise, sent an African on a promotional tour of the Byelorussian wilderness. When he appeared in Botchki, the inhabitants of the township showed that they were not to be taken in. The Gentiles crossed themselves and spat over their shoulders at the unholy apparition; Jewish parents grabbed their young and shut them indoors, away from the Evil Eye, and muttered the prescribed blessing on seeing a black man for the first time: "Blessed be Thou, O Lord, for creating a diversity of peoples." Except for a few loafers and Wolf the village atheist, none dared to approach the stand which the hapless African had put up in the centre of the market. Only when their first shock had worn off did they attempt to inspect the apparition properly, but by then the man's cart had almost disappeared on its way to Byelsk.

Omniscient Botchki delivered its shrewd verdict on the affair: the man was not black but an ordinary mortal disguised by his own boot polish. An urchin was ready to swear that beneath the man's coat he had seen *tsitsis*, the ritual tassels on the edge of the *arbeh kanfess*, the four-cornered undergarment worn by every faithful Jewish male. If this were indeed the case, he must have come from across the Bug, for no self-respecting Jew this side of the river would paint himself black even if he had ten children and they were all starving.

The prejudice against everything and everybody that came from the western side of the Bug was not confined to the Jews. The Byelorussian peasants also regarded the far bank of that river as a foreign and therefore a bad land, the domain of infidels and invaders, of Germans and Poles. Thence came their *pans*, their masters, who owned the land and of whom the less said the better.

The Jews of Byelorussia were chary of Polish Jews chiefly on sectarian grounds. The Bug demarcated the two main currents of contemporary Judaism: the *Chassidim*, with their cabalistic mysteries, dynastic wonder rabbis, and vehement style of prayer, dwelt west of the Bug, while the domain of the formal Talmudists, the calm and studious *Misnagdim*, who were sceptical of latter-day miracles and suspicious of rabbi worship, began east of the river and extended far into the Russias. At one time, the war between the sects had been so fierce that their rabbis excommunicated each other, but now only milder prejudices remained: a Polish Jew was a "Polish abomination" to his Lithuanian brother and replied with the insult "crucifix-head".

Yet Byelorussia of the czars with its dark forests, low-lying meadows, and flaxen-haired peasants remained a land of benighted peace. The few small towns were populated predominantly by Jews. The landowning nobles, the pans, were Polish. The *parobki*, serf-like labourers who tilled the land, felled the trees, and tended the herds, were mostly Byelorussian. The pans worked them from an hour before daybreak to an hour after nightfall for a platter of potatoes without fat. Polish peasants kept to their own villages, of which there were fewer the more one went east, towards Byeloviezh and Pinsk.

We looked upon our Polish neighbours as tormentors, who set their dogs on Jewish peddlers and who – themselves oppressed by the Russians – readily took up the blood call *"bij Zhidow"* ("hit the Jews") whenever the czar needed a pogrom. The Byelorussians saw their landlords as slave-drivers and all, oppressors and oppressed alike, had a common foe in the czar's policemen and tax collectors. Fear of pogroms and political persecution did more for our link with the world than the railway, but the traffic was one-way. Every year, we sent a few of our sons to America. In return, some of us received affidavits, and others occasional dollar bills, letters, and photographs. A letter from abroad – America – was always an event in Botchki. The proud mother, after staining it with her tears and carrying it in her blouse for a period proportional to her fear of the Evil Eye, took it round the town: first to relatives, then to neighbours, and in ever-widening circles until the epistle reached all who cared to read it. As the years went by the intervals between letters grew longer until only the New Year's greetings continued. As people said in Botchki – though usually only at funeral orations – the branch was irreparably severed from the tree.

# 3

# *The Gods Got Along*

Botchki's four hundred households were about equally divided between Christians and Jews. There was little trespassing among the religions and the nationalities: the Jews prayed in their two synagogues, the Poles in the Catholic *kosciol* and the Russians and many Byelorussians in the Orthodox *tserkov.* In the synagogues God was worshipped three times daily, but in the churches only on Sundays and saints' days. The Christian churches were more crowded, for they also served a dozen churchless hamlets and villages nearby.

Botchki was the best market town in Podlasie, thanks to its position as a "free" town for hundreds of years. On local saints' days in particular, thousands of peasants from the surrounding countryside flocked into Botchki to pray, drink, shop and meet their cronies. The carts thronged the marketplace, the streets and the backyards overflowing into the orchards and fields. These were great days for the local shopkeepers and for the stall-holders, who journeyed even further than their customers to sell their wares. The shops had to remain closed during the long hours of Divine Service, though trading went on briskly enough through the back doors. The sole policeman could do nothing against the offenders for from the windmill to the watermill the streets were clogged. Kerchiefed peasant women in their Sunday brightest, men in coarse grey homespun and greased top-boots, bewildered youngsters, all squatted on and beneath the carts, spreading their meal on a coloured cloth. The men fed heartily on chunks of ham and rye, consuming tremendous quantities of food washed down by pints of vodka, while whole salt herrings disappeared head, tail and all down their throats. After a meal of this nature a man might feel in need of some bodily function and this he coolly proceeded to fulfil behind the cart. If the horse moved in the middle of it all there was mirth but no fine …

Most of the Christian families were small farmers, a dozen or so were hired hands and a few were tradesmen: a tanner, a boot-mender, and a couple of shopkeepers. Of the Jews only about a score were part-time farmers, orchard keepers or vegetable gardeners. Most were shopkeepers – butchers, bakers, a candle maker, and a dozen gallanterie shopkeepers who also sold everything from sweets and haberdashery to funeral requisites. There were a sewing machine agent, two ironmongers, one or two itinerant peddlers, and four innkeepers. The tailors, boot-makers, blacksmiths, carpenters, turners, oil pressers and the two carters were all Jews.

Christians and Jews were more or less equal in number of clergy. The rabbi and ritual-slaughterer-cum-cantor-cum-circumcisor had their parallels in the Catholic *ksiondz* and the Orthodox priest, whom they called the *pop*. The Jewish and Orthodox clerics were bearded, the priest was clean-shaven. One apothecary was a Jew, the other a Gentile, but the Jew had only a limited licence; the windmill belonged to a Christian, the watermill to a Jew; and each community was represented in the ancient calling of horse stealing.

Botchki boasted more horse thieves than any other town its size in the Grodno gubernia, which is saying not a little. The story was told of a Botchkivite who, when asked by a stranger whether he indeed came from Botchki, retorted testily that the enquirer was a horse thief himself…

All the same, horse stealing was a time-honoured profession. It came down from father to son like other occupations. The Botchki horse thieves styled themselves horse dealers, which was true enough in the daytime.

To steal a horse – or rather a *sooss*, since Jew and Gentile alike used the Hebrew word for horse if it was come by dishonestly – the thief mingled with the owners and bona fide dealers on market day. When he came across a fine animal, he ascertained who its owner was and where he lived. Then, unless the stable was within the township, the thief set off on horseback early enough to get to the owner's home by midnight. The night had to be a moonless night with no snow about. If there was a dog it was settled with a lump of poisoned meat and the thief went about his work picking the lock. Pieces of felt were tied round the horse's hooves, a bag of oats was hung round its neck to keep it from neighing, and the thief removed the horse to a place of safety for a few days, along with other horses which had been "soossed" on similar expeditions. After the hue and cry was over, the whole pack was taken on a dark rainy night to the East Prussian frontier and disposed of at a fair price, or exchanged for other horses stolen in Germany.

Some Botchkivites defied classification. Among them were Yanchuk the quack and three females who augmented their livelihood by their skill as "knowers": they practised such arts as talking away the Evil Eye, pouring wax over the ailing, reading the cards for peasants on market day and generally exploiting the supernatural. The most versatile among them was old Meite, who was not only midwife but tended the female dead, cutting their hair, cleaning their nails, and washing their bodies, and engaged in a not dissimilar fashion in the preparation of brides, ministering to them and shaving their heads; it was also she who was in charge of the *mikveh* on Thursday nights, when good Jewish wives went for their ritual baths. Some other professions and crafts such as wig maker, *shammes* or beadle, and barber were part-time only.

Intercommunal relations were good in those days. The Jews lent their mikveh to the Gentiles, presented them with unleavened cakes at Passover, and treated Christian beggars no worse than their own. In return the Gentiles allowed the Jews' cows to graze on the common pasture, sometimes brought their Jewish cronies gifts of eggs and cheese when visiting town, and on occasion even provided food and shelter to Jewish wayfarers lost in the snowdrifts. Many Jews who dwelt among the peasants in remote hamlets, either as ploughmen or small traders, visited Botchki for festivals and the occasional Sabbath only.

Most Botchkivites gave way to ancient prejudices only halfheartedly, and even then more as a matter of tradition than conviction. The Jews turned away their heads when passing a sacred statue, while the Christians did the same when walking past the synagogue. The more fanatical even spat three times on such occasions – the Jews rather discreetly, the goyim more brazenly, which made the old Jews say: "What can you do? We are in exile!" Polish, and sometimes Russian, children made their shirt-tails into a "pig's ear" when a Jew passed a non-Jewish street and squealed "Zhid" or "Bayliss!" Yet even as Botchki still reverberated with the echoes of the ritual murder trial, few of our goyim believed that we used Christian blood for Passover. Jewish and Gentile homes were too close to one another for mystery: everyone knew what everyone else had for dinner, whose baby was ailing and why, whose father suffered with a hernia and whose daughter was going to marry whose son. There were no great secrets, nor could any have been kept, within the confines of Botchki.

Neighbourliness, if not love, was the rule.

# 4

## *Botchki Album*

Most strangers who arrived in Botchki in the winter were captivated by it. Snowed in, it possessed the white radiance of a peasant
bride.

The Botchkivites, once reassured that the stranger was neither
come to spy out the land, nor an agitator in the pay of the anti-
Semitic Black Hundreds, nor a tax assessor, allowed themselves to
be explored without hindrance.

The sledges of the two Hershes emerged from the forest into sight
of the township half a mile away. The visitors watched as the horses
plodded belly-deep in the drifts, their sleighbells tinkling in rhythm
with their trot, and were enchanted – until they came with a jolt
upon Nitko's "cemetery". Nitko, an old Byelorussian bachelor,
collected stray dogs and moribund horses for skinning, and though
his hut was hidden in a clump of birches, the stench would force the
passengers to turn their heads away, for Nitko would not stoop to
burying his carcasses. This was dangerous, too, for in the summer
the rotting carcasses could bring disease and in the winter tempted
hungry wolves, but since Nitko was always drunk, he could not be
reasoned with and was left to himself.

On the hillside to the right of the road rose the three graveyards
where dead Botchkivites dwelt in peaceful neighbourliness:
rounded tombstones over the Jews, stark crosses over the Poles,
dual crosses for the Russians. To the left, where the road turned
sharply to meet Cemetery Street, a clay Christ, intended to watch
over the fields, seemed more concerned with balancing on His
toppling pine cross than with keeping watch. Beneath the cross
was the boundary stone.

19

With Byelorussian frankness, Botchki unfolded its half dozen streets, its marketplace and houses of worship, its two bridges and its fire barn, all standing out white against the wintry landscape.

The first homesteads were thatched, low-roofed; icicles beneath the eaves shimmered in the oblique rays of the winter sun like multicoloured pendants which children snapped off for play swords. Smoke ribbons rose from snow-loaded roofs true and straight into the blue. Cottage, shop, and inn alike were one-storeyed, only the churches and the new synagogue being loftier. Except where its gods were concerned, Botchki was not pretentious.

The houses straggled, haphazardly spaced, haphazardly faced. If one cottage was thatched, its neighbour was tiled; if one store faced the street, the other turned sulkily sideways and showed a slanting roof; since the Orthodox cupolas were gilt, the spire of the Catholic church was grey-slated and the roof of the synagogue pine-shingled.

Orchards, kitchen gardens, fowl runs and beehives flanked the farm houses and outbuildings. Under the snow, autumn-sown rye germinated in the womb of the earth, with the promise of black bread nine months ahead.

The Hershes, like most carters, were chatty fellows, ready to volunteer more information than the most curious traveller required. They conscientiously described each home they passed and good-naturedly slandered the people who dwelled therein.

In the rambling cottage nearest the boundary lived Jasiek, a Polish freeholder who owned many acres of good wheatland, sandy potato fields and a strip of forest. Everyone took his cow to Jasiek's bull. Jews paid a rouble a time and Gentiles a bushel of grain. In front of Jasiek's gate one might see a farmer in yellow sheepskin coat, astrakan cap and gigantic felt boots, struggling with a short-horned cow, her tail twitching sideways for all to see but pretending not to know where she was being led and pulling backwards with bovine obduracy.

A dozen houses down the street, the low wooden fence of the *eruv* stood folded against the wall of Akiveh the oil presser. The eruv marked the limit of the township for purposes of Jewish ritual. All outgoing streets had their eruvs without which the township would be ritually "open" and the carrying of anything on a Sabbath, even a handkerchief, would be a sin. At one time the eruv was a wire suspended high overhead between poles on each side of the road, but after a number of Jews were dragged to Byelsk on suspicion of laying telephones for espionage, the wire eruvs were replaced by symbolic golden gates. Rabbinical reasoning found dispensation for the substitution, and even the czar could not object. No Jews lived beyond an eruv except Sheike Drum, the water carrier, and Yoodl-Mordechai Pontz, the road-mender.

Turning into River Street, the traveller discovered with some surprise that the river was crossed at its widest – and in three stages – from a bridge on to a dyke and thence on to another bridge. Botchki always had plenty of time and did not believe in shortcuts. The flow of the river, regulated by a primitive system of sluices, drove the wheel of the watermill with much clatter but little speed. Every fourth year or so the river swept the bridges and earthworks down to the river Bug, tossing timber piles like matchwood among the ice floes. By some miracle the willows lining the dyke were never uprooted, so that we could promenade pleasantly along the river when the new dyke was laid.

It was the river that put Botchki on the map. Indeed, a river was essential to a Jewish township. For instance, in case of a divorce, the prescribed text of the decree reads "In the town of … on the river …" Not that this affected us very much: wives in Botchki might curse their husbands and husbands might beat their wives, but apart from this they lived happily enough and never divorced. But it was good to feel that it was possible. Without the river there would have been no watermill, no peasants coming from afar to grind their grain, and fewer customers for innkeepers, storekeepers and produce dealers.

When the ice over the "black pit" of reputedly unfathomed depth was thick enough to bear the weight of horse and sledge, Feivel the *kvas*-maker rounded up masterless parobki and hungry tenant farmers to hack ice for the village's needs. The men grunted in unison as they stood in a ring swinging their great axes and marked out blocks to be heaved with boat hooks onto the sledges.

In the marketplace, a few sledges stood in front of the inns; storekeepers yawned on their doorsteps, sending out puffs of silver vapour into the freezing air; an enterprising tradesman swept a path in the snow for hoped-for customers. A solitary horse ambled up to the middle of the square toward the pump, knowing that his master would follow him. Botchki's winter life, indeed the whole of Byelorussia's resigned hibernation, was reflected in the rhythm of his nodding head.

The snow around the pump, transformed by much water drawing into a slippery mound of ice, took its daily toll of bruised limbs. Heavily kerchiefed women lost their foothold and slithered before falling, skirts and flannel drawers up in the air. This spectacle was a source of considerable glee to idling storekeepers and passers-by and was known as the *srakopad* – the "bottom-bumper".

Right next to the pump, the fire barn dominated the centre of the marketplace. It housed the fire engines, hoses, axes and brass helmets of the "brigade". Of the entire paraphernalia, the helmets, and not the engines, were the most important, as the carters eagerly explained. They were needed for all town functions. A Catholic procession, a reception for a civic or military authority, even a welcome for a new rabbi, was not thinkable without the fire-fighters of Botchki, arrayed in their glittering helmets, marching to the roll of the drum.

The Botchki brigade did not discriminate against Jews, and many a diffident storekeeper was turned into a veritable fire-eater the moment he donned his helmet. Subscriptions to the brigade funds were voluntary, yet nobody refused his fair share, for setting and extinguishing fires were equally within the scope of Botchki's firemen.

The three fire engines had names: the Red Machine, the Green Machine, and the Little Machine. Only the Little Machine functioned at real fires, but it was a pathetic hand pump with a garden hose. The bigger machines, which were each operated by eight pumping hands and were fed from the nearest well, worked admirably at parades, as the storekeepers whose goods received their misdirected jets could attest. At the cries of *"Pajar!"* announcing a fire, all three machines clattered down the streets with gusto, pushed along by scores of helpers, but when they reached the scene of the conflagration they almost invariably failed. Eventually, if there was no wind and nothing combustible nearby, the fire spent itself.

Twice – the Hershes would tell with some pride, winding up

their monologue – Botchki was practically levelled to the ground, and a street or two went up in flames every few years. Mostly the fires broke out in the autumn, when the barns were full and the buildings tinder-dry. Then the "red cock" spread its wings over our town.

So, between fires and floods, life was not devoid of interest in Botchki – even for those who, like Israel Zhager, my father, did not particularly appreciate scenic beauty or drama.

# 5

## *My Parents . . .*

My entrance into the world may be traced to a small jute bag full of egg-cakes. It was a custom in many a Jewish household to have two commodities on hand for an emergency: raspberry preserve and egg-cakes. The former was an infallible remedy against a cold, if taken with many glasses of scalding tea, while the latter were an indispensable item for families with marriageable daughters. The marriage agent, the *shadchan*, might turn up unexpectedly, bringing with him an eligible young man who would, of course, have to be entertained and given the best possible impression of the family's social standing and the bride's virtues. And how else was this to be done at a moment's notice than by a generous supply of egg-cakes, which remained fresh for a long time and could always be kept handy?

Carts passing from Byelsk to Semiatitch stopped at the market square. The shadchan, always on the alert, might persuade the father of some young passenger to come with his son and take tea at Reb So-and-So's to discuss the possibilities of a match. The jute bag would be taken off the beam hook, the samovar put on the table, and the necessary impression of well-being created. The young swain sat, his nose buried in the tea-glass, while the maiden, shyly conscious of being inspected from the other end of the table, nervously twisted the corner of the starched cloth or made unnecessary journeys to the kitchen. While the two stole only occasional glances at each other, the parents, encouraged by the ever-resourceful shadchan, soon fell to discussing their genealogical trees, the qualities of the respective candidates and, of course, the dowry.

No Jewish girl without a marriage portion could seriously hope to find a husband. Sometimes the conference ended in a quarrel. The guests might be outraged by the offer of an insultingly low dowry and walk out in a huff, leaving the tea-glasses half full. Then their hosts would follow after them shouting, leaving the slighted bride in tears.

If things went well, though, the tea-drinking continued for hours. It was a grave discourtesy to refuse yet another little glass.

There is the story of the young suitor, unfamiliar with the art of match visiting, who had been warned by the shadchan to act like a man of the world and to speak to the prospective bride of the eternal themes: love, family, and philosophy. When the fateful day came, he made a valiant attempt. Did she love prune tzimmes? No, she didn't. Undaunted, he tried again. Did her older brother love prune tzimmes? She didn't have a brother, came the answer. Well then, he persisted, if she *had* had an older brother, *would* he have loved prune tzimmes?

On a midwinter day in the 1880s Israel Zhager passed Botchki on his way to his job in the Orlovka forest. He was coming from the paternal home in the timber region of Lithuania and had been engaged by Reb Kalman Masur to supervise the felling at the Orlovka concession, on the fringe of the Byeloviezh Wilderness.

Israel, or Srolke as he was affectionately called, didn't find the Botchki scene overly fetching. The truth is that after travelling a hundred miles by sledge, he was glad to have Leser the shadchan waylay him and pronounce him, after a brief examination, a worthy suitor for Feigl, the daughter of Reb Leibe Kossomski. This sort of thing meant hot tea, egg-cakes and a rest.

Thus Israel Zhager, seventeen, restless and curious, followed Leser to Reb Leibe's to found the house of which I was to be the fourth child. He was thin, short and had only a few hairs on his chin.

Feigl was petite and olive skinned, and she carried her raven hair in a chignon on the top of her head. Her eyes were of a blue so dark that they seemed blacker than the traditional Jewish black eyes, which, indeed, are really dark brown. She too was seventeen – the dangerous age separating marriageable maidens from spinsters. The dowry was small indeed, the egg-cakes a trifle stale, the sugar on the table used sparingly, and the prospects of an inheritance on her parents' death "after a hundred and twenty years" slight. Two boys and several girls older than Feigl were already married, but the dowries for a number of younger, unmarried children still had to come out of the gallanterie shop run by her mother which, even at the best of times, yielded little more than was needed to feed and clothe the family.

But Feigl's eyes won the day. A dowry of four hundred roubles, pitifully insufficient for a suitor of Israel's prospects, was proposed and accepted by the young man subject to his parents' consent, another parley being arranged for the next holiday when Israel would have a break from his job. By the time the disapproving reply arrived from Israel's father, the engagement had been entered into, duly recorded on parchment by the ritual-slaughterer-cum-cantor-cum-scribe, a tea-glass smashed for luck, and the whole thing irrevocably concluded, bringing joy to the hearts of Feigl's parents and mixed pleasure and uncertainty to the young couple.

The disapproval of the groom's father, old Reb Ber – a small, frail man with a long, thin beard and side curls – took a tangible turn when he descended, shouting, remonstrating and threatening, upon the quiet of the bride's household. There was, as the saying goes, plenty of thunder but no lightning. Reb Ber, for all that he was a blustering little martinet used to driving hard bargains with Byelorussian fur trappers, was a good man at heart and a good Jew. He did not really go against his son's choice, and he would rather have seen his son sign a divorce than "tear the parchment" upon which the betrothal agreement had been made. Moreover, the bride's ancestors – men of profound Talmudic learning – were a greater source of gratification to old Reb Ber than extra hundreds of roubles. Reb Leibe was a direct descendant of Reb Yankev Schorr – he of the "Shproong" – and had himself graduated from a fine yeshivah. He had been ordained into holy office by several great rabbis and pronounced fit to teach, dispense the ritual law, and take religious charge of a Jewish community. Reb Ber's greed extended beyond the confines of the material world: a place in the Garden of Eden thanks to his new family connections was worth something, after all. There was yet another consolation: Reb Leibe and his wife Soreh-Enie were scrupulously honest and would count out what they had promised on the eve of the wedding. Israel might have been promised more elsewhere but received nothing in the end. As the folk ditty goes:

> *Ot azoi, un ot azoi,*
> *Nart men op a chosn –*
> *Men sogt im tzu a sach nedan,*
> *Un men git im nisht kein groshn . . .*

> This is how, oh, this is how
> A bridegroom to entrap:
> You promise him a pile of dough
> And pay him not a rap!

After a week in Botchki, eating at the frugal but much blessed table of the Kossomskis and witnessing the esteem that Reb Leibe enjoyed in the synagogue, Reb Ber Zhager left for home, outwardly maintaining his disapproval but in reality well pleased.

# 6

## . . . and Grandparents

Reb Leibe was a remarkable figure, even for Botchki. He was deemed a trifle eccentric by the worldly, a saint by the pious, and a godly man by all. Upon his marriage to Soreh-Enie in 1866, he had brought with him the *smicha*, the coveted parchment pronouncing him a rabbi, but no other contribution to their partnership, not even worldliness enough to distinguish between a three-kopek and a five-kopek piece.

Their home was a single-storey, two-room dwelling, the front room being the shop and the other serving as living room, kitchen, nursery, scullery and bedroom, all in one.

Soreh-Enie had taken command from the first. With her dowry she had started the tiny gallanterie shop and here she ruled, while her husband, incapable of anything practical, sat against the far western wall of the synagogue, poring over holy books nineteen hours a day. From the outset, the family depended upon the labours of Soreh-Enie, who set herself diligently to the task of nest building.

It was but an ill-feathered nest and became more and more crowded as the years went on. By the time I was old enough to know, my grandmother had been eight times bereaved, with two of her surviving children unmarried.

At eighty she was still behind the counter, perched on a high stool, her many skirts draped over her charcoal pot, winter and much of the summer, to direct its heat upward and bolster the sluggish circulation of her frail body. The Byelorussian winters were so intense that a bucket of water set outside the door became a block of ice within minutes, and Soreh-Enie could hardly have survived the cold without her fire pot. When the live charcoal was reduced to ashes, she lifted the pot up on to the counter, refilled it, then blew upon the cinders until the glow was reflected on her wizened face. Sixty years of blowing had given Soreh-Enie a cherubic expression and the pot a sheen and life all its own.

When a customer came into the shop, she jumped down with surprising agility. But people rarely came, so she was able to doze off for long intervals.

Soreh-Enie was an ordinary person in every way; a good wife, a pious Jewess, a frugal housekeeper, a fond and dutiful mother. There was nothing saintly about her, unless courageous plodding and unceasing drudgery throughout a very long and very hard life qualify one for sainthood. Reb Leibe's was the life of the hermit; hers was the life of the humble servant and provider for a still humbler servant of God.

She was torn between two conflicting selves, each making equal demands upon her. The first was the loving mother and devoted wife of a saintly man, who was content to serve him in this world and in her anticipation of bliss in the world to come. Was it not said in *The Way of the Righteous* that a devoted and God-fearing wife shall inherit the next world with her husband? She, too, was something of a savant, if only in the humble Yiddish texts accessible to Jewish women. She was sure to attain everlasting happiness, even riches, in the Garden of Eden, for distinctly it said, "the righteous shall sit on golden thrones, crowns on their heads, listening to the Torah from the mouth of God Himself and enjoying the lucidity of His Presence", while their wives, if worthy, would sit at their feet on golden footstools. Some sages, indeed, had it that the footstools would be only of silver, which was no small source of worry to Soreh-Enie. Through years of honest trading, she had a developed sense of fairness, and she could not see why her portion should be inferior both in size and quality to her husband's.

Soreh-Enie's other self harped on grudges. That self was a practical, sharp little woman who knew the ways of this world and had a keen nose for a deal. Was it fair that she should stagger under the load of both bearing and providing for her children? And why should she bear yet another child every twelve months, even if the texts did prescribe the direst punishments for those who shed their seed in vain? At such times she felt that the texts contained much injustice: "What is God's is God's, but what is man's should be to man," she reasoned, uneasy at her own heresy. The devoted Soreh-Enie showed the world a blessed, almost childlike expression; the other Soreh-Enie rebelled and sneered so that the right corner of her mouth lifted at a derisive angle towards her ear. As the years went by, the two selves learned their parts, their arguments, and their standpoints exceedingly well, but were never reconciled. They followed on each other's heels, more and more rapidly, until the cherubic and sneering faces replaced each other so fast that Soreh-Enie acquired a disfiguring tic.

Reb Leibe never suspected the violent struggle raging within his wife. To him she was always "dear Soreh-Enie"; inner battles never disturbed his mind. Not for him to question the ways of God. His contentment was permanent and his faith unshakeable, even though he never knew the meaning of joy; joy was something reserved for a later and better life. In this world a Jew had to study the Torah, pray and suffer; God in His mercy saw to it that His flock should not want for suffering – there was poverty, illness, death and, at intervals, reports of greater calamities befalling the Jews elsewhere in the world – in Syria, Bessarabia, Poland, or the Ukraine.

Reb Leibe's world was walled in by the huge volumes of the Babylonian Talmud, its commentaries and subcommentaries. He rose long before the sun to pour fresh water over his fingernails, which banishes the unclean spirits that cling to them overnight, then he said his first short prayer, for it is a sin to take more than three steps from one's bedside without a prayer. When he had attended to his human needs, he washed again and said another, somewhat longer prayer; no food or drink would touch his lips before morning service when he strapped his *tefillin** onto his arm and forehead in the synagogue. Every day was a half fast for Reb Leibe, for he stayed behind till midday, studying the holy Law for several hours after the last worshipper had gone. A brief interval for an abstemious lunch at home and then again to *shul* to

---

* Tefillin or phylacteries: two small, black, leather boxes containing parchment with four biblical passages, which the male Jew wears from the age of 13 for certain prayers.

continue his labours till sunset brought evening and night services. At home, after a spare supper and some more study by the light of a kerosene lamp, came bedtime prayers and a short sleep among the family before *chatzot*, midnight prayers.

He seldom looked at those who addressed him. His pale eyes seemed to be ever contemplating his own beard. From puberty to his dying day my grandfather never looked upon the face of any woman but Soreh-Enie. It was sinful, not only to look at a woman, which deflected one's mind from the holy pursuit of the Law, but even to listen to a female voice, especially one raised in song. From the moment he left home, Reb Leibe obstinately cast his eyes down to the ground and raised them only upon gaining the shelter of the synagogue. Throughout the two furlongs separating his house in the market square from the synagogue he continued to recite holy texts softly to himself, gesticulating with his thin ivory hands as his mind wrestled with the dialectical problems that occurred to him. On market days he departed at sunrise, as usual, leaving word that his food be brought to him at the synagogue by one of the children, for he could not have passed the crowded streets without looking up and seeing what no God-fearing man should see. The folk song *"Der Zeide oon di Bobbe zeynen koorts oon klein"* misses them by very little:

> Grandpa and grandma may be short in height
> Yet as a pair they are spright and bright
> They have just passed a happy jubilee
> When seventy was he, and eighty she.

These were my grandparents, who begat Feigl.

# 7

## *Arrivals and Omens*

After their wedding, Srolke and Feigl moved into the house of Isser the capmaker. The low house in Bransk Street, with its pine-log walls, grey with age, was divided into three two-room apartments, each with its stove but no other amenities. The Zhagers occupied the middle section; the capmaker, his wife and his parents-in-law lived on one side of them; the piece-goods merchant Solomon and his wife on the other. The sharp-angled roof hid beneath two great willow trees that stood like sentinels before the house. Through the back doors the residents had easy access to the old well whose stark outline of timbers and dangling bucket brought to mind a leaning gibbet.

Srolke worked in the forest throughout the week and came home only for Sabbaths and holy days, while Feigl coped with the raising of the children. My brother Chaim had preceded me by seven years, Basheh by four, and Ethel was two years old by the time I arrived.

While Feigl carried me in her womb, the family moved for the summer to my father's cabin in the forest to get the benefit of the pine-forest air. By then their position permitted her to indulge in such luxury. Three months after her return home, I put in an appearance in the early hours of a winter morning, blowing in with a snowstorm.

Frowsy old midwife Meite lamented that she had been dragged out of bed in the dead of night and had had to wade thigh-deep through the snowdrifts. "It was murderous!" she fulminated. "I even saw the blizzard tear away a roof!" She grumbled through much of the night, forecasting through her toothless gums that the ungodly hour and ungodly weather boded no good for the new-born.

If the whistling of the wind was the uplifted voice of an outraged spirit, all precautions had to be taken to disperse the evil influence. Old Reb Leibe himself had hung appropriate spells over all the doorposts and chimney-vents. Written in Aramaic in exquisite Hebrew characters, these spells besought each good angel to guard over the child-bed and explicitly warned every evil spirit, from the redoubtable Asmodai to the most obscure imp, to keep away from the precincts. Moreover, throughout the eight days between birth and circumcision – a period fraught with special danger, since the new-born had not yet entered into the Covenant of Abraham – vigil was kept over Feigl's bed by members of her family who took turns to watch and pray.

Every evening a score of little boys from the *cheder* were invited to the house. Joining hands, they formed a circle around Feigl's bed and chanted in shrill piping trebles the most hallowed of all incantations, the *Shemah*: "Hear O Israel, The Lord is our God, The Lord is one."

After this, the children were given handfuls of sweetmeats and spiced peas and, having reaped the reward of their labours, ran into the street, calling back in unison to the new mother and her child:

"A good night to the new-born! A good night to the *kimpe-torin!*"

On my eighth day I was the central figure in the picturesque, if painful, ceremony of circumcision. My father was now a well-to-do man – he had two thousand roubles beneath his straw mattress and was a candidate for the honour of first warden of his congregation. The morning of the circumcision he attended synagogue as usual and was expected to – and did – invite everybody present to his house for the *briss* and banquet.

The various ceremonial functions were allotted to relatives, close friends and the most prominent members of the community: the rabbi himself handed me, laid upon a silken cushion, to the ritual-slaughterer-cum-cantor, who, since he was skilful with his blade and sang in a tearful quaver, performed the circumcision. I was placed on the traditional guest chair of Elijah the Prophet – rigged up for the occasion by Uncle Shmerl, the carpenter, who also served as my sponsor – and offered up for the sacrifice. The *mohel* pinched my prepuce between two fingers and swiftly sliced it away, all the while intoning the blessing of Abraham's Covenant. To my grandfather, Reb Leibe, fell the greatest honour: he recited the prayers and tended my wound by the time-honoured custom of aspiration, *metzitzah*.

I registered my first protest in a drawn-out howl. My mother, too, shed tears, but whether of bliss that her youngest had entered the Covenant or of sorrow for his pain, who can say? A *mame's hartz iz shver tzu farshteyn*: the heart of a Jewish mother is unfathomable.

The efforts made at my birth to place me under the protection of supernatural forces may or may not have done me any good. Without the intervention of the angels, Grandfather, the cheder-boys and the amulets, I might well have come out a good deal worse.

The omens, in any case, had not been very encouraging. When my parents married it rained day and night for a week, an augury of tearful times to come which neither my mother nor grandmother ever forgot. Was I going to be as wild as the blizzard of the night of my arrival, or turn out to be as ungodly as its weather? According to legend, the unborn baby possesses all knowledge until its head emerges from its mother's womb, when the jealous angel flicks it all away with a finger, thereby creating the dimple on the upper lip that we all have. Did I, too, know what the future held for me before the angel's flick?

# 8

## Toddler's Troubles

Of infinite interest to me, once I had learned to crawl, were the occupants of the neighbouring apartments: Ber the feather merchant and Solomon the fabric merchant. Ber and his wife, Yente, lived with their daughter and their son-in-law, Isser the capmaker. Both Isser and Solomon were childless. Isser, the Botchkivites joked, could not bring children into the world because he never laid hands on anything without turning it into a cap, and Solomon had a dried-up wife, good for nothing but giving people the Evil Eye.

To call our neighbour Ber a feather merchant may be an exaggeration. Actually his calling was as lowly as it was ancient. He made the rounds of the outlying hamlets on foot, mending the peasants' homespuns, and returned home every Friday afternoon with his payment – bulky bales of feathers and occasionally a few eggs or a chicken.

Ber's weekly load kept Yente plucking eiderdown for the six days of his absence. She squatted on a low three-legged stool, among the sorting sieves and bags, plucking the quills to get the down for the great *perenes*, the huge down-filled counterpanes which formed the basis of every Botchki bride's trousseau.

This place was my wonderland: Old Yente, nestling among the billowing feathers at the dark end of the room; Isser, her son-in-law, rattling his sewing machine; Mashke, her daughter, hovering in the background, hopelessly trying to keep the peace, the eternal mediator between husband and mother. The slightest disturbance – a door opening, a sudden movement – sent up clouds of feathers, which twirled for a time near the ceiling, settling down on Isser's

35

bushy brows and beard and, worse still, on his new caps. His spleen aroused, the capmaker raced his machine even more vigorously, setting the whole roomful of feathers, bags and sieves a-dancing, and the old woman's teeth a-clattering. These goings-on were an exciting change from the orderliness of my own home.

Solomon's side of the house also had to be explored and I can still remember propelling myself there on all fours and the soothing sensation of the large cool glass beads that fringed their tablecloth caressing and tickling my head. I can also remember – less fondly – the occasion when I was treated by Solomon and his wife to what I thought was the best carrot-tzimmes in the world. But this marvel of a tzimmes gave me such a tummy-ache that I soon lay writhing on the floor. Mama sent for the "knower" to "pour out wax". The crone held her lump of beeswax over a candle flame to make it drip on to birch twigs and form the figures of the evil spirits which were thus driven out of my body. This was the last Solomon tzimmes I ever ate. From then on, Mama watched out for the "Solomon woman" and quickly covered my face whenever she passed, to protect me from the Evil Eye.

But soon two, more serious, blows shook up my happy infancy – the death of my sister Ethel and the forest fire.

When I was two Ethel contracted scarlet fever. The doctor was called from Byelsk but his sledge became snowbound on its way to Botchki, and he arrived too late.

Imprinted on my memory was a scene which was to haunt my childhood – although whether it ever happened or was a hallucination I shall never know – of my father bent over Ethel's death cradle, helplessly feeling her burning forehead under the icebag, and wailing, "Why does it have to be Etheleh? Why couldn't it be the boy who has the heat?"

The effects of the forest fire were less immediate but in the end even more devastating. One night – a Friday night, since Father was at home and I was in my cot rather than curled up at the foot of my mother's bed as usual – I was awakened by an urgent rapping and saw the dim form of a man on horseback, silhouetted against the window. It was the overseer of our lumber concession, shouting to wake my father. I have never forgotten his words – although they were in Byelorussian, which I did not yet understand – hoarse, urgent words:

"Srolke, Srolke, *lyess goret*! Israel, Israel, the forest is on fire!" The sky to the east was bright red.

Father dressed hurriedly, groaning all the while, shouting at Mama and scaring me, but I only half understood his agitation. How could such a pretty red-coloured sky, lighting up the black horizon of the forest, put such fear in the faces of the parents?

He returned on Sunday covered with soot, his hair and eyebrows singed, woebegone and defeated, though much of the concession, the off-wind part, had been saved.

That evening Father waited for Reb Leibe after services and confessed his qualms about having rushed to the forest to supervise the sawmill workers' digging of firebreaks. He had been sure that the fire threatened lives, but could he really be sure? Could not Satan have lured him to his destruction by thoughts of saving lives to lead him to the life-forfeiting sin of desecration of the Sabbath? He could not rest, he said, without submitting to an examination by the Beth Din and its ruling.

The Rabbinical Court met in due course, found that Father had acted for life-saving reasons, and suggested that he donate a nominal eighteen roubles to charity (each Hebrew leter has a numerical value and *Chai*, which means life, has a value of 18). Had the Beth Din found him guilty of abusing the Sabbath to save his property, he could have been sentenced for breaking the Sabbath (*Chilul Shabbes*), and to be subjected to the eternal fires of *Gehennem*, Hell. In biblical times the penalty would have been death by stoning.

The Beth Din exonerated him, but in his own zealous conscience, did he exonerate himself? From this time on he gradually turned from a doting, if often hot-tempered, parent to an often morose stranger. I could not understand that he was really angry with himself rather than with Mama and me, and I felt hurt and baffled. My mother, the daughter of an ordained rabbi, could understand his dread but found his sin, if sin there was, pardonable. If sucking one's teeth on the Sabbath to remove food particles was *ossur* – forbidden; if one couldn't extinguish or remove a candle that was about to set a room on fire; if one couldn't write with one's finger on a moist pane; if one couldn't eat an egg laid on the Sabbath; if one wasn't allowed to take an emetic or get an enema or have a tooth pulled except by a Gentile; if one couldn't rattle a cup of nuts on the Sabbath to pacify a crying infant – if a thousand such minutiae were ossur on the Sabbath – how could anybody but a saint escape sin?

# 9

## The Angel's Kopek

In Botchki the usual age for Jewish children to start school was four-and-a-half. School was called *cheder*, which literally means room but was actually a class where a teacher, often aged and bearded, sat drilling a group of anything from four to forty boys. Botchki's five cheders covered religious knowledge from the alphabet in the primary or *prepl* cheder to Talmudic dialectics in the most advanced.

Because my grandfather was Reb Leibe, I was obliged to shoulder the yoke at three-and-a-half. Precedent was not wanting; my grandfather quoted instances of scholars such as the Gaon of Vilno who had been initiated into the Torah at so tender an age that they recited grace over their mother's milk.

One sunny July morning I found myself on the bony arm of Zeide, my grandfather, for the first time in my life. This unwonted physical touch felt strange. The pungent smell of snuff which hovered about *Zeide* tickled my nostrils, and the yellow-streaked, silky grey beard brushing against my face disturbed me. I was glad that Zeide had considered my first trip to cheder a fit occasion for wearing his yellowing black-and-white striped prayer-shawl, or *talless*, and that he draped it not only over his own head but also over mine, because I did not want to be seen carried in so unusual a manner along the length of Bransk Street.

Once in the cheder of Reb Isaac, my grandfather handed over his charge. In appreciation of the double honour – getting a visit from Reb Leibe and having that pious man's grandchild entrusted to his care – Reb Isaac welcomed me with an extra painful nip on the cheek. After a little bargaining, they settled the fees at a rouble a month and Zeide set me down next to the rebbe at the head of the table, so that I faced a score of gaping boys.

Rebbe took a large card displaying the square characters of the Aleph-beth from the hook and laid it before me. As I couldn't see over the edge of the table, Reb Isaac lifted me on to his knee.

"Now," he said kindly, "if you are a good boy and repeat after me without mistake, an angel will drop you a kopek from heaven. Listen well."

He led with a long wooden pointer across the first line, "Aleph, beth, gimmel, daleth. Aleph, beth . . ."

I could not speak. The schoolboys, who were all older and bigger than I was, stared at me. The rebbe's beard was a foot wide and came down to his lap. Its rusty copper, streaked with dull grey, was not at all silky and well-kept like Zeide's. The smell of rebbe's snuff was more pungent than my grandfather's and, worst of all, his trousers were grimy. My own clothes were of fine black velvet, and my curls had been brushed for the occasion by my mother.

Urged on by Zeide to repeat the Aleph-beth after rebbe, silently harassed by the boys around the table, and torn by such conflicting demands, I burst into tears. But Zeide came to the rescue. "Put the boy down, rebbe, and let him stand on the bench," he suggested. This was better, and I repeated half the Aleph-beth without prompting.

"You are a fine boy," said the big beard. "Now repeat after me: 'Kometz aleph, O; kometz beth, bo; kometz gimmel, go.'"

I repeated.

A shiny kopek plopped on to the alphabet card. I looked up, but the angel was gone. All I saw above me were the moist, benign eyes of my grandfather.

Cheder was pleasant enough and full of surprises. Reb Isaac was seventy and corpulent. At frequent intervals he dozed off, pointer in hand, snoring resonantly through wide-open mouth and nostrils. It was midsummer and the flies sought out these spacious apertures. The boys, ever eager for some diversion from the monotony of kometz-aleph and kometz-beth, watched fascinated, scarcely daring to breathe for fear of waking rebbe and bringing the reprieve to an end.

Not so Willie. Willie was a stocky bully of about twelve, more than five years older than the others, and was nicknamed "Willie the American" because his father, Arke, was in America. Arke, a famous horse thief who got into trouble with the authorities, had had to leave Botchki rather hurriedly. Willie, progeny of a stock known for brawn rather than brain, had been in the prepl cheder for six years without getting beyond the alphabet board. Reb Isaac only tolerated him because the dollars from America came regularly and in advance.

Willie, an expert strategist, waited tensely for the right moment to attack. When he considered rebbe's mouth sufficiently fly-beset, he'd slam a book on to the table, and rebbe would wake up with a start and snap his jaws shut. Few flies were agile enough to escape. Reb Isaac would hurriedly resume where he had left off, dissembling his momentary lapse, but the flies which he spluttered out with his words bore witness against him. In his drowsy mind probably buzzed the disquieting text: "He who falls asleep over his lesson forfeits his soul ..."

By that time Willie's preoccupation with his book was too artless to be convincing. Retribution fell upon him swift and abundant. Held down across Reb Isaac's knees, he received as many strokes on his bare bottom as rebbe could mete out before his breath failed him.

The instrument of punishment varied with the gravity of the offence, the strength and status of the offender, and on what was at hand: a cat-o'-four tails, referred to by the boys as "macaroni"; rebbe's own belt or braces; or the cover of an old prayer-book. When the offence was mild, rebbe used only the palm of his hand, and supplemented with a few slaps and pinches, which Willie used to get most days. Reb Isaac never failed to wind up Willie's subjection to the approved rod with the goyish ditty:

> *Yaki stav, taki mlyn;*
> *Yaki oytietz, taki syn ...*
>
> Like the pond, so the mill;
> Like the father, so the son ...

For the first few weeks I did too well in my lessons to please Willie or, for that matter, any of the other boys who followed him. Willie was the acknowledged "czar" and received tribute in buttons. Woe betide him who was not sufficiently ingenious or dextrous enough to raise the weekly levy from home. After a short interview, the czar took his button tax by force, and the rebel found himself holding up his pants with his hands. I objected to losing the fine glass buttons from my velvet suit and threatened to tell. Things might have fared badly for me had it not been for Meyerl. Meyerl was only six but already "Viceroy" and rival-in-chief to the czar, a position he got thanks to a strong elder brother. Whoever Willie disliked, Meyerl took under his, or rather under his big brother's, wing. Meyerl was also popular with the more imaginative boys because of his stock of stories of witchcraft, spirits, ghosts and charms. He was the cheder's authority on all aspects of the supernatural.

Whenever rebbe left the cheder for evening prayers at shul and warned us that his wife and daughter would keep an eye on us, we would position ourselves around Meyerl, crouching in the twilight to listen spell-bound to his hair-raising tales of ghosts, will-o'-the-wisps, werewolves and the dead.

# IO

# *Experiment in Metaphysics*

The dead in Meyerl's world led an eventful existence, not unlike that of the living. "At midnight," he'd recount in a scary, hoarse whisper, "the dead rise from their graves. The elders wake first and softly tap the message to their neighbours, waking the still drowsy and the new dead. When the tombstones move aside, they wriggle out of their graves. Their hands and faces are hidden under their shrouds. Any human who sees them on their secret procession to the Old Synagogue would surely be struck dead. To the synagogue they come, and they tap three times on the door to warn of their arrival. If any living man, woman or child be there, the dead cannot enter and, bent and shaken, must return to their graves. But if the synagogue is empty, the door opens of its own accord.

"Then they enter and seek out their seats of old. Their *chazan* shuffles forward to lead the prayers. He chants, 'Yea, faithful art Thou to quicken the dead. Blessed art Thou, O Eternal, who restoreth to life the dead.'

"They must return before daybreak because at the first cock's crow their graves close up and the tombstones move back into place."

I am not sure how afraid of the dead I was at the time, but I was filled with a deep pity for their wretched bondage and penance. Old and long-dead Jews shouldn't have to shuffle surreptitiously through the fields to the synagogue, I thought. And they must be walking barefoot, too, even in the snow – but maybe one didn't feel the cold "afterwards".

Meyerl was a master of his craft. Not satisfied with the terror he wrought among his listeners, he continued with his necromantic tales in which the living, too, played a part. His own grandmother, he claimed, had once disturbed the praying dead by coming to wash the floor of the synagogue before the cock's crow. As she opened the door, she beheld hundreds of lit candles darting about in mid-air. Carried by invisible hands, the candles were lining themselves up and moving towards the doorway, where she stood rooted to the spot; each was extinguished as it reached the threshold.

The beadle found her in a dead faint, Meyerl concluded triumphantly. Hundreds of half-burnt candles lay in a heap by the door, and Meyerl's granny lived only long enough to tell the tale.

From Meyerl I learned that the soul was a blue flame breathed into the nostrils of the new-born by the Angel of Life and sucked away through them by the Angel of Death. Meyerl swore that he saw the blue flame emerge from his grandmother's nose as she died. It had singed the feather they had laid over her lips to make certain that she was no longer alive.

I decided to investigate. First I meant to find out whether cats, too, had souls. This was easy, for who would be better able to say than Grandfather?

"Zeide," I asked, "do cats have souls?"

"Certainly, Dovidl, every living thing has its soul."

"And is a cat's soul blue?"

There was no reply.

Next to cheder was a foot-wide blind alley between two tall fences. Even by day little light penetrated there and I believed this to be the best place to see the blue flame. I had set my mind on the victim already. Gruneh, rebbe's unmarried hunchbacked daughter, had a large tomcat which basked on the oven opposite my seat in the classroom where I watched it and speculated on its soul. The cat's blue eyes were a good omen. For days I collected bricks and used every minute of my free time building a trap in the alley.

At last all was set. I lay waiting at the open end of the alley. When the cat ambled past, I pushed him into the hollow of the pyramid I had erected and closed up the entrance. One kick, and the whole contraption of bricks and stones fell with a crash, sending the poor animal to its death.

I flung aside brick after brick until the lifeless shape lay revealed.

I had seen no blue flame, and I was torn between pity for Gruneh's tomcat and anger at the cheating Meyerl.

That day I got my first belting, but it hurt me less than the look on the disconsolate face of Gruneh, the haunting reproach in her eyes. Yet it is an ill wind that blows no good. My early delving into the anatomy of the soul boosted my standing at the cheder. Once belted, I was accepted by the boys as one of them and in time, when Meyerl left the prepl cheder for Reb Alter's reading class, I stepped in to his viceregal shoes.

The supernatural continued to fascinate me. It also scared me, especially when I was alone in the house when Mama was out visiting neighbours, Chaim was still in cheder and Basheh was out playing forfeits or hopscotch with the girls. Then, with only the shadows crowding in on me from the corners, the flickering kerosene lamp, and the desolate chirping of the cricket in the oven for company, Meyerl's stories assumed a powerful reality. At such times I found a sanctuary in the Book of Psalms; I read its pages laboriously and devoutly, tears streaming down my cheeks, my heart torn between physical terror and faith in a benevolent God.

> *Borchi nafshi ess adoinoi*
> *V'chol krovay ess shem kodshcy.*

> Bless the Lord, O my soul:
> And all that is within me, bless his holy name.

When mother, who had no idea of her child's anguish, returned and found me on my footstool under the lamp, in tears over the Psalms, she felt much gratification. Smiling happily to herself, she would sigh:

"Praised be God! Our Dovidl will grow to be a fine man."

# I I

# *Sabbath Was a Bride*

These were fine days. My father was the *gabbai*, or first warden, of the New Synagogue. His appearance before the Rabbinical Court had made him more respected than ever and this, along with the community's growing honours, seemed to have persuaded him at last to exonerate himself. His abuse of Mama and me grew ever less frequent and less violent.

The election of a gabbai was simple but efficient. When dissatisfaction with the officiating gabbai became too strong, his opponents called an assembly of the synagogue for a vote. Only men voted. Each put a slip of paper with the name of his favourite on it, into the beadle's skullcap, and whoever got the most votes became gabbai.

Even at the best of times an *assifeh*, as the assembly was called, was a primitive affair marked by the absence of orderly debate and by much shouting, recrimination, and often a few blows. Words like "chairman" and "rules of order" had yet to be invented in Botchki.

Among the gabbai's chief functions were the collection of synagogue dues and their equitable disbursement among the rabbi, cantor, beadle and various synagogue accounts. One of the principal sources of synagogue revenue was the "Torah auctions". During the morning service on Sabbaths and festivals, the scroll of Law was solemnly brought forth from the Ark to be read from the *bimeh*, the reader's platform, in the centre of the synagogue. The gabbai "called up" members of the congregation to mount the bimeh and make the blessing over one of the portions of the week's lesson. For this honour the member was expected to contribute an agreed sum to the treasury. The gabbai had to memorise the exact pledges and collect them later, since neither writing nor handling money was permitted on holy days. The most coveted portions were often auctioned and fell to the highest bidder.

The gabbai also fixed the price of yeast. This second biggest source of communal income was a congregational monopoly and the mainstay of the rabbi's living. Under pain of excommunication, no one but the rabbi's wife could sell yeast to a Jew, nor could a Jew buy it elsewhere. Botchki approved of the arrangement, which taxed parishioners according to the number of Sabbath loaves they could afford.

Finally, the *shochet-mohel*, or ritual slaughterer-cum-circumcisor, was entitled to so much for a hen, a little more for a duck and quite a lot for slaughtering an ox. Whenever the synagogue funds were low, the community would suddenly find that the shochet was making too much and demand a share of his income under the threat of engaging an extra slaughterer.

The gabbai mediated the interminable squabbles, chiefly those relating to status in the synagogue, and much of this mediation took place in our home, often continuing till the small hours. When I grew tired of listening, I would go to sleep in Mama's lap. But I heard enough to comprehend very early in life the intricacies of the gabbai's life.

Every Friday afternoon, when Father returned from the forest for the Sabbath, he took me, his youngest, to the communal baths, the *mikveh*. Thursday was women's night, reserved for the good wives likely to be required by their husbands on Friday night to fulfil God's commandment. According to the holy texts, relations between husband and wife on Sabbath eve was auspicious, since evil forces were kept at bay by the holiness of the day. The women came singly, stealing furtively through the lanes and averting their eyes from passers-by.

Not so the men. "Katherine" the grave digger began stoking the furnace at daybreak on Friday for them. By midday the boiler was full and heaps of stones heated white in the furnace. To the centre of Botchki he went and, assuming the duties of town-crier, with uplifted face thundered into space: *"Yidn in bod arain ... in boooood aaraaaaaaaaain!"*

"Jews, into the baths ... into the baaaaaaths!"

The male community turned out by the score, fathers leading their sons and carrying their clean linen in bundles under their arms. Young and old undressed in the entrance room before going into the steam room. Steam was raised by throwing pails of water over the heated stones. The bathers chose their places on the benches that were arranged in tiers, from floor to ceiling. I saw nothing but pink perspiring bodies and was repelled by the slipperiness of the men's glistening flesh. I never ventured above the lowest bench; my father went a little higher; only horse dealers and other tough members of the community climbed to the top. The heat near the ceiling was unbearable. This, I thought, must be how Gehennem felt.

I watched the men pair up for the "smiting". Smiting was carried out with the passive partner lying on his belly on the highest bench he could brave, while the active partner flayed him with fresh birch twigs. When the victim was about to faint, a bucketful of ice-cold water was poured over him. The recumbent partner then rose, beard and hair dripping, wiping the water from his eyes and emitting gasps of satisfaction. The process then reversed and the smitten turned smiter.

The men strolled home from the baths with leisurely tread, their stiff collars gleaming white against their dark Sabbath garments. Faces were flushed and eyes shining with the light of the approaching Sabbath, the "Bride". Friday sunsets were endowed in my imagination with greater beauty and depth of colour, and my eyes were also bright with more material expectation – fresh white Sabbath bread, tea and preserves waiting at home.

Shortly before sunset, the grave digger closed down his steaming mikveh and, returning to Market Square, announced to the faithful in no mean voice that it was time they went to prayers: "*In shoool araaain . . . In shooooool araaaaaaaain!*"

Prostchuk, the Sabbath goy – the non-Jew who was allowed to assist Jews on the Sabbath – was posted at the bridge at the top of River Street, and answered the grave digger like a faithful echo.

For serving as assistant beadle, for burying the dead, stoking the furnace of the baths, and for a host of other jobs, "Katherine" received a chunk of fresh Sabbath bread from every housewife, though the more grasping expected him to bring a bucketful of "tea-water" from the special spring near the Gai. He brought it in a wooden tank drawn by a lean horse – an animal usually en route to Nitko the Skinner – or by his daughter.

After tea, the Sabbath spirit enveloped Botchki. For me, Sabbath was the best part of the week, and Friday night the best part of Sabbath. I couldn't take my eyes off Mama, beautiful in her best dress, new *sheitl* or wig, and fob-watch, standing up to light the candles, whispering the Blessing, and, removing her cupped hands from her eyes, greeting us through happy tears: "Goot Shabbes, Yisroel. Goot Shabbes, my children. Now, you three men, it's time for shul."

We walked proudly through the twilight on our way to meet Sabbath the Bride – Father, in his wedding-day tail-coat and *surdut*, Chaim in his new fringed *arbeh kanfess* and side-buttoned shoes, and I, carrying their prayer books and flaunting my new velvet suit, bringing up the rear.

On special occasions, even a small town like ours invited a real cantor to lead the Sabbath services, but mostly it was one of our locals who led the prayers. Only an invited cantor was dignified by the name of Chazan. A folk song tells of such an event, *A Chazandl oif Shabbes:*

> *Iz gekoomen a chazandl in shtetele,*
> *davenen a Shabbes.*

> Came a little cantor to the little shtetl
> to lead the Sabbath prayers . . .
> Came to hear him the shtetl's finest gents:
> One a little tailor,
> One a little cobbler,
> And one a little carter.

In the song, each registers his enthusiasm in the terms of his trade: the tailor compares the singing to the stab of the needle; the cobbler to the tap of the hammer; and the carter to the tug of the reins.

Visiting cantors had to get to Botchki days ahead of time to make up a choir in a hurry from cheder boys and men cajoled away from their work. The song about the makeshift choir's tribulations is called T chiri-biri-bom.

When I say, *Leicho deidi*,
You must answer, *Tchiri-biri-bom!*
*Noo! Leicho deidi, likrase kalloh*
(Go my friend to meet the Bride),
*Tchiri-biri-bom-bom-bom.*

Whether led by a cantor or an amateur, the congregation swayed backwards, forwards or sideways, in or out of rhythm with the melody, like so many ears of corn waving in an erratic wind.

The Sabbath candles in their silver sticks shining over the twin loaves, the kosher wine carafe and the porcelain dishes made our table wondrously festive. There usually was *gefilte* fish with fresh horse-radish, baked chicken, and a prune-tzimmes or a carrot-tzimmes. Formal declaration of the sanctity and purpose of the Sabbath, the *Kiddush*, had to be made by the head of the household. The prayer bearing witness to the world's completion on the sixth day was intoned with widely varying degrees of enthusiasm and musicality, from the mediocre performance of my father to the impassioned delivery of our *shochet-baal-tefilleh*, whose trills were heard several houses down the street. After the blessings over the wine and the loaves had been made and both partaken of by everyone at table, infants included, we would proceed with the meal.

Though my sister was given her share of everything at the table, I felt sad that, as a girl, she had to miss out on shul, though I did envy her missing out on cheder.

Often we had a guest for Friday night, mostly a homeless mendicant but occasionally a *meschulach*, a charity collector, or a *maggid*, an itinerant preacher. But welcoming all guests – *orchim* – is a solemn duty, and if the guests take too much on their plate or are a bit unwashed, that too must be borne.

The morning prayers were followed by the *tcholent* – the special meal sealed with bricks into a very hot oven the day before and taken out at midday. With the removal of the first brick, the smells of stuffed derma or *kasheh, kugel* pudding and other tempting delicacies fused to overwhelm the house. We all over-ate and the parents welcomed the traditional nap.

If Sabbath afternoon was a time of rest for adults, it was one of boredom for children. It was our playtime, but after cutting out games prohibited by the Sabbath laws, as well as noisy ones, there was not much left. As we grew older, we did have the Saturday afternoons and evenings to ourselves – within limits, of course.

More often than not, at least until I was ten, Father made me stay in sight. Whenever he could not keep his eye on me, my scrupulously observant brother, Chaim, did. Even when I was a boy of three or four, he would watch me closely and denounce me for the smallest sins. One Sabbath, when he "told" on me for writing with my finger on the moist window pane, my father for once objected: "But this isn't writing, Chaim, is it?"

But Chaim scored again: "It certainly is, *Tatte*. It says so in the holy text of the *Chayeh Odom*. Look for yourself." Father looked. And he never questioned Chaim's denunciations again.

Sabbath was a tyrant bride.

# 12

# A New Rabbi Arrives

At the end of the summer my father was summoned from the forest for an emergency meeting of the congregation.

The old rabbi had come to the conclusion that Botchki's housewives baked too few Sabbath loaves for his yeast monopoly to provide his several unmarried daughters with dowries. True, many a shopkeeper or tradesman might waive the dowry for the prestige of having a son married to a rabbi's daughter, but then a rabbi generally aimed higher too.

When the rabbi left Botchki, the congregation found itself a flock without a shepherd, as the men said, or a ship without a rudder, in the idiom of the women. For in Botchki even secular life without a rabbi was unthinkable. Every Jewish household had to own six sets of kitchen utensils and tableware; meat set, milk set, *pareveh* or neutral, and three Passover sets. Contact between a milk set spoon and a pan of meat soup barred both from further use. In such a contingency only the rabbi could decide whether the contaminated utensil could be cleansed with hot stones or had to be thrown away. Dishes made of china or other breakable materials, of course, were beyond saving.

Or, again, the Sabbath chicken might be found to have a needle in its gizzard and therefore be pronounced *treife*, or unkosher, by the rabbi. Two merchants might fall out over a deal. A woman might be in doubt whether she was fit for marital duties or for entry into the synagogue. All such problems required the judgement of the rabbi, to say nothing of major events such as marriages, circumcisions, divorces or burials.

In this crisis, my grandfather Reb Leibe, who for forty years had let nothing draw him away from his saintly pursuits, came to the rescue. He was persuaded to serve as temporary rabbi while the search for a permanent successor went on.

While factions formed and dissolved, while candidates from the "four corners of the earth" descended upon Botchki with sample sermons for the congregation's critical ears, the fate of the rabbinical chair was being decided by two men – my father and the gabbai of the Old Synagogue. The two dignitaries scoured every yeshivah between the Polish river Bug and the Lithuanian Niemen. One day they telegraphed the glad tidings to Byelsk, whence they were conveyed by horse cart to Botchki, that a rabbi had been found: Reb Hannan from the village of St John, a hundred miles away.

The new rabbi's arrival is still vivid in my memory. It was an auspicious occasion. All the township Jews and many Gentiles advanced in a body along the Byelsk route to greet him, the Jews clad in their Sabbath best and their women decked out in their finest dresses, wigs and what trinkets they possessed. When the carriage reached the windmill, the crowd stopped it, and in the first rush of welcome, nothing could be heard save the cries: "Peace be unto you! Unto you be peace!"

The men swarmed round the carriage to shake hands with the rabbi; the women hardly contained their impatience to get a glimpse of him.

As he stepped down to greet his *kehilleh* or congregation, the men whispered, "What a stately and goodly man!"

"What a kingly face!" the womenfolk echoed, "and what a princess-like figure of a rebbetzin!"

Rabbi Hannan was tall, olive skinned and lithe. He was only thirty, but his clerical alpaca garb, his cascading black beard and high ivory forehead gave him the presence of a dignified scholar. So great was the crowd's enthusiasm that the horses were unharnessed and the carriage drawn into Botchki by the élite of the community. I was on the edge of the procession, among the marvelling children and Gentiles, and I saw the rebbetzin, a tall, thin lady with a white veil over her wig, and her three children – the youngest asleep in her lap, the middle one a curly-haired girl of about three, and the oldest a boy about my age, very shy and a bit fat, whom I liked right away.

On the way to the residence, the rabbi and most of the men who had gone to meet him at the entry of the shtetl stopped over at the new shul for the Mincheh or afternoon service, and immediately thereafter at the old shul for the Ma'ariv, the late evening service. Here Rabbi Hannan, before he gave his sermon, walked across from his official chair on the immediate right of the Holy Ark in the centre of the East wall to the far end of the West wall to shake hands with my grandfather. He addressed him as "my teacher and my guide". Zeide had refused to be disturbed from his studies for a minute longer than was necessary and had not gone to meet the rabbi's carriage.

The local ladies, including my aunt Bashke, were in the receiving line to welcome all who might wish to get a look at the refurbished rabbinical residence and a taste of the delicacies hastily prepared for the occasion by our bakers, butchers and grocers. The rebbetzin graciously undertook the serving and Rabbi Hannan offered tiny glasses of vodka and kosher wine on the table of the courtroom, the Beth Din, which was located in the rabbi's house – gestures that were much appreciated as proof of their unpretentiousness and desire to be both welcomed and welcoming.

Later in the evening Botchki revelled. Led by its drummer, the Fire Brigade paraded until midnight. For the first time ever, our skies were lit up by the magic showers of exploding fireworks, and we children were allowed to stay up to witness the breathtaking spectacle.

The next Saturday afternoon, the new rabbi sent for me and asked me whether I'd like to "play and learn" with his son Avremke, "for children," he smiled, "need friends. Just be good to each other." As if on signal, Avremke came into the courtroom and stood facing me, quite close and not at all shy. "Don't just gawk at each other, children," the rabbi suggested. "It's the holy Sabbath and there's no cheder, and I won't make you study at home this once, so just say 'sholem-aleichem!' and leave me to my Ethics of the Fathers. When you are a little older, children, you'll discover how great is the wisdom of this book."

The *Pirkei Ovess* which the rabbi was studying was a collection of ethical principles and counsels which it was customary to study on Sabbath afternoons, instead of the Talmud. It was full of such pearls as "Be tail to lions rather than head to foxes," and "If I am not for myself, who will be for me? And if I am only for myself what am I? And if not now, when?"

"Let's go, Diodie," Avremke said, "and you call me Avremke, not Avrom." I promised, proud to have a friend. I knew that my parents would be proud, too.

Avremke took me out by the back door.

We investigated the garden at leisure. The crab-apple tree and the pear tree were flanked by rows of berries and flower beds on either side of the cobbled walk leading to the privies at the far end. It was these which made the biggest impression on me. They were as superior to the latrines of other houses as the rumoured indoor toilets of the nobility were superior to them. Two adjoining green-painted cubicles, with tiny heart-shaped cut-outs in doors that closed properly, were kept spotless and odourless with carbolic and lime. Outside, in a waterproof box, were towels and jugs of water. As far back as I remember, no outsider ever got access to these super-toilets, except me. Facilities like these surely justified the polite term *"beyss-ha-Kisseh"* – "House of the Chair" or "Throne Room" – used for all privies.

I was shocked to see Avremke reach up and about to pick a pear and shouted: "It's Shabbes! Desecration of Shabbes merits death by stoning, burning or garrotting, though I'm not sure which." Avremke looked at me quizzically as if to say that no one could see us behind the high fences.

We returned to the house at five for *shalosh soodes*, the "third meal", and a treat of pastries which the ladies of Botchki had brought for the Rabbi's first Sabbath, and then set out again to explore the house itself. On one side of the corridor were the Beth Din, the dining room and the kitchen. On the other were the main bedroom, the children's room, and the "salon", a living room also used as a guest room. For Botchki the house was palatial, twice or even five times the size of other Jewish habitations.

True, I had already seen an even more imposing place, the mansion of our *poretz*, the landowner of Andreyanki, to which my father had taken me on one of his business calls. But, while Andreyanki was unreal, unimaginable and unfriendly, the rabbi's house was familiar and real. It had no carpets, no tapestries, and only one servant girl, but it also had no dogs to chase the visitor long before he got to the tradesman's entrance, no frowning steward to address him by the contemptuous "*ty*" and keep him for hours before letting him see the landowner, and no haughty Pan Andreyanki to bend the knee to. Here all was more like home, the floors and ceilings were bare but spotless, the walls were lined with rabbinical books, and the rabbi and rebbetzin were friendlier than one's own parents.

One morning very early, Avremke came running to cheder to tell me breathlessly about the wonderful thing he had seen, wonderful and terrible too, he admitted. "These St John relatives are visiting us but we haven't yet got beds for them, so they sleep on straw mattresses on the salon floor while my parents and us three children sleep in the main bedroom. Very early this morning I was tiptoeing through the salon on my way to the privy and came upon my cousin Leyke – she's fourteen already – spread out on her straw sack without anything on. She does not look at all like you or me. And I'm almost certain that she didn't really have her eyes closed."

"What was it like, Avremke," I asked.

"It was," he hesitated, "it was a little bit like in the Song of Songs. But better. She had the twin gazelles, but her tummy did not look much like a sheaf of wheat and it was not garlanded with lilies of the valley." I suggested that Leyke might have thrown off her bedding in her sleep because of the heat, but if he thought she did it on purpose when she heard him come through the connecting door, I said, then maybe she would let us both look.

Nothing came of it, but it was exciting stuff for the two weeks of Leyke's stay. I wondered what Avremke's father would do if he knew; I knew only too well what mine would do. I was relieved by the sinless ending to our temptation and, with the approach of the Days of Awe, was glad to return to the flock, not a chastened, but a wiser lamb. Avremke, a more rebellious lamb, though not quite seven yet, was sure to learn more about girls than I, and much sooner.

# 13

## Weekdays in the Synagogue

Father liked to take me along whenever he went on gabbai's business to the synagogue, usually after the evening meal, when Mama might go to visit Grandmother and he might wish to show me off to his friends on the committee.

"Tonight," he said as I lit my lantern before returning to Reb Isaac's, "you should come straight from cheder to the synagogue. If you listen in, you may learn something. If you prefer, you may join Zeide in the old synagogue. Either way, in God's house, you can roam about safely, maybe with Meyerl or some other chaver."

What a good father I had, to think of letting me bring a friend along! Maybe Meyerl would show me the traces of the nocturnal synagogue visitations of the dead. Maybe he'd let me in on other secret things that went on there, like the appearance of his recently deceased grandmother. Would Meyerl tell whether the grandmother had already spoken to him and what she told him about the other world? Had she found out where the goyim were and whether they had souls? Were the worms eating her already?

"There's not much to do here tonight, Diodke," Meyerl explained when we met at the new shul. "Let's go to the old shul. Once the regulars are gone, it can get interesting."

With only single candles lighting the nooks and recesses of the old prayerhouse, I let him lead the way. Zeide was of course there, as always, but we roamed as far away from his pew as we could, curious only about strangers and anything different they might do.

The first unusual personage we encountered was a corpulent, benevolent-looking old Jew with an unremarkable greying beard but enormous sidelocks, braided like thick ropes and reaching to

57

his lap. He was leaning on the long table at the other end of the hall and holding forth to some half-dozen fascinated *batlonim*, the loungers who liked to hang about during the evenings in the synagogue discussing politics, and to some chance passers-by.

He claimed to have arrived recently from the Holy Land and took from his worn briefcase document after document – in Turkish, Hebrew, Aramaic, Yiddish and Russian – attesting to his credentials as the authentic *meshulach* or emissary of the great rabbis of Jerusalem to their opposite numbers in Poland, Lithuania and Russia, on a mission of charity.

His document of appointment certified that this reputed Jerusalem scholar, Reb Boruch Porush, was charged by the renowned charity named after the *tzaddik*, or sage, Rabbi Meir of the Miracle, to solicit contributions from "our generous brethren in the lands of the exile" for distribution among the pious starving Jewish community of Jerusalem. It was an impressive document, written in a scribe's hand on a broad sheet of paper over several rabbis' signatures and personal stamps. The red wax and blue ribbon seal of the charity dispelled all doubt.

A dozen other certificates and appeals followed this document, all folded concertina-fashion into a black flannel shawl and topped by the "authorised, sealed, locked and guaranteed" collection box itself – an iron contraption secured by a great brass lock and artfully fashioned to prevent coins from being removed.

In a letter which he fished out from one of the bottomless pockets of his moulted squirrel-lined overcoat, Reb Boruch asked the reader in plain Yiddish for personal or communal help in procuring board and bed and a little travel money, since "it was not permitted nor even possible, to take a single groschen out of the box". The documents were virtually illegible from long use, the paper was cracking on the folds, and the ink was smudged.

But the meshulach had come from across the Great Sea and had doubtlessly much interesting information to impart about the lands, seas and communities he had crossed. Meyerl and I listened to his conversation with the batlonim, hanging on his descriptions of foreign cities, especially mosques and bazaars, and the ways of their people.

The batlonim wanted above all to hear how the Turk got over his difficulties with the Italian, whether the Sultan was actually about to sell Palestine to Lord Rothschild, blessed be his name, and whether he had visited Kishinev since the great pogrom of 1903. The meshulach seemed to be able to tell them anything they wanted to hear, I thought, except late in the conversation, when he cautioned them not to put their trust in the self-proclaimed "half-price Messiah, Theodor Herzl." One or two batlonim nodded, but most cooled off visibly.

The only question I asked Reb Boruch was how he managed to cross the great boiling river, the Sambatyon?"* He did not reply.

The meshulach was suddenly troubled and tired and inquired where he could find a charitable evening meal and a bed for the night. On being told that he would have to see the rabbi the next morning, he moved away to the bench by the stove, said his bedtime prayers loudly while securing his papers and collection box for the night, putting his talless and tefillin sack under his head and covering himself with his greatcoat. He had no personal luggage and stuffed his linen, underwear and the like into his greatcoat pockets. His damaged umbrella he put next to him, in a pathetic bid for self-defence.

The next evening we were all to be taken by Reb Isaac to listen to the *maggid*, or itinerant preacher, of Plotzk.

"My father," said Meyerl, "heard him when visiting some far-away town and he said that the Plotzker made the synagogue windows burst at certain points in his sermon."

A great crowd was expected, so the event was moved to the new synagogue and my father had to act as host to the Plotzker himself and to handle the collection plate. Meyerl and I stood unobtrusively behind Father, not two feet away from the maggid, and got the full force of his intimidating voice.

Next to the Plotzker, Father looked diminutive. Both men had straggly little beards sparsely covering their chins and faces, but the maggid's face was as heavy-jowled as Father's was lean. The Plotzker was six feet tall to Father's five and his weight around two hundred pounds to Father's one hundred. When the Plotzker donned his talless and let loose his first summons, "Satan, I have

---

* A legendary river beyond which the ten lost tribes of Israel were thought to remain in exile. Crossing the river was impossible during the week as masses of rocks were thrown up. The river came to rest on the Sabbath.

come to do thee battle!" Father and us children literally jumped and both men and women both broke forth in deep sighs.

The homily went on for well over an hour, its appeals to the Uppermost mingling with threats to Satan, and its thunderous menaces alternating with words of comfort, raising and dropping us at his will.

When he finished on a barely audible note, "Repent, repent forthwith and so that you shall know what awaits you, sleep nights in your shrouds, Amen!" people held their breath for many seconds before letting it out in one piteous groan.

At the last moment, the Plotzker pushed a mighty pinch of snuff up his hairy nostrils and gave a gigantic sneeze while descending from the bimeh.

To show that they wouldn't be held to repentance for long even by the great maggid, the Botchkivites revealed – or maybe invented the story – that he was looking about for a pious well-to-do young widow with a view to matrimony. His power over pious young women was great and people wondered whether he did not look for them in the many other towns and villages where he preached.

One was not, of course, allowed to engage in commerce in our houses of worship except for selling religious books and sacred objects. If an itinerant book-seller, a *moicher-sforim*, wanted to make a living, he had to have a horse and cart because a volume of the Talmud might weigh fifteen to twenty pounds. A beginner who came on foot brought his stock of small volumes such as prayer books and light articles such as tallessim, tefillin and *mezzuzehs**, to one of the long tables in the back of the old synagogue and kept shop till late at night. In one case, the bookseller was known to have had a secular novel or two inside his backpack for sale to our young agnostics.

Meyerl and I kept up our explorations for a good while. The old synagogue was seldom unoccupied for long, for it was always open to the lonely and the lame, to all whose homes were too degrading, too depressing, or simply too cold. It served as a sanctuary from almost any kind of wretchedness. It was like a club in which both children of five or six and people of seventy or eighty felt at home.

* Mezzuzeh: a small scroll of parchment containing biblical passages from Deuteronomy, placed in a case and affixed to the doorpost of a Jewish house and of every room in the house.

Exciting things happened all the time, some good and comforting, others that gave me gooseflesh and made my locks creep at the base of my neck, but nothing I witnessed during my first year of cheder was as eerie as the ritual Priests' Blessing of the people.

I remember an early summer day on Shavouess, or the Festival of Weeks, the festival we children remembered best for its cheese blintzes and for our first barefoot excursions to river and forest. Father led me by the hand to the synagogue for the festival service, but he stopped just before entering:

"I have to tell you about something that did not matter before, but now that you can read psalms in praise of the Uppermost One, I have to caution you about the Priests' Blessing. Do you remember it from the last holiday, Diodie?"

"No, Tatte," I said. "Last time, it was on Passover. You sent me outside on some errand, an excuse, I thought."

"Well, this time you stay with me, right through the service, but we are forbidden to look at the priests. God's spirit rests upon their heads and hands, and we may not lift our eyes to behold the Spirit of God."

"I know, Tatte, we just had the portion about God's spirit in cheder not long ago, and it said 'no man may see God and live'."

About an hour into the service, the Cohanim – male descendants of Aaron, the first High Priest – about one tenth of the congregation, left their seats and walked solemnly across the prayer house towards the east wall on each side of the Ark.

They mounted the two tiers of stands – one made up of the benches and the other of the tables behind them. There was a gasp from one of the elders when a youngish priest inadvertently touched his shoes in the process of removing them, and a Levite, assistants to the Cohanim, rushed to pour water over his hands to purify them. The congregation remained very quiet during the disruption.

The priests took their positions on the tiers and faced the east wall. Each carefully stretched his talless forward like a ghostly tent over his head, body and arms, extending his hands at shoulder level.

Now Father and I lowered our eyes to receive the Blessing, "Just," Father explained in a whisper, "as it would be in the Temple."

A hushed silence descended on the congregation, and I shivered. We heard, but did not see, the priests turn to face us and await the deep bass summons of the prayer leader: "Cohanim!" And the priests answered: "Thy hallowed people." The whole Blessing was most solemnly intoned, one word at a time, "Yevorechecho! May He bless you . . ." Some fifteen words in all, but they seemed to last an hour, while I held my breath and felt transported back to our destroyed Temple in Jerusalem.

After the service, Meyerl told me some of the rules governing the Priests' Blessing. "Did you know, Diodie, why some Cohanim did not take part?" he asked. "The stutterers, the insane, the crippled, people with running noses, and the young ones unable to present evidence of maturity by two pubic hairs. Nor may the father of a whore or one married to a divorced woman participate."

And I did peep, and I did live, and I was not struck blind.

Though trembling with the fear of discovery, I still told myself how good it was that no goy could hope to take part in this blessing.

# 14

## *Days of Awe and Days of Joy*

The Ten Days of Awe, or Penitence, began on Rosh Hashanah, when we had to eat apples and honey and pray for a sweet year and when the whole congregation had to go to the river Nuretz to cast away their sins on the running waters to the far seas.

It was about this time that Rosh Hashanah or New Year greeting cards would reach us from America, and my Aunt Scheine in Bridgeport sent one to me. The good wishes were embossed in the brightest colours including gold and silver and were very pretty. Even prettier were the plump ladies on the pictures, all of whom looked like twin sisters of the beautiful girls on the tea canisters.

Long before daybreak on the eve of Yom Kippur, the family was already busy with the *cappores*, or forgiveness birds – a hen for a woman, a cock for a man, and an appropriate young bird for a child. Each bird was tied up, taken to a corner, and twirled three times around the supplicant's head to the incantation:

> This be my substitute
> This be my forgiving offering,
> This be my atonement
> This bird go to death
> And I to good life and peace.

I watched excitedly through half-closed eyes, pretending to be asleep. The cappores had to be slaughtered lawfully and served for the last meal before the fast. Women sought to buy white chickens for better forgiveness. A pregnant woman, unable to predict the

63

gender of her unborn child, sacrificed three birds – one for herself and young birds of both genders to meet either contingency.

The shochet, who was not only our ritual slaughterer but second to the rabbi in authority over rituals, condemned these practices: cappores were not genuine expiations; keeping him awake all night was inconsiderate, even risky, for in a tired hand the ritual knife might slip and cause Jews to eat an unkosher bird; and the demand for white birds sent prices soaring.

What was important to me was that after I finally woke up, Father let me perform my own capporeh with my own cockerel. There was the pretty bird that was to die for me and I was near to tears when I felt its warm shanks in my fingers. I refused to take my cockerel to the shochet and I cried until they let me off and sent Chaim instead.

Once, I saw Zeide wrap the price of his capporeh in a kerchief and twirl the money as a proxy before giving it to charity, and wished I could do the same.

It was an eventful day for Father and me, crammed with important things. Father had many things to see to, both as a pious man and as gabbai, and I meant to be in on them all. We had to supervise the spreading of fragrant grass on the synagogue floor and to put in a reserve of smelling salts and reviving spirits for emergencies – with hundreds of candles lit for the high occasion and the great crowd of worshippers, there would be many faintings. The service and the fast were going to last some twenty-seven hours without pause – sunset to sunset with enough margin – with an hour or two sleep for those who could not stay the course.

There were precautions to take about returning home even for a short spell. Husband and wife had to avoid conversation and stay fully dressed. I savoured every bit of the great meal on the eve of the fast, though I hadn't quite forgotten my cockerel. Forbidden on this occasion were eggs and garlic.

Approaching the shul at sunset, when the Gates of Mercy were opening to our prayers, Father and I stopped for a moment. "Now," he said, "is the best time for the paternal blessing."

As he put his hands on my head, I saw behind us the long line of worshippers coming from their houses at a sombre, shuffling pace in their loose shroud-like white vestments and cloth slippers, as required.

Our prayer leader, Reb Gershon-Ber, was in stockings. I shivered in my slippers at his powerful whisper through the Kol Nidrei, the evening service.

When we got to the *Chotonu*, the acknowledgement of our sins, I looked down the great hall from my perch behind the raised gabbai's pew and saw that only a few worshippers were in their normal prayer positions. The majority were in their great tallessim, stretched to cover them completely from outside view – like the tent cities in the Egyptian desert, I thought. Some of the "tents" were shaking with their trembling and sobs.

Whenever I saw adults crying, I tried to fathom why. But when I looked at the talless-covered men, my father and Uncle Shmerl included, beating their breasts and sobbing, I strained to hear words, to catch sight of faces. What were the people underneath thinking, feeling? Could good people be bad, too?

The distressed women's moans reached us from the gallery. Father sent me and Meyerl over to the aperture with a small tray of reviving remedies.

Towards midnight, I found myself under Father's talless, shivering with cold. Through the chilly drizzle in the street, he carried me all the way home.

When the ways of God's judgement are presented like the ways of terrestial courts, they can be understood by a child, and I was that child. Heaven was a court in three instances and with a court calendar: from Rosh Hashanah on, the people were sentenced by the primary court, but they had ten days to appeal. On Yom Kippur, the middle court heard appeals until the hour of *Neyileh*, the final service held at twilight, when the third court confirmed or reduced sentence.

Through the high windows, I watched for the rays of the sun to touch the tops of the tall trees by the old cemetery, signalling the Neyileh service and the convening of the supreme court to hear the last minute appeals. At the end, a solitary blast on the shofar, the ram's horn, clanged the gates of the court shut. Pardons and denials were now final. One almost expected the decisions to appear on the gates forthwith. The unbearable tension of the Ten Days of Awe was gone.

Upon the appearance of the three stars, Father and I – to let no time pass between two good deeds – proceeded with the construction of our reed-covered tabernacle, the *sukkeh*, in which we took all our meals for eight days to remind us of the Exodus from Egypt. I asked Zeide why God did not order Sukkess to be celebrated in the spring, like Passover.

"That is an excellent question, and one that has already been asked by some of the rabbis," Zeide answered, eyes shining with pleasure. "It is because in the spring it is hot and we might live in our sukkeh for the coolness. In the autumn, it rains, and so we go to the sukkeh to show that it is in memory of God's guidance rather than for the comfort."

Since children were allowed to return to their house in bad weather and every move created arguments, I enjoyed Sukkess more than I pretended. I was sorry for the *sadovnik*s, the Jews who rented orchards from the landowners for the season, whom the rabbis excused from living in a sukkeh on account of the danger of raids by neighbours who knew that they would be absent from their watchmen's job. For myself, I enjoyed eating the evening meals under the stars, even if it rained a bit.

Sukkess itself was the commemoration of our forty years' sojourn in the desert, but it was best appreciated for its ninth and last day, *Simchas Torah*, which was the most joyful day in the year as well as the last day before the dreary months of unceasing rain and mud-choked streets.

Unlike other holidays, Simchas Torah was more the children's day than their parents'. We had few chores and many exciting tasks in synagogue and home. Father came in for special praise for his management of the synagogue's affairs on that day. Simchas Torah was the feast of "rolling back the scrolls", from the end portion of the last Sabbath of the year to the first, and Father had to call for volunteers – and how happy these were – to bring out not only the scroll in active use that year, but every scroll in the Ark, "to take part in the joy of their sister scroll". The festivity lasted throughout the long evening and the next day, and we all joined the procession of all the scrolls; we circled around each scroll in turn and kissed its velvet jacket and tinkling bells as we danced seven times around the bimeh.

At mid-morning, the *sefer-torah* in use was displayed on the reading stand and its continuous parchment was rolled back in strict ritual steps until the beginning of the scroll – *Bereishith*, Genesis – was exposed for the honoured "call-up" of the day, the "Bridegroom of Bereishith", for which Father would collect a most generous donation. This Simchas Torah harvest of sold and auctioned "call-ups" was the richest of the year. Every Jew in the congregation had to receive the honour of a call-up, even if it were only a portion of a line or two.

My own excitement rose to the sky when Zeide made me his personal assistant for the ceremony of *Eem-Kol-ha-Neorim*. Zeide called up all the boys, including infants, that he could get under his talless and who could be trusted not to set it on fire when carrying the plaited candles ensconced in red apples. The whole unwieldy mass circled the hall seven times, too. People went a little wild on this occasion, and it even happened that little girls full of envy, big girls green with it, and even a grandmother or two invaded the men's hall to dance with the scrolls. And who could deny them?

There were treats for us children, gifts of cardboard flags with burning candles on their flagstaff, cakes with honeyed beet-filling, and for me – my reward for protecting Zeide's vestments – a call-up to the Torah on the bimeh, like a grown-up, though Zeide had to intone the adult blessing for me. Even my shy, self-effacing Mama looked down through the gallery aperture to shed her sweet tears of happiness.

Zeide too made merry on this one day. After the first glass of brandy – in honour of the Torah, far be it from any good Jew to drink brandy or relish anything other than in honour of God or His laws – the pious Reb Leibe's pale blue eyes filled with tears; his parchmentlike cheeks glowed purple and benign within the grey-white frame of his beard. Joy was so foreign to the old man that when he honoured the Torah with such rapturous emotion, he appeared to me like an overgrown child. At these times, my respect for him may not have been at its greatest, but it was then that I really loved him most.

God is good to us Jews and He can also be good to the goyim, in fact to all people, when He wishes. By the time the Festival of the Candles, *Chanukah*, came around about two months later, Botchki had exchanged her black, wet, muddy autumn garb for a dress of white linen. Instead of being sucked in up to our knees by the slippery mud on our way to and from cheder, we now walked or skated on the hard squeaking snow, and in our rare free hours were given sleigh-rides from friendly Jews and Gentiles.

The rabbi introduced us to Chanukah by a homily rather than by a sleigh ride. "Remember, boys," he urged, "that Chanukah is not for our pleasure but for God's. You have to learn and obey His commands and prohibitions. The lighting of the Menorah is so holy a duty that if a man is too poor to buy the oil with which to light it, he must sell even his only coat to buy oil. We may not use its light for any purpose other than to celebrate God's miracle\*, not even to read from a prayer book."

We nevertheless relished every minute of the eight days of the festival. At home – we had half-days off from cheder – we gambled in buttons and hazelnuts, rolled down an inclined board to hit the "big one" below. We even bet an occasional groschen from our parents' and friends' Chanukah-money gifts. I was partial to gambling with *"dreidlach"*, spinning a wooden or leaden top, with the Hebrew letters NGHS (nes gadol haya sham) carved on its sides, meaning "a great miracle happened there". It was a game combining virtue and sin. But I was proudest that my Uncle Shmerl had taught me how to carve a wooden top and how to pour lead through a hollowed-out piece of wood.

I thought Chanukah the best festival of them all until Purim, the Festival of the Persian Jewish Queen Esther, came around.

Even the chant of the reader of the special Purim scroll, the *Megilleh* of Esther, was jollier than all the others from the first words: "And it came to pass in the days of Ahasuerus who reigned from India unto Ethiopia, seven and twenty and one hundred provinces!" Though the reader must chant the scroll text solo, the entire congregation chimed in victoriously, "Seven and twenty and one hundred provinces!"

The scroll of Esther, more than anything I had hitherto read in or out of cheder, carried me for a long time on the wings of its

---

\* The miracle occurred when, in 167 BCE, the Maccabees defeated the Syrian Antiochus who had profaned the Temple of Jerusalem and wanted to impose Greek culture in the land of Israel. When the Maccabees rededicated the Temple, they found only enough oil for the candles for one night but, by a miracle, the oil lasted for eight nights. The memory of this miracle is preserved in every Jewish home at Chanukah when candles are lit for eight nights.

fantasy. I swore to myself that I would one day see all one hundred and twenty-seven provinces.

On Purim I got my sweet tooth indulged more than ever – fruit from one of Queen Esther's provinces, perhaps – an orange wrapped in pink tissue like gossamer – all because God had wrought a miracle, causing King Ahasuerus to stop his viceroy Hamman from exterminating the Jews of his Kingdom, and to order instead the pious Jew Mordechai to hang Hamman and his ten sons on a high gibbet. How is it possible, you may ask? For God everything is possible.*

We commemorated Purim by the wonderful custom of *Shalach-monnes*, or gift distribution, to one another and to the poor. That is how I got the orange, but it was so precious that I kept it and kept it, until it died from mould in its pink shroud.

Lesser miracles came in the wake of the Purim miracle: the banquet; the invention of *Hamentashen*, the best cakes one could dream of, all poppy seed and honey; Jews getting drunk in line of duty that one day in the year in synagogue; and my brother Chaim's mishap. As a help to the Reader, he had to chant the names of the eleven hanged Persians, according to tradition in one breath, without taking in air. Because these Persian names were cumbersome and my brother was of choleric disposition, he turned red, then blue, and had to be led down from the lectern.

Purim was indeed a wonderful festival.

---

* Queen Vashti, Ahasuerus's first wife, disobeyed her husband's command to appear before guests at a banquet and was banished from the court for this disrespect. Ahasuerus decided to take a new wife and chose a beautiful young woman called Esther, a Jewess who later saved her people by revealing Hamman's plans to kill the Jews.

# 15

# *Law and Order, Czarist Version*

Those were idyllic days for Botchki. It was still good to be a Jew, so good indeed, I heard the old people say, that it couldn't possibly be expected to last. The pogrom at Kishinev and the Bayliss Trial, though still fresh in the memory of the people, had passed into history, as had the pogroms and upheavals of 1905. The nearest Botchki itself had come to a proper pogrom had been in that year, when more than a hundred Jews were slaughtered in the streets of Byelostok by the hirelings of the anti-Semitic Black Hundreds. The Byelostok pogrom was set off by the accidental explosion of home-made bombs in a suitcase that was being taken to the railway station in a Jewish droshky.

Wave after wave of terror swept over Byelorussia, but Botchki remained immune, thanks to its horse thieves. However incensed by agitators against the "enemies of God and the czar", however encouraged by the authorities, the local Christians could rarely be drawn in. A deep respect for the horse dealers' competence in taking an eye for an eye, combined with neighbourly feeling, assured the peace. Although pogroms took a frequent toll of Jewish life, some sturdy communities successfully warded them off. On market day in Botchki, an altercation between a Gentile and a Jew might grow into a dangerous brawl as the supporters of each formed into factions, especially if the day was well-advanced and the goyim, filled with vodka, were ripe for trouble. But at the cry of "Kill the Jews!" the horse dealers came out wielding their cart-shafts, the butchers their axes, and the blacksmiths their hammers. The sight of them sufficed.

Law and order were represented in Botchki by the *strazhnik* and the *uradnik*, respectively. The strazhnik, whom we nicknamed Order, combined the offices of police sergeant, night watchman, and beater-up-in-chief. The uradnik, nicknamed Law, was the local adviser to the "higher authority", who was the *pristav* in Byelsk. The uradnik also served as Justice of the Peace. His justice was summary and simple. He imposed fines for offences real and imaginary and collected them on the spot, saying *"charosho* – fine, fine, thank you" by way of a receipt.

The short, fat strazhnik had a red complexion; the uradnik was tall, dry and pale. The former carried a rifle and the latter wore a sword and spurs. Both were autocratic bullies, each in his own style. Nevertheless, Jews and Gentiles regarded them as good men, for there were few concessions that they would not grant for a few roubles and a bottle of vodka. "As soon as they open a bottle, they turn a blind eye" was the tribute Botchki paid them.

The most common offences were trading after hours, neglecting to sweep and weed the stretch of road in front of one's house, and failing to report for military service. Law and Order were never known to interfere with the horse thieves or rioters. When there was trouble in Market Square, neither was to be found. In 1905 gendarmes had to be sent from Byelostok to arrest the enemies of the czar – Motl the Pisser and Olek, the son of Marcinova, our laundress. Law and Order conveniently considered these two a pair of innocents – only a bootmender and a labourer – perhaps because the 1905ers were said to own firearms.

I made my first acquaintance with Law and Order after my promotion to Reb Alter's prayer classes. Reb Alter's cheder shared what used to be the *hekdesh*, a shelter for paupers supported by community funds. Ever since his own place blew away in a snow-storm, Reb Alter himself occupied the less derelict half of what was by then a hovel. A cheerless, stuffy place, it was stacked to the ceiling with grimy bedding, chipped crockery and torn prayer books. A leaking bucket stood handy to the right of rebbe, who sat at the head of the table. The boys sat on benches on either side, while the lowest part of the table was kitchen territory. Rebbe's digestion was poor: he had an unquenchable thirst which he vainly tried to allay by continually dipping the heavy, double-handled copper tankard into the bucket. The tottering kitchen stove faced the lower end of the table and belched clouds of smoke and fetid odours over the pupils.

Rebbe's wife, Beladinneh, eternally peeled potatoes. Every time a new pupil was admitted to the cheder, Reb Alter shouted across to his spouse, "Beladinneh, Shove-thee! Shove-thee and make room."

She was duly nicknamed Beladinneh Shove-thee.

Enthroned on top of the tower of bedding were several silent shapes: Pinchos, rebbe's idiot son, and a litter of kittens. My association with Pinchos was limited but humiliating, for the diminutive, Pinke, became my own nickname whenever I was disgraced at home.

Once a month, Order, the strazhnik, raided the cheder, and Reb Alter, who was too poor to pay for a teaching "licence", was forced to pay his periodical penalty in silver and copper.

One day a Polish urchin stopped outside the window to listen to the Children of Abraham chanting their prayers: "How goodly are thy tents, O Jacob, and thy tabernacles, O Israel ... glorified and magnified be the living God, the Infinite Being ... Evil shall slay the wicked and they that hate the righteous shall be desolate."

The urchin did not seem to think Reb Alter's tent particularly goodly, nor did he fear being slain for his wickedness by the infinite Being. He picked up a chunk of brick and flung it through the glass pane – the only glass pane in a window otherwise stopped up with cardboard and cushions.

Beladinneh ran as fast as her legs could carry her in pursuit of the wicked, but she was no match for him. Her complaints, meant to pierce the heart of Heaven, reached instead the ears of the Law and brought that worthy official to the spot.

"How dare you disturb the peace, Jewess?" he raged.

"Boy come, window smashed. Darling uradnik, write protocol," Beladinneh pleaded in broken Russian. The Law demanded thirty kopeks.

I was nearly five years old and understood enough. My little fists clenched, I thought the Law despicable.

# 16

## Summer 1915

The days of accommodation were coming to an end. Rumours of trouble between "the German" and "the Russian" had reached as far as the Byeloviezh forest; and when the moon started to move across the sun in the summer of 1914, we hurried into the streets with pieces of glass smoked over by candles to watch what we all knew to be a certain omen of war. It was, moreover, the most fateful day of the Jewish year – the Ninth of Av, the anniversary of the destruction of both our Temples.

It was said that Czar Nicholas was the sun and Kaiser Wilhelm the moon. After craning their necks and blinking their eyes for a good while, Botchki's "politicians" gave their verdict: Wilhelm would be victorious. "It is a sure sign," they said, "the moon is moving in front of the sun, blocking out its light."

This was a calamitous prophecy: if the Czar lost, it meant that war would inevitably reach Botchki.

True, none of us had much love for His Czarist Majesty, and although we said weekly prayers in the synagogue for the entire Imperial family, each member mentioned by name and title, this was not entirely by choice. Most Botchkivites secretly shared the sentiment of "*daloi Nikolai*" "down with Nicholas", some even repeating it, though only under their breath. "*Sol ich asoi kein tzar nit hobn*" or "may I be spared affliction" carries a double meaning in Yiddish since "tzar" means both "affliction" and "czar", and this common expression was used more often than legitimate business required until Chineh, the plumber's wife, was arrested by the uradnik for uttering it. She was not set free before a five-rouble bribe was paid. Nevertheless, the czar was the czar, and a known devil is less terrifying than an unknown one.

I approached the excited eclipse watchers, among whom my mother had lingered in hope of further "news". I pulled Isser the capmaker by the sleeve: "Reb Isser, did you say that people all over the world can see the eclipse?"

The capmaker, a cousin of Wolf the Atheist, was somewhat of a philosopher himself: "Yes, Dovidl, that's true."

"Well then," I piped up, "the czar must have seen it too, so maybe he will not go to war now."

The people stared at one another in amazement, taken aback by this irrefutable logic.

Mama blushed at the wisdom of her son. Yet that same evening, when I refused to finish my milk, she called her six-year-old logician "Pinke!"

In late summer of 1915 the calm was broken. Day and night, army carts rumbled over the cobbled streets on their way west; the tramping infantry and the clatter of horses' hooves and gun carriages portended imminent evil. Dispatch riders galloped through the town like whirlwind messengers of disaster, gone almost before they were seen.

One day the Cossacks appeared. They were already at the tollgate before the warning came through, so there was no time to get off the streets before they swept across Market Square on their long-tailed ponies, trampling an old woman to death. Meyerl was standing on his porch when a passing Cossack picked him up on the tip of his lance. As a result of this drollery Meyerl's shoulder was wrenched off, maiming him for life.

When the first goggled devil whizzed past on his motorcycle, the Botchkivites thought it time to prepare for flight. Under cover of night they dug pits in their cellars and courtyards and buried what valuables they could. Father returned from the forest and, to my great excitement, he brought a piebald horse and four-wheeled cart.

As there was no cellar in the house, my parents dug a pit in the woodshed, while I held up the lantern. When everything we could find room for was buried – the Sabbath candlesticks, the linen, Mama's squirrel furcoat and a few other valuables – we covered the pit with logs and firewood and snatched a few hours of sleep.

The next day, a Friday, we spent making bundles of the things we would need for the journey, which might last weeks or even months. All we knew for certain was that we would travel east through the wilderness of Byeloviezh toward the marshes of Byelorussia, away from the front. By noon the booming of heavy guns became audible, and we were filled with dread: would the Russians hold out on the Narev River until the Sabbath was out?

The people, my father included, went to seek the rabbi's advice. Rabbi Hannan pensively stroked his beard and pronounced, "The Sabbath is indeed a holy institution. The Fathers have said, 'If his choice be to desecrate the Sabbath or succumb, let him succumb and not desecrate.' However, in the holy Torah it is also written 'and he shall live by these commandments' – a passage interpreted by many of the great to mean that one shall not die by them. I, therefore, add the weight of my humble authority to the side of leniency and herewith enjoin you: Go, harness your horses upon the holy Sabbath, that you and your children may flee to safety."

At home, Mama, Chaim and Basheh were anxious for Father's return, for the desolation of our empty home weighed upon them. Whenever they broke the silence, their words reverberated through the empty rooms, then sank like pieces of lead among the bundled-up belongings of a family going into exile.

I vaguely guessed the portent of Mama's sadness, but I was not inclined to join in the lamentation. My mind was elsewhere, preoccupied with my own crisis: How do I save my violin?

The violin was the only toy I'd ever had. I valued it specially because it was a present from Aunt Feineh on one of her annual visits to Botchki. I worshipped Feineh. My mother's sister embodied for me all that was most glamorous, most in contrast to the peasant stolidity of our own women. She came from the big town, was smartly dressed and her voice was magnetically husky. Unlike any other adult I knew, Aunt Feineh was spontaneous. She was not ashamed to laugh out gaily or to cuddle me whenever the fancy took her. The others believed that too much kindness spoiled a child, and that joy was improper.

I feared that in the hustle my violin might be forgotten or that Father might ban it from the cart on the pretext that the horse was already overloaded. He had made a sour enough face when Aunt Feineh had removed the pretty tissue paper from the shiny brown violin, grumbling, "Money thrown away. Fiddles, shmiddles."

To save the violin, I had to get it into the cart before it was filled up. I slunk out of the house and put my treasured possession on the bare boards at the bottom of the cart. Thus I was sure it would be taken along, whatever else was left behind – but I never saw my violin again.

As the silver Sabbath candlesticks had been buried, Mama stood two candles into scooped-out potatoes on top of a crate to signal the beginning of Sabbath. She leaned over the fitful little flames, her blue eyes welling with tears, and spread her hands before her face in blessing. I was ashamed of my own lightheartedness and suddenly I no longer cared about the violin or anything or anybody else.

Her prayer was scarcely audible: "Blessed art Thou, the Eternal our God, King of the Universe, who hath sanctified us with His commandments and enjoined us to kindle the Sabbath lights."

Father quietly entered the room. Sensing his presence and not daring to let him see her tear-stained face on the holy Sabbath, Mama cast her eyes down as she greeted him, striving to sound cheerful: "A good Sabbath to you, Yisroel; a good Sabbath to you, my children."

Father, always reluctant to betray the slightest emotion, took refuge behind a severe exterior. He replied curtly, "Good Sabbath. The rabbi said we may harness," and with these words he hurried outside. There was no time to receive the Sabbath in congregation; the men of Botchki said their prayers as they harnessed the horses and the women as they stacked the carts.

Late that night the Children of Jacob reverted to their forefather's strategy when warned that Esau was drawing near. They divided into several columns. Our family, like most of Botchki's Jews, fled through Byelsk toward the safety of the great Byeloviezh forest. Others who were too poor to have a horse and cart or too rich to abandon their homes hid in the woods, the latter to be close enough to keep an eye on their property. Rabbi Hannan, who had sent his wife and children with our column, stayed behind to guard the Scrolls of the Torah hidden deep in the woods, and Zeide's family and a few others who insisted on submitting to God's will joined the rabbi. There were even some who stayed in their homes out of sheer obstinacy.

Like the poorer members of the Jewish community, the Byelorussians stayed in their houses during the two days Botchki was shelled. The more prosperous among the Poles awaited the coming of the Germans with glee, regarding the defeat of the Russians as a victory for themselves and a promise of new and better things. Other Poles had stalked the Jewish shopkeepers for days to see where they hid their wares. Prostchuk, the Sabbath goy, followed the Jewish congregation into the woods and commiserated with us when the smoke over the trees told us that our homes were burning. Only Botchki's richest freeholders and the strazhnik and uradnik fled to the interior of Russia.

Chaim and Basheh were perched on either side of Father on the high front seat, while I sat with Mother in the lowest and safest part of the cart. Because of our piled-up possessions, I saw few of the vehicles, in front or behind, that formed our exciting caravan. It was a dark late-summer night and, over-awed by the rustling of the giant trees of the Byeloviezh forest closing in on us, I fell asleep on Mama's lap.

# 17

# I Go "Queer in the Head"

Agitated voices awoke me. A weak sun lit up the yellowing crowns of the oaks and the slim shapes of the evergreen pines. The caravan had stopped in its tracks. During the night the last two carts had been caught up in the vanguard of a retreating Russian division. When passing through Orla, they were separated from the rest of the party and came under German shelling. Solomon, our neighbour the fabric merchant, had both legs torn from his body, and Chineh, the plumber's wife, was killed.

The preparations for her funeral had woken me up. I was not allowed to get down from the cart, but I watched Chineh's grave being dug in a small clearing by the road. In a broken voice, her husband Yosl chanted the Kaddish over the mound of yellow sand. Chineh was buried dressed as she was at death, and the straw from her cart and a bundle of linen stained with her blood went into the grave with her. There was no oration, for there was no one qualified to deliver it, and no ablutions, for there was no water, but tears were not lacking.

Accompanied by Solomon's agonised moans and the creaking of the ill-greased wooden axles, the bereaved community continued on its way. By noon we had penetrated deep into the stillness of the forest.

"Father Byeloviezh", as the woodmen called it, stood dark, silent, awe-inspiring in its primeval mightiness. The boom of great guns disturbed its quiet no more than had the twang of crossbows in the past. Had it not been for Solomon's cries, the little company would have found it difficult to believe that war and destruction had been left behind only a few miles back. The strip of blue high above the narrow track was the only reminder that there was a world outside.

One or two carts caught fire for want of grease on their wooden axles; otherwise nothing untoward occurred that day, or the next. At night, the horses were unharnessed and left to graze. Shortly before moonrise the next evening, our caravan emerged on the outer fringe of a forest clearing and stayed the night with a hospitable Jewish dairyman. He offered the hungry, thirsty wanderers churns full of milk and an oven full of warm rye bread, and he placed his lofts filled with fresh hay at our disposal.

After travelling for three days, the Botchki refugees arrived in Pruzhene, a forest town the size of Byelsk, where, for the first time, I saw paved sidewalks and horse carts holding to the centre of the cobbled streets.

Here my family found hospitality with a timber dealer whom my father knew. Many other Botchkivites were quartered throughout Pruzhene in synagogues, barns and haylofts. Still others, including the wife and children of the rabbi, continued "into Russia", determined not to be caught by the German advance.

I'm not sure how long we were in Pruzhene and I remember little about that time because I had undergone an acute crisis. The sight of Chineh's body being lowered into the pit haunted me. In the blackness of the night the straw between my fingers seemed to be soaked with blood. I tossed and turned ceaselessly. Waking in a sweat, I freed myself from the wisps of straw that had strayed over my face. Afraid to call out, I sat shivering till daybreak, wrestling with my terrors. In the daytime, unable to rid myself of my persistent nightmare, I wandered about the Pruzhene streets in a daze. My parents began to suspect that their boy was going "queer in the head", but amid their greater worries, they paid little heed to me, and I was left to go my own way.

This must have been a very strange way, for years later Chaim and Basheh still taunted me with the phrase "Go and walk under the horses, Dovid." Apparently I had been so distracted that I used to cross the streets of Pruzhene right under the bellies of the Russian cavalry horses.

From that tormented time one image stands out in the blank of my memory like a dark spot on a snowfield. I saw a stocky *Katsap* from Great Russia in huge top boots, his sheepskin cap pushed back from his forehead, take potshots with a rifle at the sky. The Katsap leaned against a post and spat out angrily after every shot. I looked up and saw two specks moving through the late-summer clouds in the blue above. At first sight they looked like big birds, but they passed across the heavens with a loud drone, and their wings did not move. People said they were German aeroplanes.

One night we heard shooting over Pruzhene. We lay pressed against the thickest walls of our quarters murmuring prayers, but in a few hours everything was quiet once more.

The Germans had entered the town, though no one saw them up close. For us their arrival meant the war was over. Nobody knew the significance of the change of masters that had taken place. Our Jews and Gentiles alike had always considered "the Authorities" as Heaven's punishment for their sins or the sins of their fathers. For the Jews, a new regime might or might not alleviate persecution. That same afternoon Father harnessed the horse and we set out for home. The caravan which made the return journey was smaller than the one that had set out from Botchki. Some refugees had continued their trek toward Minsk, while several others, whose horses had been commandeered by the retreating Russians, were having to make their way back on foot, walking beside the carts of those more fortunate.

Our journey back was devoid of incident, though several times we had to draw in to the side of the road to let a German detachment pass. From my seat on the bottom of our cart I could just see a line of grey-blue uniforms filing past on horseback, the spikes of their helmets bobbing arrogantly.

On a rainy morning in mid-autumn our travel-worn column made its way through the mud of upper Byelsk Street into Botchki. The men lowered their eyes and the women sobbed: half of Market Square and most of Byelsk Street, Bransk Street, and Synagogue Street lay in charred ruins. Only a few precariously tottering walls remained of most of the brick buildings, and hardly a trace of the wooden houses in the centre was left. An occasional chimney raised its orphaned head above the debris. The strangest spectacle was the gutted shop of Yoel the ironmonger. The long iron bars of his stock in trade lay twisted amid piles of crushed pots, buckled pans and cracked cauldrons. Most of the Gentile huts, in the outlying streets, were intact.

Among the ruins, some of which were still smoking, Christian children rummaged around for the spoils which fire and shrapnel had spared. Their elders, barefooted, trousers or skirts pulled up to their knees, stood by with open sacks. As the caravan approached, the urchins fled and their parents moved away reluctantly, dragging their sacks behind them through the mud.

Our silver candlesticks were gone. So was Mama's squirrel furcoat and much else. Luckily though, Soreh-Enie, or Bobbe as we called her, had had the foresight, before escaping into the forest, to leave her cow with Marcinova. Pani Marcinova, the loveable hunchback who was also Mama's laundry help, had agreed, crossed herself and prayed to Jesus to let Mistress Soreh-Enie and her family return safely.

We were reunited in Bobbe's home which had escaped destruction, and together we shamed the looters away. Marcinova came to meet us, holding on to the cow's neck as though ready to fight the whole world for her. She greeted Bobbe crying and laughing all at once. "*Bozhe moi*, my God, you *have* come back, you've *all* come back to your Marcinova. May God bless you – your God, my God, makes no difference. But you see, Mistress," she got back to crying now – "the stable has gone. These chazeirim, these mamzeirim" – Marcinova liked her bad words in Yiddish – "the pigs, the bastards, have torn it apart, board by board, just for pleasure. So what are you to do now?" she asked into the air, not addressing anyone in particular.

Zeide was almost useless. Through Bashke, his unmarried daughter, he could speak to the woman without looking at her and without knowing any "star-worshipper's" tongue. He asked for the loan of pliers for pulling out the old nails that were needed in the reconstruction, and a hammer and saw. We retrieved part of the lumber, maybe a third, and embarked on what Zeide referred to as the "sacred work" of building a shelter for the cow. "Sacred," he explained, because the cow would provide them with food, and they would provide her with grass to feed on. "Beware, children," he said, "lest you cause *tzaar baalei chaim*, suffering to living things."

His brief homily over, Zeide began straightening nails, for he now had almost enough lumber to knock together a minuscule shed, just big enough for the cow to squeeze into, though not to exit, except backwards. The first blow of his hammer came down on his fingers. There were cries of pain, not Zeide's but the women's, and a hurried application of home-made bandages, while our angelic laundress ran home for iodine.

Thanks to the accident, neighbours, both Jews and goyim, volunteered to help and put up the stable in a few hours. Digging up what was left of their caches, Zeide had found a padlock, and by nightfall the cow was fed and locked in.

Zeide didn't go to shul for evening prayers that day. His strength seemed suddenly to have given out. He looked faint with hunger, for the women were busy with the looted shed and fouled-up house and in no better condition than he. Father had gone to look for a place for us to live in, so that Zeide and I were alone and sat on piles of lumber detritus in the dark yard.

It was pitch dark now, except for the fireflies and occasional tongues of fire and puffs of smoke breaking the darkness. The township felt more threatening now than in the daytime, shelled buildings and charred tree-tops looking like misshapen monsters. I felt safer talking to Zeide than gazing into the dark terrors surrounding us.

"Zeide," I said, "Why are people less decent to human beings than to dogs and cats? I remember the laws about animals. One forbids us to cook a kid in its mother's milk. Another prohibits the muzzling of an ox on the threshing floor. Now it seems that the soldiers are muzzling everybody, for I see few signs of food around."

"We must go to sleep, my Dovid. You have a good head for your age, but you must rest it now."

"I'll be seven come next Purim, Zeide."

Zeide rose for *chatzos* – the midnight visit to shul made by the strictest observers – but was held back by the frequent passage of soldiers or field police. He woke again at daybreak and took me along to *Slichess* – the prayers for forgiveness which precede the Days of Awe. Both synagogues were virtually undamaged and we stayed on in the old shul for morning service. "Thank God for leaving us the shuls," I said piously. "Don't raise the High One's name in vain," Zeide corrected me. "It is a grievous sin."

# 18

# *Law and Order, Prussian Version*

Although half of Botchki had been destroyed by fire, many of the returning refugees were lucky and found decent quarters, mostly in houses left empty by people who had gone on to Russia. But we were not so lucky. Our place of refuge was probably the worst, for we were now paupers. The Orlovka forest, into which my father had put his savings shortly before the outbreak of the war, had been confiscated by the Prussians, who had taken over the timber trade. Our bagful of czarist banknotes, called assignations, had only the value of wallpaper.

Our new "home" was given to Father rent-free by his Byelorussian friend, old man Stolkowski. "Don't feel bad about it, Srolke," he said as he led us to the derelict hut behind his own house. "You are young, hard-working and clever, and you'll soon rise in the world again."

The hut, which had not been used for years, was a one-room, dirt-floor shanty, without a stick of furniture and only a makeshift cooking pit surrounded by a few raised stones.

Pan Stolkowski wouldn't hear of payment. "Potatoes you can dig up right here, firewood is all over the place. That is about all I can offer but it is yours for the taking. You'll need to keep the fire going in the winter, day and night. You'll have sacks of straw to sleep on, so it won't be so bad once you get used to the smoke. Tell you the truth, which even my wife doesn't know, this is where my father lived when I was born."

The hut stood in a small orchard in Starosielo Street on the outskirts of the town. The fruit trees round the main cottage were laden with ripe apples and pears and Hungarian plums wrinkled from the night frosts. The garden behind it was filled with vegetables. Most important, there was the potato patch that Stolkowski had mentioned.

For my part, I was delighted with the new order of things. I had an orchard in which to play, a garden with sweet, ripe poppyseeds and tasty carrots, a little hayloft in which to hide wild pears "for ripening", ploughs and harnesses and toolsheds to examine – and no cheder. Adversity had drawn the family closer together. We all squatted on the floor for the meagre meal Mama prepared in her only utensil, the one we had taken on our flight – a two-handled copper pot. The stress and sadness of our new condition made the parents speak with tenderness in their voices. Mama's soft words combined with my own sweet wave of self-pity: "My poor child, so young and delicate, and I have nothing for you but these stodgy potatoes. Not even a drop of fat to make the swallowing easier."

The longer the potato lumps stuck in my throat and the more pained my mother's look, the more was I elated in my martyrdom. When, at last, tears did appear in my eyes, it was not because of the poor fare but because Father did not lavish upon me an equal amount of attention.

But poverty, once come, stayed even after its novelty waned, settling down with the family like an old, toothless female relation. I could see it grin at times, cruelly and spitefully licking its blue lips: "Yes, yes, I have come to stay, children."

By midwinter all Stolkowski could spare for us were potato peels. The hut felt snug enough, thanks to the fuel from Stolkowski's woodshed, but the hopelessness of our situation grew upon my parents as the snow reached the roofline and we could get to our neighbours only by tunnelling a path between the door and the snowbound street.

The soles of Father's boots gave out. Mother had used them on her daily excursions through the snow to get what little she could from her parents. On their return from the woods, Zeide and Bobbe had found most of their gallanterie stock gone. Among the few things which escaped was the shiny enamel sign displaying a dancing African who proclaimed, "only Bonn's chicory is as good as coffee": the sign was bullet-riddled and the Negro looked upon Market Square with the sadness of a blind man, for both of his eyes had been shot through.

Bobbe nevertheless resumed her seat over her fire pot, dozing through the days amid the virtually empty shelves and waiting for customers who rarely came. She had conjured up sufficient stock to cover the bare front shelves – some lengths of Brussels lace, grey with age, a few cards of needles, a tin of senna leaves, and some pairs of English rubber heels. There was little that Bobbe could do for her daughter and grandchildren, for she had several hungry mouths of her own to feed; yet when every other resource failed to fill the copper pot, my mother would give in and go to Bobbe's, for wasn't blood thicker than water after all?

One morning Father rose from his straw sack and informed us that he was going to Andreyanki. The larder was empty. Even the previous week's potato peelings had been washed, cooked and eaten. Father hoped to prevail upon the landlord of the Andreyanki estate, with whom he had had dealings before the war, to part with a few sacks of potatoes in payment for an outstanding debt. He borrowed a sledge from Nossen-Aaron next door, harnessed our piebald horse, and made ready to go. The problem of boots was solved with Stolkowski's help using an age-old Byelorussian device – they cut a jute sack in two and filled each half with hay, tying them with string around his feet. "They won't let me in like this," he said, "they'll set the dogs on me." But he went nevertheless. Without food the family spent the short winter's day waiting.

In the evening Father returned, his sledge laden with potatoes. The family came out to meet him. The bulky, muffled figure of a man in the driver's seat next to Father disquieted us. The man was Andreyanki's "econom". After helping my father unload, he rode off without so much as a "goodnight." There were plenty of potatoes and even a bag of rye, but the horse was gone.

Others, I heard say, were in no such straits. The Prussians, from the moment of their arrival, had regimented Botchki's population for all manner of military labour. Throughout the winter their gendarmes made the inhabitants work from daybreak till nightfall, clearing roads through the ice and snow for their advancing troops. In the summer they laid new roads and built bridges. Every able person "from fourteen to seventy", as they put it, was dragged out into the streets and made to join the teams. My mother escaped service, since they would not force her to leave her three small children unattended, and my father was disqualified because he looked too frail. Thus we did not receive the rations that sustained our neighbours. This was no great loss, however, since my parents, like some of those that did get pressed into the work gangs, would rather have submitted to torture than partake of the pork-contaminated meals prepared by the German field kitchens.

The slow winter months passed in great hardship, but with the arrival of spring, life in the hut became more cheerful. Father went into "trade", which in those days meant that he had become a smuggler. During the occupation, all commercial transactions were *verboten*, and buying and selling commodities such as sugar, salt and tobacco became severe offences. Men and women called on surrounding farms with small packets of these forbidden articles padded in flat layers round their waists, and returned with a bag of rye or oats.

Grinding the grain into flour was also verboten and had to be done by hand at home, since both the windmill and watermill had been commandeered and were strictly supervised.

The gendarmerie tried to stamp out smuggling, but the *schmoocklers* carried on at night, taking devious, unfrequented forest tracks that did not appear on the Prussian ordnance maps. These nocturnal expeditions were perilous, and every month one or two smugglers lost their lives. If a smuggler became trapped in the treacherous swamps around the Nuretz's upper reaches, there was little chance of rescue since no one passed that way: the mud would swallow its victim with slow relentlessness. In the winter the river ice sometimes gave way under a smuggler's horse and both of them fell to their deaths. Occasionally a desperate smuggler refused to halt when challenged by a gendarme and risked being shot rather than part with his bag of grain.

In our family, my father's excursions meant bread and some-times butter and cheese, although the bread was almost always mildewed and the butter rancid. Only the smallest supply of anything edible could be kept at home; the rest had to be buried to elude the gendarmes' frequent raids.

The Byelorussians were not strangers to the art of harbouring food in the earth from which it came. The traditional way to protect potatoes from frost was to bury them in a vast circular bed of straw under several feet of earth. These flat pits were called *kopitzes*.

Under the new regime, when every day brought some new order, when requisitions and confiscations followed one after another, the koptizes were dug further afield and became hiding places for rye and fruit as well as for potatoes.

When the gendarmes discovered these caches, the peasants bore the succession of lawful robberies stolidly. They looked on while the gendarmes unearthed their children's food. But even Byelorussian patience was exhausted if a family's only horse was commandeered, leaving the plough idle in the empty barn. Then a gendarme would be found clubbed to death in a lonely byway in the marshes. Retribution followed, and more confiscations.

The Prussian authority, unlike the Russian, took no bribes: it confiscated everything, decently and lawfully, and sent it to the Reich. For the rest, law and order in Botchki hardly changed. Whereas before the war the townspeople had needed a licence for the most trivial things, now the same things had become entirely verboten. Instead of the strazhnik and uradnik, Botchki now had Law and Order in one. No loss was sustained by welding strazhnik and uradnik into one very fat *Landjäger*, called appropriately enough *Schmalzgesicht*, or Fatface. Schmalzgesicht was more efficient than the two czarist dignitaries combined, and if, by comparison, he lacked downright cruelty, he excelled in a ruthless Prussian devotion to duty.

Like his predecessors, Schmalzgesicht waged war against the cheders. The schools that used to be licensed or tolerated for a small bribe were now forbidden. But the rewards to be expected in the next world for the clandestine study of the Torah grew with the hazards.

# 19

## *Rebbe versus Fräulein*

I was now a *Gemoreh* boy in the cheder of Reb Lippe, setting out on that sea of Talmudic law, rite and tradition that fills the sixty great volumes of the Gemoreh and its hundreds of commentaries and subcommentaries. Because cheders were now illegal, Talmud instruction could be risked only at nightfall; by day I, like every boy under fourteen, had to attend the *Zwangsschule*, the compulsory German school, where little Jewish boys were made to sit bareheaded and mix with girls and Gentiles. Cheder had become another form of smuggling. Even with shutters tightly closed, with heavy blankets on the doors and windows to shut in sound and light, and with his wife guarding the front door and his daughter the back, Reb Lippe shook whenever footsteps sounded in the street.

"If an ox gores a cow, and the cow be with calf, the owners of the ox shall pay for both cow and calf," I repeated eagerly after rebbe. I was keenly interested in what I learned. The knotty problems and convoluted reasoning of the Gemoreh appealed to me more than copying out Gothic calligraphy at the Zwangsschule. My eyes smarted from the fumes of the kerosene lamp, and though I was hungry and cold, I nevertheless felt real satisfaction at mastering the seemingly insuperable. It made me feel a thrill similar to that I experienced after leaping a wide ditch.

The top boy in any cheder is not popular: he is quoted by rebbe to the slower-witted, who in turn associate him with their whippings. I feared rejection by my schoolmates even more than a beating, so I found a way into their favour. Since the Gemoreh boys were thankful whenever they went home early, I saw to it that we could do so frequently: through my broken front tooth, I propelled spit with perfect aim on to the glass shade of the kerosene lamp while rebbe's attention was diverted. The glass cracked, the cheder was flung into darkness, and the boys were sent home.

However, other boys did show interest too, sometimes. The very passages of the Gemoreh over which Reb Lippe tried to skip with the greatest speed made the less industrious boys wake up and ask for explanations. On page 84b of the second volume of the tractate on Damages, a purely legalistic argument was interrupted by an account of the prodigal dimensions of Rav Pappa's bodily attributes. The Gemoreh related in the style of *The Decameron* that that great Babylonian rabbi was exceedingly fat, as was his spouse, so that when they stood facing each other in the market a sheaf of hay could pass beneath their touching bellies. To a Roman matron who inquired of him, "How can thy children be thine?" the dialectician replied, quoting the words of King Solomon, "Love compresseth the flesh."

The crippled Meyerl halted Reb Lippe's rapid mumbling with a sleepy innocence: "Rebbe! Could not God have blessed him with offspring even if he did have a great belly?"

Rebbe brought his short-sighted eyes closer to the page and mumbled on: "The limb of Rav Pappa was like unto a gourd of nine gallons' displacement."

"Which limb?" persisted the indomitable Meyerl. Reb Lippe could not beat him, because of his deformity, and the boys gloated.

At the Zwangsschule I found favour with Fräulein Zack, the pretty, fresh-faced headmistress, because of my progress in arithmetic and geography – fascinating new subjects to me. Still, my handwriting was my nemesis, and I received many whacks of her ruler during penmanship hour as I copied out lines. The German school was more efficient than the czarist two-class school, and the teachers were stricter. School no longer took second place to the parents' needs at home, and truancy was paid in fines – a mark for the first time, two marks the next time, and so forth.

Arithmetic, nature study, history and reading were pleasant enough, though unlike the rigorous cheder, the Zwangsschule spoon-fed its pupils. Progress was determined by the slowest rather than the brightest. But there were other aspects of the Zwangsschule which I did enjoy. There was a spacious courtyard behind the Orthodox church where Fräulein taught gymnastics for half an hour every day, and there were even ten-minute intervals after each class. Standing in the corner was the usual punishment, but if a student became too unruly in class, he had to spend half a day in the woodshed. Once I was shut up in the woodshed for describing Botchki as a "Russian town" in an essay on "Our German Township."

My happiest memory of the Zwangsschule was the school play. As top boy I got a leading part in *The Bandit Hauptmann and the Princess*, though I had no acting ability whatsoever. I forgot half the words, trod on the prompter's head, but managed to brazen out the rest. The gorgeous costumes were made of crinkled paper and Eya, the plumber's little girl, sang superbly. The photograph taken after the play included the cast, Fräulein Zack, Schmalzgesicht, the Catholic priest, and two Landjägers stationed in nearby villages. Every pupil had to buy the memento for forty pfennigs on pain of *Strafe*, or fine.

Between cheder and Zwangsschule, I spent at least fourteen hours a day away from home. School was from eight to four, with an hour for lunch, which seldom consisted of more than bread and an apple; cheder took place from five to ten; then back home through the dark streets, lantern in hand. The chief meal was taken at home at half past four: a single portion of potatoes, either dry, baked, fried, in a soup, or dipped whole in herring brine. The ditty in which the Byelorussians laughed at their own misery ran:

> Sunday – potatoes
> Monday – potatoes
> Tuesday – potatoes
> Wednesday and Thursday – potatoes
> Friday – baked potatoes
> Saturday – stewed potatoes
> And Sunday, oh Sunday – potatoes again

Pestered by her youngest for something to go with the bread, my mother sometimes forgot herself and retorted, "What shall I give you with it? My heart? Here, take my heart and eat it: you'll poison yourself . . ."

When in a calmer mood, she'd answer me with good-natured mockery, "If bread-and-nought isn't good enough, have bread-and-bottom, your own bottom."

Or: "You can have bread-and-tongue. You have a nice, smooth little tongue, Dovidl."

But her actions belied her words: she often went hungry, telling us that she had already "eaten while cooking", so that her family might feel the pinch of hunger a little less. She grew pale and thinner – more from worry that her children had not had enough than from hunger itself.

But hunger, as they said in Botchki, is like a shrewish wife: you get used to it.

And just then, when Father began bringing an occasional loaf from a smuggling trip and poverty at last appeared to be relinquishing her hold on us, the great fire came.

# 20

# *The Fire*

It was market day, the streets were teeming with peasant carts, wedged tightly one against the other. Either from malice or carelessness, a client of Judah the horse dealer threw a lit cigarette into the straw on the stable floor. Within minutes wooden walls and thatched roofs were an inferno from which the flames, fanned by the wind, spread, kindling nearby cottages like so many Sabbath candles.

We were all away from home that day: Father out smuggling, Mama and Chaim helping Grandmother in the shop, Basheh and I at school.

The cry "Pajar!" went up in Market Square. Since an easterly wind was blowing, the smoke spread to one side so that people thought upper Bransk Street was burning. Instead of hurrying home, my mother and Chaim stayed to help Bobbe pack in case the wind turned the flames toward Market Square. Confusion spread in the market even farther than the fire in Starosielo Street, and in the centre of it all Schmalzgesicht vainly tried to restore a measure of calm. In his hoarse voice he thundered out orders above the bedlam of shoving peasants, carts and excited Jews, for the people to clear the road for the fire engines.

Fräulein Zack dismissed classes. Blinded by the thick smoke that hung over everything, I pushed my way to Bobbe's. People ran to and fro carrying buckets and household pans. Caught in the chaos, frightened horses bolted, neighing wildly and dragging their carts behind them with a terrifying clatter. Had the fire reached the market at that moment, scarcely a soul would have escaped, but the wind blew steadily east.

Inside the gallanterie, behind doors shuttered against looters, Bobbe took charge, for she alone remained cool. Old as she was, she climbed on a chair on top of the counter to conduct operations. Under her direction, we spread out the bedsheets on the floor and filled them with the contents of shelves, home and kitchen. Within minutes every portable object had been bundled up and the white packs stood ready, their dog-ears erect, prepared to bolt as soon as the signal was given.

After an endless hour Market Square was sufficiently cleared for the fire engines to pass through the gates of the fire barn. Under the command of Schmalzgesicht, the "Commando" donned their brass helmets and manned the engines, which they wheeled at a lumbering speed toward Starosielo Street, pointlessly shouting "Pajar".

We started on our way home, intending to pack our belongings in case the fire spread, but as we approached Starosielo Street, we saw that our hut was gone – the last one devoured by flames before the wind changed direction. I stared at my mother who stood there, pale and shivering in the hellish heat, and thought I noticed the same twitch of the mouth, half despondent, half protesting, that I had so often observed in my grandmother.

I did not share the glee with which the other children and some of the adults witnessed the "Brigade" unroll the hoses and set the hand pump into action. The well across the street was dry, the pump couldn't be filled, and the hose was punctured.

Questions gnawed away at my faith: "Why? Why did He not send a good wind to turn the fire away from our little hut? He could so easily have changed the wind one house earlier." Engrossed in thought, I stood alone in the midst of the crowd. The sounds around me came muffled and only half read, as through a glass wall.

Suddenly, Mama's legs gave way. As I watched her, I recalled our calf, Pooza, helplessly shaking on its thin legs the night it was born – the night I had been roused from my bed to hold the lantern in the cowshed and watched my father ministering to the feeble creature. Even Pooza, I thought, had been sustained and cared for when she was weak. Why had my mother no help or comfort? Where was the mercy of God about which there was so much in the prayer book?

As Mama sank down on the charred grass facing the burned

hut, large drops of warm midsummer rain began to sizzle on the broiling dust of the street. Soon the rain was falling in a torrent, damping the subsiding flames into yellow smoke and hissing over the smouldering beams which the firemen had dragged into the roadside. Forlornly we sat by Mama without a word, crying, while a pool of rainwater formed around us.

My tears were of resentful protest. God and His rain were mocking us.

Sosie, the eight-year-old orphan granddaughter of our next-door neighbour Nossen-Aaron, came out into the twilight. Their house had escaped with only a blackened porch and cracked window panes. Old Nossen-Aaron had been resourceful. He, too, had made use of the sheets from his bed, but not for packing. Soaking them in the water butt with the help of Sosie, who could climb like a squirrel, he had spread them over the thatch. Nossen-Aaron was a humble peasant Jew, with little claim to God's personal interest in his welfare; he thought it wiser to follow the example of the goyim.

Although he was glad to have escaped disaster, Nossen-Aaron felt sorry for our family and perhaps guilty at his own good fortune, and he sent Sosie to offer hot food and shelter. Mama was stiffly rocking to and fro and made no sound. She was too ill, too numb to speak. Indifferently she allowed Chaim and Basheh to help her into the house.

Under the bright light of the big kerosene lamp, Mama awoke with a start: was she now reduced to charity?

After supper Sosie sat beneath the lamp doing her homework. She had to write an essay on a subject set by Fräulein. It was "Rain". She asked me what she should say. "Say that rain is a wondrous thing," I advised. "Sometimes it may happen that we stretch out our hands and find rain falling on one but not on the other. This must happen when we stand under the edge of a cloud, for rain does not fall all over the world at the same time." I felt pleased with my own discovery, which had come to me in a flash, though had I dared, I would have added that rain was a thing by which God mocked His victims after a fire.

# 21

## *My Sanctuaries*

If Father actually accepted the evidence of his innocence and lived for some three years in peace with himself and with us, that peace turned out to have been merely a truce with his own conscience. The calamity of his impoverishment was God's unsparing punishment and proved that he had committed a mortal sin. Again he raged against himself for the deed and against Mama and me for whose sake he had done it.

I recall how on the morning after Father received the final order to quit the concession, when I greeted him with "Good morning, Tatte," he hissed:

"Beggar-boy in blond curls and velvet suits, get out of my sight!"

But his bitterest taunts were aimed at Mama, and I prayed to God to let me get even with him.

When things at home were particularly tough for us two, we ran for shelter to Bobbe's, pretending to be needed to help with the shop. There, even in the hardest of times, I was given some soup or a potato dipped in herring brine.

Bobbe's was more than a shelter: it was a place of sanctuary. What made it so were the walls of the little brick building and the dwellers within these walls. It had been Bobbe's dowry upon her marriage to Zeide in 1866. It was ancient because it resisted the fires which destroyed the surrounding timber houses every few years, comforting and ever open to those in need.

I saw Bobbe as the sanctuary priestess who, single-handedly, enforced safety since Father would not dare question our pilgrimages to her establishment, let alone enter and check. Here, threats, shouts and commands were forbidden to anybody but Bobbe herself.

The power behind Bobbe's throne was her last unmarried daughter Bashke, called "Bashke der Bobbe's" to distinguish her from my sister, who was "Basheh Feigl's". She was Mama's younger sister and at 22 already counted as an old maid. But for all that, she was the unchallenged second-in-command of the establishment – directing the shop, dealing with the tax collectors, and travelling to the city to do the buying.

Bashke was more like her beautiful sister Feine – the aunt who had given me my toy violin – than like Mama. She had a healthy appetite for life, laughed easily, and was ever interested in people and full of curiosity about their virtues and vices alike. She had many friends among the Gentile girl customers of her own age. She loved me and was unstintingly proud of me, and I loved her for it, especially for her disparagement of Father and Chaim as dry sticks. Just to be near her lent me a measure of her self-confidence and strength.

It was easy and natural for me to take my troubles to Bashke, but I would never take them to Mama, who was too fragile. From as far back into my childhood as I recall, I was obsessed with the need to protect her. Mama was diffident, tearful, ineffectual, unable to argue even in self-defence – in a nutshell, to communicate at all.

The solace and protection that Mama and I found at Bobbe's sanctuary were largely due to Bashke's merit. But Yeilke, too, helped make us feel welcome.

Bobbe had always complained against everything and everybody, though one suspected that she intended only to ward off the evil eye. But she did feel unjustly punished by the burden of Yeilke, her weak-minded son who had spent each day of his forty years standing on the same spot in front of the glass door that led into the shop – never saying more than a word or two at a time. He watched the same water pump in the centre of the Market as long as there was daylight. At dusk he crossed the one yard between the door and the table for his dish of soup and bread or potatoes. He never went to synagogue. The local experts who knew about such things could not agree about his case. Some said Yeilke was a mongol; some said he was just a common idiot; and Wolf the

Atheist held Yeilke to be as bright as any of them, maybe brighter, but hiding behind his simpleton's appearance to avoid house work and the taunts of the Market Place. Having been privileged to watch Yeilke since my infancy, I never saw any evidence that he was unable to understand what was going on. When Bashke was too busy or too tired to lug water from the pump, my Uncle Yeilke shouldered the yoke with the two wooden buckets as skilfully as anybody and negotiated the return without spilling a drop. "He's good at this one thing," said Bobbe. "And may well be as good as we are at a lot more things," I thought. I also could not decide whether to be pleased or insulted that Yeilke singled me out as most worthy of his affection. Sometimes he actually talked to me about his distrust of people.

My visits to Bobbe's helped me escape the wrath of my father, but I still needed shelter against the fear of God's wrath which held my home in its grip, and relief from the gloom generated by Mama's intermittent fever and Father's ceaseless scoldings for my neglect of the study of the Torah.

This I found with Motl, son of Diodie the oil-presser, and his atheist uncle Wolf. I sought him out to share my mutinous feelings at Father's unfairness. Reb Lippe's cheder stood sealed, with the German eagle embossed in red wax. The long battle of wits between Lippe and Schmalzgesicht had ended: the Holy Law was defeated by the Prussian Law, and its volumes lay shamefaced on the long table in the middle of the desolate room. Motl recalled how I had climbed on his back to peep through the window and had seen the abandoned Gemorehs lying open as we had left them on the night of the raid. I could not help thinking that the defeat of the Jewish God in his battle with the German Kaiser served Him right: He should not have destroyed our hut and should not have made Mother ill, "the God of Victories!"

Motl agreed enthusiastically, giving simple, conclusive evidence: "Look at Sirota and Abramek. They eat pork like Gentiles and never go to shul. They work for the Germans and they shave their beards. Aren't they healthy? Haven't they got the best horses in town and more money than we do?" To hear Motl speak like this both terrified and thrilled me. It was like pilfering ripe plums from a high-fenced, guarded orchard.

Motl was only eleven, but his uncle had had his influence over him. My admiration for him was reciprocated, and we soon became so inseparable that people called us David and Jonathan.

Motl was in many ways more like a Gentile boy than a Jew. His father, Diodie, was the nearest to a goy that a Jew could be. He owned his vegetable gardens, berry patches and orchard, and these he cultivated with such magic expertise that Gentiles came from far and wide to consult him on soil preparation, crop rotation, irrigation, frost protection and even grafting.

As well as being Botchki's farming wizard, Diodie was an important member of the township's linseed oil extracting trade. His plant had three hand-operated mills with great wooden wheels turning metal rollers to grind linseed into powder, and a gigantic contraption called the press to extract the oil from it.

The press, which since the German occupation had acquired an architecture, history and personality of its own, in fact consisted of two parts: the press proper, called the "female", and the huge wooden hammer called the "male". The press was a primitive structure of about twenty by thirty feet across and about seven feet high, made up of logs and hardwood crossbeams above a box containing the linseed powder, beneath which stood a deep tray to receive the oil. The hammer head was a half-ton tree trunk, some five feet in diameter, held horizontal by a long pole, the "handle", hooked to the centre beam. Two muscular men swung the hammer with increasing force against protruding wedges deep into the interior of the contraption to extract the precious oil.

The customers sometimes received their pay for seed and labour in cash, but more often in kind – a quarter of the oil yield and the entire residual cake, used as cattle fodder. Constant association with their peasant customers rendered the oil pressers "coarse" and "peasanty", according to Botchki's fancier Jews, but for me it was an escape from my God-fearing cage of a home.

Because the oil press was now verboten, the work had to be carried out in secret, usually in the early hours of the morning. Schmalzgesicht had put a seal on each of the three mills: he deftly tied a spoke to the sidebar of the wooden tank under the rollers, and then joined the rope ends with the wax seal. Deftly, too, the oil presser loosened the bar from its joints each night, lacing it back in position each morning. Whirling the embossed Prussian eagles in dizzy circles, the great wooden wheels turned silently round their greased axles. It was not easy to run the press clandestinely – its great hammer boomed – but Diodie's wife, Gita, had doctored it with a heavy padding of rags, blankets and feather pillows. The work had become harder, the yield of oil lower, but it was still worthwhile. The press was Diodie's livelihood while for the peasants linseed oil was as important as was olive oil in sunnier lands: linseed oil made the potatoes palatable, and linseed cakes fattened what cattle remained.

For his immunity to Schmalzgeischt's periodic raids on the oil presses, Diodie had the David and Jonathan Intelligence Service to thank. The two of us recruited our friends, taught them our secret signals, and deployed them at night at strategic points. Whenever Schmalzgesicht or one of his informers was spotted, a coded message would be whistled down the dark street and bring the press to a standstill. This gave Diodie time to replace the beams and sidebars under seal and empty the tanks of powdered seed. Then, hiding the bags of linseed under their straw mattresses, Diodie and his family went to sleep on top of them, while their frightened customers escaped through the back door into the stable or ran into the fields.

While waiting for seed to be milled, the peasant folk amused themselves hugely, which they did much more successfully than the Jewish villagers. They set a carafe of home-made vodka on the table and sang the sad, high-pitched songs of the Byelorussian field workers. Sometimes, when a good deal of vodka had been consumed, there was horseplay. The men would lift a screaming girl into one of the large wooden troughs which stood in the room to receive the ground seed from the tanks. Covering her with another trough, they paraded her round the house in triumph, rocking and buffeting her until she was black and blue or until her torturers were exhausted. Frequently, the younger folk made off in pairs to seek the dark seclusion of stable or orchard.

In the shade of the thatched tent in the centre of the orchard where Motl and I kept watch for pilferers, I first read the precious volumes lent by his uncle, the Atheist. Wolf was the only Jew in Botchki to receive a newspaper from Byelostok, and he had a library of "atheistic" books. At the age of nine I thus read Yiddish and Hebrew translations of Kipling and Zola, Verne and Spinoza. These books opened exciting new vistas, though I understood little of their contents – indeed, none of Spinoza. Their added thrill lay in that they were forbidden and, like all explorers' paths, risky, for had my father caught me, my life would "not have been worth a broken groschen," to quote him.

At Motl's, too, I learned to pick fruit by climbing to the highest branches, tend a hothouse, prune and gather honey. Here, also, I got to know about animals, birds and plants and the kind of goyim I didn't know existed, indeed a whole world I didn't know existed.

# 22

# *Tisha b'Ov*

My father was worried about my behaviour and the fact that I now no longer benefitted from the cheder. A family council was held to devise a scheme to stop me from mixing with the peasants at the oil presser's, and Zeide offered to instruct me privately. I submitted without protest, and henceforth spent every available hour in the old synagogue. I was told to consider myself the luckiest boy in Botchki, since no other boy had such an erudite grandfather to instruct him while the cheder was sealed.

Zeide and I spent afternoons and evenings within the crumbling old brick walls of the House of God. Here grandfather and I were on our own, except for the brief period of evening prayers. Zeide was a kindly and understanding teacher; he gave me full credit when I deserved it and was sympathetic rather than angry when I failed to grasp a difficult text. I had already learned to ask frank and searching questions that habitually centred on the subjects of guilt and punishment, free will and the creation. The age-old plaint, "a righteous man yet cometh upon evil days, whilst the evil man findeth good days", was a source of perplexity to me, and I resisted Zeide's every attempt to justify it. I seized upon every contradiction in the texts, arguing, for example, that if Providence preordained the actions of man, the entire edifice of reward and punishment upon which everyday Judaism is based had to be either illogical or unfair.

My magnanimous Zeide reasoned with me patiently and at length, but when I asked diffidently who created God, I received the same reply as I had once in Reb Alter's cheder – a smack in the face.

My grandfather's main interest in the holy texts was that of the jurist, the debater, and the dialectician – *Halacha*. I too found pleasure in speculative reasoning, but I was really absorbed only when we came upon those passages in which Zeide showed little interest – Talmudic lore and history – *Haggada*.

I was already at odds with God, but our religious and communal observance – our rituals, fasts and festivals, joyous and sorrowful alike – captivated me. I felt the same joy as the God-fearing on Simchas Torah, Chanukah or Purim, but also the same awe and sorrow as they did on Yom Kippur and Tisha-b'Ov. In fact, I was more fascinated by the sad occasions than by the happy ones. The prostrations, breastbeating, and sobbing that characterised the Fast of the Destruction were powerful drama, fearsome and frightening, but also exciting.

I awaited the Ninth of Av, the anniversary of the destruction of both temples, even more impatiently than the joyous occasions – the Feast of Tabernacles, the rejoicing of the Law, or Passover. The fast did not worry me, for I was used to fasting even on ordinary days, and Tisha-b'Ov was a day fraught with drama.

On the evening of the eighth of Av, after partaking of bread sprinkled with ashes to commemorate the Destruction of Jerusalem, the community gathered in the two synagogues to hear the Lamentations of Jeremiah. The women's gallery was as crowded as on Yom Kippur, for the ninth of Av was a day of tears. Few of the women could read, but the less they understood, the more they wept – perhaps not so much for the destruction of a strange temple in a faraway past as for their personal grief: a sick child, a dying relative or simply hunger. The common women gathered in little flocks round the more learned ones and laboriously repeated after them in Hebrew:

> How doth the city sit solitary ...
> How is she become as a widow! ...
> She weepeth sore in the night, and her tears *are* on her
>     cheeks: ...
> Judah is gone into captivity because of affliction, ...
> The ways of Zion do mourn, ...
> And from the daughter of Zion all her beauty is departed: ...
> mine eye, mine eye runneth down with water, ...
> The Lord was as an enemy: he hath swallowed up Israel, ...

The elders of the daughter of Zion sit upon the ground, *and*
keep silence: they have cast up dust upon their heads;
they have girded themselves with sackcloth: the virgins of
Jerusalem hang down their heads to the ground.

For once text and reality were as one. The daughters of Zion
almost extinguished the flames of their candles with their tears. As
for the men, even if they had not all cast dust upon their heads and
girded themselves with sackcloth, they had nevertheless shed every
mark of pride on entering the house of God. They came in the
poorest of their clothes, in their socks, to testify their mourning
and contrition. They sat on overturned prayer stands, leaving the
benches unoccupied, throughout the night and most of the next
day; no dialectical texts were permitted to intrude upon the mourning on Tisha-b'Ov. Zeide had sprinkled ashes on his forehead and
left arm and on the bread of his last meal on the eighth of Av, and
put a stone in place of the pillow on his bed. That day Zeide
confined my instruction exclusively to pages recounting the story
of the Destruction. The tales of Roman emperors, of their governors in Judea, of deeds of Jewish heroes, and of the siege and
storming of Jerusalem held me spellbound.

We children stamped even the most fateful days with our
exuberance. Tisha-b'Ov, for instance, we dubbed "Titchke-Bob" or
"beanpole," and we nicknamed its fast "Shishke-b'Ov", or the
Burrs of Av, to mark the Battle of the Burrs which we fought on
that black day. All the boys between six and sixteen, except for
good, over-obedient "Mama's boys", slunk away from the synagogue sometime during the chanting of the *Kinoth*, the Lamentations, and ran to the weed patch by the old burial ground.

There we organised ourselves into two camps, Roman legionaries and Jewish patriots, to enact the Battle of Temple Mount,
which we impiously called the Shishke Battle and fought with
compressed balls of the burrs that were always in abundant supply
during the month of Av. Although I was mostly on the losing
Jewish side, I fought like one of my forefathers on that fateful day,
"falling on my sword" rather than surrendering, so that by battle's
end I needed hours to remove the enemy burr-balls from my hair
and clothes, and the skin on my hands, legs and face was bleeding
and scratched.

During our battle, the adults looked the other way. They did not punish us young warriors for sacrilege, preferring to see our Battle of the Burrs as sharing our elders' pain in marking the day.

# 23

## Pooza's Passing

A month after the fire Mama was still feverish and bedridden in our new quarters – a ramshackle place between the Catholic Church and the old Jewish cemetery. Now, my father moved heaven and earth to save her: he converted his illicit stock into money and brought in a doctor all the way from Byelostok. Shaking his head gravely, that worthy Russian examined her, adjusted his pince-nez, and gave his verdict, with melodious, almost caressing gentleness: "It would be best to operate, but as you cannot find the money or she the strength for treatment in the city, we shall have to put our trust in God. She must have good nourishment, good nursing care and, above all, no worry. The illness comes from the bad bread and lack of fat. You people in the villages live like starved pigs. It's disgusting."

After writing out his prescription, he washed his hands in a basin of hot water that my father held out for him.

There was a steady commotion at the door. Half the town, Jews and Gentiles, were besieging our house for a chance to see the doctor. In a short hour the doctor had examined a score of men, women and children with complaints ranging from headaches to cancer of the throat, filled his pockets with mark and half-mark coins, and was driven off in his droshky.

The doctor's visit changed the household and made us all walk on tiptoe, as it were, including our father himself. His rebukes to the children were now softer and mostly meant to enforce considerate behaviour towards Mama. He went to see Marcinova, our onetime laundress, and begged her to take over the care of our mother. "I can't pay you more than a pittance right now," he told the tiny Polish woman, the one who had fought off the looters and saved Bobbe's cow for her, "but with God's help I'll pay you soon."

"Pay? shmay!" she snapped at him. "I'm going to save your poor Feigl, my poor Feigl" – she switched into the Yiddish for "little bird" – "if it kills me." In she moved to the rescue, nursing Mama day and night. Herself destitute, she would rush to the aid of others, sometimes not quite as distressed as she was herself. Marcinova's devotion transformed our gloomy dwelling into the semblance of a home, and by spoonfeeding her – often with soups smuggled in from her own unkosher kitchen and eggs she had begged from her Polish neighbours – she got Mama back on her feet.

My sister Basheh had taken on the full burden of the household on the day after the fire, never taking a break, like an ox on the threshing floor, I thought. But Chaim would not interrupt "God's chores" of his religious training to give a hand at home and delegated the hardest and most unpleasant tasks to me: shouldering the two heavy water-buckets on the wooden yoke all the way from the pump, emptying the slops, chopping wood, greasing the cart, and one task I did not object to, feeding and caring for Pooza.

Pooza was my particular ward. Indeed, she owed her life to me. In the days of Starosielo Street when she was just a helpless calf, Father meant to sell her to Tanhum the butcher, since he thought that his wife and children had prior claim to her mother's milk. My tears and screams raised the roof, but got me nowhere.

When Tanhum arrived to take possession, he found Pooza gone from the cowshed. So was I. The butcher spat out angrily, slung his rope around his waist again, and left.

For two days and nights we hid in the woods near Andreyanki. I filled my stomach with acorns and blackberries and Pooza filled hers with grass. On the third day a peasant picked us up in his cart; I was exhausted and violently bilious. Pooza was not much better, and she followed the cart with docility, indifferent to the rousing welcome she and her saviour received as the little procession wound its way down River Street to Market Square. I was ill enough to have my punishment deferred, and for Pooza the escapade, having weaned her, ended in total reprieve.

Henceforth Pooza followed me faithfully wherever I led her.

After the Germans confiscated her mother, Pooza had become

our sole provider. In the winter I spent every free moment in the cowshed – spreading the floor with fresh straw several times a day, mixing Pooza's fodder, and fetching her water warmed in the oven. Banned from my mother's bedside, bullied by my brother, and constantly chastised by Father, I lingered over Pooza much longer than was necessary. From her large brown eyes effused the warmth I missed at home. Lovingly I stroked her brick-red, silky coat. Whenever I felt a lump rising in my throat, I would run to Pooza, and there in the darkness of her shed find relief in tears.

In the summer I rose to the sound of the shepherd's horn and took Pooza to join the herd. Barefoot in the chilly dew of the meadows, I would saunter after her, imitating her antics and giving myself over to joy as fully and carelessly as my charge. Each evening I went to meet her as she came back with the herd.

The common pasture land was the poorest in the region, since the rich meadows belonged to neighbouring landowners. During holidays from the Zwangsschule I would take her to the woods, to distant clearings known only to me. There Pooza grazed the rich grassland at her ease, while I lay on my back, face to the sun, singing whole chapters from the Song of Songs to my Pooza, to the green pines and to the blue skies; the fields seemed to sing with me.

At such times Reb Lippe's allegorical interpretation of the love song was unconvincing. For him, Thirzah's breasts were not breasts but the teachers Moses and Aaron, and the beloved of the Song no beloved, but the holy Torah. To me, the orchards of Andreyanki were the vineyards of Ein-Gedi; the humble forget-me-nots of the Byelorussian bogs were roses of Sharon and lilies of the valley; and the voice of the wind in the pines and birches, the voice and shape of Shulamith herself. How could the voice of Shulamith, singing in the pine-boughs and humming in the stream, be the drone of the Torah, which issued monotonously from the huddled shape of Reb Lippe, rocking under the kerosene lamp of the cheder?

Whenever cattle theft was talked about, I would spend my nights in the cowshed. Summer thunderstorms and winter blizzards swooped down over the shed like sinister flapping wings. At those times I dreaded that the dead of the cemetery nearby might suddenly rise. What if they knocked on the door of the cowshed? When Wolf and his "atheistic" books denied the existence of the other world and its spectral legions, I was not convinced, least of all during the ungodly midnight hours. I reassured myself by the thought that if the dead avenged themselves on those who doubted their afterlife, surely they would visit Wolf first, and then there would still be time for me to repent.

With Pooza in the cowshed, there was milk for Mama, skimmed milk for us, and butter and cheese to pay for the medicine. But as Mama's illness dragged on, despondency settled down on us more persistently than ever. How often did Father repeat, "If it weren't for the cow, bless her, there would be no way out but from the bridge into the river."

When the gendarmes came to take away Pooza, our household went into hysterics; Mama screamed and fainted and even Pooza, despite the rope lassoed across her great horns, dug her hind feet into the threshold and refused to move. Father kissed the Authority's hands and, pressing a few marks of ransom into them, saved Pooza for a while.

But she did not escape the wrath of God that had descended on our home. One late-summer morning I found Pooza, with bloodshot eyes, lying on the straw breathing heavily, her belly distended and the joints of her legs swollen and soft as jelly.

I ran for Yanchuk, the "knower", who lived way down across the river. I hurt my toes against the cobblestones, tearing a toenail off as I ran, but I did not even know it. With difficulty I panted, "Quickly, father Yanchuk, Pooza is dying!"

Yanchuk did not hurry. With slow deliberation the old wizard collected his herbs and instruments – an awl and a little wooden mallet. But as soon as he saw Pooza, he knew that she was not suffering any flatulent disease, and that knocking holes into her skin wouldn't help.

Yanchuk made a solution of hot linseed oil and a powder that he concocted from a variety of herbs. For three days she would allow only me to give her the mixture. But on the afternoon of the third day, Yanchuk pronounced the dreaded verdict that there was no hope. In a last effort to save her, my father asked several neighbours to help him raise Pooza on her legs. They passed planks under her belly, which had become as hard and round as a drum. Attaching ropes to the planks and slinging them around the beam overhead, they hoisted Pooza until she was suspended in mid-air, groaning pitifully. She stood a moment, then flopped down again, this time on her side, her legs stiffly thrown upward and her eyes glazing over. Yanchuk hobbled away.

The neighbours helped carry the dying cow into the barn. Father went to call Lukas, the Polish "nobleman" who had licked the boots of the Prussians so successfully that he had been appointed purveyor to the Baylsk garrison. Lukas bought dying cattle which he turned into bad meat for the Prussians and good profit for himself. After examining Pooza, the tall, bewhiskered Lukas offered twenty-four marks and the return of the hide, but only if the meat were drained of its blood. He had had too much trouble with carrion already and refused to pay a pfennig unless Pooza's throat were slit before she breathed her last.

In consternation my family and neighbours looked at one another. We knew that the ritual-slaughterer could not lay his sacred knife on an animal in that condition. Unperturbed, Lukas sharpened a long knife on a black slate-stone. The last crimson rays of the sun played with ghastly brilliance upon the steel blade. I could not avert my eyes from it. In my stupor I heard Lukas remonstrate: "Well, Srolke, you had better cut her throat. I am buying meat from you and not a cow. Good healthy cow's meat, as far as I am concerned."

My father's hand shrank back. No Jew, except the shochet, was allowed to slaughter an animal. With an unusually gentle and faltering voice, he turned to me: "You are well learned, my child, and know that none of us may do it. But Mother is ill and needs medicine, and you are not yet bar mitzvah. God will forgive you."

"You must listen to your father," he added.

Wooden hammers pounded in my head; my hands trembled as I tried to press the knife into Pooza's throat and pushed it wide of the mark into her shoulder. Pooza was dead but still warm when my father pressed his boney hand over mine, and the knife deeper into the yielding flesh. The clotting blood crept from the gaping slit like a dark-hued snake. My ears buzzed. When the snake curled through the grass round my bare feet, my strength gave out, and I fell to the ground.

The touch of a beard brushing across my face woke me. I felt my father's lips on my forehead and, looking across the room, I saw that my mother's bed stood empty. Terrified, I looked at

Father with a mute question, as my head began to swim again. My father understood and hastily called across to the kitchen, "Feigl, Feigeleh, come in quickly, the child wants to see you."

Walking slowly as if counting her steps and holding on to the walls, Mama stammered softly, "My good boy. You are better, you are going to get well soon. I could not stay in bed and you so ill. We shall both be well soon, with the mercy of God. The bad times will be gone like an evil dream."

I saw snowflakes falling gently against the double panes of the window, hesitating in the evening air. Bits of coloured wool amid the white cotton and charcoal smiled at me from between the double panes. It was late autumn: I had been in a fever for nearly two months.

# 24

## *How Reb Gershon-Ber Prayed*

The three Gods of Botchki – Jewish, Greek-Orthodox, and Catholic – groaned equally under the heel of the Prussian boot. In the third year of the occupation the cheders still stood sealed; the Orthodox *tserkov* was empty even on Sundays, for their *pop* had fled with the Russians; and in the Catholic *kosciol* Mass was held in the presence of a gendarme. Although the Poles mostly sided with the Prussians out of hatred for the Muscovites, the Germans did not trust them. Russians, Jews, and most Poles regarded Lukas with contempt for accepting the office of burgomaster from the invaders and gloated when he lost an eye while duck shooting in the Nuretz with his German patrons.

The Botchkivites weren't sure whether to gloat or tremble when news of the Treaty of Brest-Litovsk* and of the Russian Revolution began to filter through. Nicholas had had his deserts, they said, and there was every hope that – with the help of God, of course – Wilhelm would get what was coming to him. But then what?

Wolf the Atheist agreed with this analysis of the Revolution, and so did many a non-Jewish veteran of the 1905 Revolution, though they doubted whether the help of God had anything to do with it. As the months passed, the news became ever more bewildering, ever more contradictory. The local politicians – the synagogue *batlonim* or time wasters, who preferred idle speculation to serious study – gathered round the synagogue stove,

---

* A peace agreement between Russia and the Central Powers signed in March 1918. Russia recognised the independence of Poland, Finland, Georgia, the Baltic States and the Ukraine. The Treaty was declared void under the general armistice of 1918.

carving and recarving Europe after their own fancy, getting the English, the Turks, the French and the Bulgarians sadly mixed up in the process. Schmalzgesicht and the gendarmes elsewhere made no secret of their uneasiness but kept the iron rod of discipline over the villages none the less.

When some of the families who had fled into the interior with the retreating Russians in 1915 began to trickle back, we were convinced that things were happening "over there". Among the returning refugees were Rabbi Hannan's wife and children, my old chaver Avremke among them. He had attended a Russian school, for the Bolsheviks had forbidden all religious instruction, cheders included.

When we met during evening prayers at the Old Synagogue, Avremke and I renewed our friendship and pledged to read books together. We had no doubt that Wolf, arch-enemy of God, synagogue and Gemoreh, would supply us with the right books. Since the contraband had to be stored and read in hiding, a third partner, Reuben of the Estate, was admitted into the conspiracy and soon Motl joined us. The foursome was headed by Avremke, who was full of exciting stories of the Russian upheaval.

Reuben was one of the younger children of Reb Gershon-Ber, a highly respected member of the community and a tenant, by long lease, of Botchki's largest farmstead, the Estate, with its eighty acres of potato fields, gardens and orchards. The Estate had once belonged to the princely Sapieha family, for centuries the lords of Botchki. It had passed through the hands of the princes Radziwil and Branicki, but its present owners were reputed to be the Potockis. Jewish Botchki still prided itself on its connection to the "Ger Tsedek" or Righteous Convert to Judaism, Count Valentin Potocki, who was burnt at the stake in Vilno in 1749 for apostasy.

The derelict mansion was three storeys tall, with brick stables and a large pond whose fish had died out long ago, but it still bore evidence of its former glory. The walls were green with moss, and bristly tufts of grass grew in the stonework around the roof. Slime covered the rooms even in the small wing which was inhabited. Crumbly stone walls surrounded the Estate, except where the river formed the natural boundary. To keep the rats out of the inhabited wing was as much as Gershon-Ber's spouse could do. She was a woman laden with more troubles than Job's wife.

The Estate was possessed of sinister mystery. The dark, slippery passages and creaking stairways of the mansion abounded with terrors and were, of course, reputed to be haunted. For us four godless delinquents and our sinful books, the Estate's stables, barns, walled orchards and hidden nooks afforded ideal cover and its very disrepute provided security from prying inquisitors.

Gershon-Ber's burly sons and meek-eyed daughters went about their tasks of ploughing, weeding, threshing and churning with an indifference bred of familiarity to their dismal quarters. Fear, which kept outsiders further from the Estate than fierce watchdogs, had no place in a household where death itself had taken up residence. Gershon-Ber's children carried the germs of death within them, from the eldest giant behind the plough to the grubbiest toddler trailing behind its mother's skirts. Consumption laid them low before they reached thirty, every new death adding another streak of grey to Gershon-Ber's leonine mane. With each burial he was held in greater awe by the congregation.

By virtue of his powerful baritone and tragic fate, Reb Gershon-Ber was always asked to conduct the Days of Awe services in the new synagogue. Fresh from the graveside, he led the prayers with an emotional power that no professional cantor could equal. Thundering out his protests and plaints before a Deity now cruel, now compassionate, but always inspiring awe, Reb Gershon-Ber's mighty voice reverberated around the blue glass dome in the centre of the synagogue roof. "O, behold me, destitute, trembling and terrified in dread of Thee, standing in Thy presence to supplicate Thee ... Accept my prayer as the prayer of a grave, venerable, and righteous person, whose beard is well grown and whose voice is sweet."

Or he chanted the prayer of the holy Rabbi Amnon of Mainz, a person of great merit and much respected in the archbishop's court. According to legend, the archbishop pressed Rabbi Amnon to abjure his faith, and in a moment of weakness the rabbi, in order to evade the prelate's importunity, promised to make his decision within three days. But, smitten by his own conscience for wavering, if only for a moment, he deliberately angered the church dignitary by refusing to come before him at the end of the appointed time. Dragged before the archbishop for punishment, Rabbi Amnon offered to pronounce sentence on himself. He begged that his tongue, which had slighted the faith, be cut off. His antagonist, though, saw fit to leave him his tongue but have his feet cut off for failing to bring him when summoned. Shortly after this – it was on the first day of the New Year – the rabbi asked to be carried to the synagogue, his severed feet by his side, and placed before the Ark. To sanctify the name of the Lord and pray for His pardon, he composed on the spot the prayer recited on Rosh Hashanah throughout the Jewish Diaspora ever since.

Reb Gershon-Ber felt much like Rabbi Amnon when he sobbed out the sanctification before the open Ark, his quavering voice rising and falling on the ebb and tide of his own sorrows. Like every *baal-tefilleh* or prayer leader, Reb Gershon-Ber's task was to demand justice and mercy on behalf of the people who sent him to address the deity for them: "Who shall finish his allotted time and who not: who is to perish by fire and who by water, who by the sword and who by wild beast, who by suffocation and who by the plague . . ."

Each of these blows had struck some member of the congregation: fire (in the barn), water (in the White Hole of the Nurtchik), the sword (in the Czar's army), beasts (torn by wolves), strangulation (a laden sledge turned over in the snow), and the plague (the dreaded consumption). The assembled men sobbed in unison with their interlocutor throughout, and individual worshippers broke out in loud wails whenever the liturgy matched their particular calamity.

And again thundering at his Maker in impassioned protest: "Verily, man's origin is dust . . . his sustenance is obtained at the cost of his life – a fragile potsherd . . . a faded bloom . . . a transient dream."

Reb Gershon's sons' sustenance was indeed obtained at the cost of their lives, and their powerful frames were fragile potsherds in the face of the consumption. As my friend Reuben spat blood from his lungs and bitter vituperation from his heart against God, I shuddered inwardly, but not with fear, for I, too, was now at war with God.

# 25

## *My Brother Was Different*

My brother Chaim and I did not hate each other, we were just competitors. Since we were nearly always famished, we competed much of the time for the best mouthfuls of food, and above all for the skin on top of the boiled milk, the *pliamme*. Mother often favoured him with bigger portions, even over her beloved Diodie, to avoid his screams. To get back at my older brother for nicknaming me *Ferdishe Fisslach*, or "little horse's legs", alluding to my experience under the Cossacks' horses in Pruzhene, I called him more sonorously Chaim Pliamme, turning his favourite titbit into ashes, teasing him more and more often as he got more of Father's approval. My brother was too fussy to be liked by any one very much, and I also suspected him of informing my father of my transgressions – though always truthfully – from the least serious, like missing a *brocheh* or a prayer, to the most serious, like partaking of milk food less than six hours after eating meat. He earned me many hidings this way, but never any favours for himself, for Father regarded him as doing only what any scrupulously observant Jew or *froomer yid* must do. My brother got most of Father's approval but I got most of Mama's favour.

When Chaim started his apprenticeship as ritual slaughterer or *shochet*, and more especially when he had developed the skill to cut the throat of an ox with the ritual knife which he demonstratively honed in front of me, I did turn from mere rival to antagonist. Chaim warned me that God would punish me and that I'd never go to heaven, and I assured him that he'd never go to the other place, but only because there was no such place.

He did, however, much more to punish himself than me,

probably in an effort to reduce the penalties when he got to the next world. To his multiple skills of *shochet, bodek, mohel*, and *baal-tekieh* or shofar blower, he added the most trying and least rewarding vocation of all, that of *baal-krieh* or reader. This skill, for which the text book is called *Tikkun* or "Correction," involves the total memorisation of the Scrolls which are written exclusively in consonants, as well as of the vowels and musical notations that are essential to correct reading but do not appear in the Scrolls; mastering it requires years of dull but sacred work and lifelong refresher exercises for each week's portions. The *Tikkun* was a permanent fixture on Chaim's corner of the table.

For years I had competed with my brother for the top place in the Kossomski-Zhager tribe, so I was happy to see his status dive when he settled for ordination in the auxiliary rather than rabbinical offices. There he had to master only the field of man's behaviour – the mass of religious prohibitions, permissions, and obligations governing a man's life, interpreted by rabbis over the centuries and covered most minutely in such texts as *Chayeh Odom*, or *Life of Man*. These texts became as dog-eared as his *Tikkun*, but he never got near to qualifying for a rabbinical chair.

One day I succeeded in forcing my pious brother to sue for peace. I had watched him through a crack in the door, dusting a greenish powder over his heavy growth of beard, and saw him again half an hour later, as smooth-faced as Basheh. "Are you engaged in magic, or shaving secretly, Chaimke?" I asked innocently. "Either way you risk forfeiting your life, or anyway your livelihood." My usually sullen enemy, suddenly turned sweet brother, shouted: "No, no, no, Dovidke, I did not violate God's prohibition against putting a razor to my hair."

"Then," I retorted, "you're bound straight for the 'other place' for the practice of witchcraft. Your *Tikkun* is no match for that!"

"*Nein*, Diodie, you're not as familiar with the *Chayeh Odom* as your clever head should have made you. I didn't apply a razor, I just used a depilatory powder from the apothecary's. But please, dear, clever brother, don't tell, or I will be laughed out of town."

I let it go at that, knowing that my brother would never call me Ferdishe Fisslach again.

As Chaim's studies progressed, it was he rather than Father who began to dominate life at home. He got up for *slichess* service in the shul long before daybreak, observed all obligatory and elective fasts, and, except for a touch of gluttony, led an exemplary moral life. He burned the family's kerosene at all hours of the night for his study of the *Chayeh Odom* and the drill of the *Tikkun*, and at the approach of the Days of Awe filled the house with his blaring practice on the ram's horn. Neither parent dared object or ask him to go easy on the kerosene, and at times even my scepticism grew a little shaky.

How was my brother able, not just to follow the path of the *Chayeh Odom* himself, but lead others on that path, to abnegate this world – *Olem ha-zeh* – and put all his hopes in the next one – *Olem ha-boh*? Could it not be that he chose the modest life of a synagogue functionary over the rabbinate for the same reasons that made Zeide refuse to accept a "chair" even after earning his ordination? We were never close enough to talk, and so I shall never know. We remained forever on the opposite banks of that dark river *Chayeh Odom*. To Chaim, *Life of Man* was literally what its title claimed: to me, it was rather the Book of the Non-Life of Man.

My life with Chaim was rendered liveable only by my sister Basheh, who liked me as much as she disliked him and approved of me as uncritically as she disapproved his every action. Even though she was older than me, we had always been close and had shared the same childhood games in our rare breaks from household chores or school – hopscotch, square jumping or bowling an old iron barrel band with a stick on the market square, usually around twilight. At the German Zwangsschule, we were even in the same class, but not in cheder, for girls don't go to cheder.

Basheh was even shorter than I and had a small head covered with a mop of tiny curls. She was a deep-feeling soul, easily hurt but as easily pleased, with an occasional flare of hot temper and a trick of turning beet-red in the face whenever crossed – the only point in which she resembled Chaim. She was well liked by the other girls and took every opportunity to show off her admired brother to her *chavertes*, as much to impress them as to please me. This was all the more precious to me since I had few friends among my own classmates, who tended to be jealous of my easy successes in school. In Botchki, where boys and girls mostly went their separate ways, Basheh and I were the exception.

# 26

## *Polonia Restituta*

Nineteen eighteen was the year of Polonia Restituta, a Poland restored after more than a century of Partition. But the Jews of Botchki knew their new masters too well to place great hope in them and their changed order of things. The Russians' lack of compassion for their Jews and the other subjugated peoples of their empire, even their downright persecution of them, was at least partly due to their never having experienced persecution themselves. The Poles, on the other hand, wanted to compensate for over a century of humiliation and oppression under the Muscovites by pitiless Jew-baiting. The Jews watched the appearance of the disorganised and motley Polish legionaries with fear. These legionaries, whose fancy eight-cornered caps attracted self-appointed militiamen from the neighbourhood, began showing their mettle by firing after the orderly detachments of Prussians who were retreating voluntarily.

The Landjägers, harassed in trying to secure a disciplined retreat without looting or fighting, made a right-about turn, re-entered Botchki, chased the new heroes out and resumed control for one symbolic day. The next morning they evacuated once again, this time without any sniping by the legionaries.

Since Schmalzgesicht had gone back to his Bavarian pig farm, Law and Order found themselves vested in the person of one-eyed Lukas; his patriotism, like that of other Polish renegades, knew no bounds. He was more difficult to bribe than the czarist strazhnik, although not quite as invulnerable as Schmalzgesicht. Lukas took large amounts only.

If the news of the 1918 armistice left Botchki's Jews more dazed than enthusiastic, the news from San Remo the previous year had sounded to them like the horn of the Messiah. The Allied Powers had accepted the Balfour Declaration of the British Foreign Secretary, Arthur, 1st Earl of Balfour, recognising the rights of the Jews to a home in Palestine. Men, women, and children flocked into the synagogues to offer the thanksgiving service *Hallel*. Botchki had never before experienced such jubilation. Jews embraced one another, some danced in the streets and many shed tears of joy. I remember my regret that we could not elect a king there and then.

The rabbi and many of the older generation remained cautious, contending that the return to Zion must come as a miracle of God, not as a favour from the Gentiles. But the young "intelligentsia" took charge and, instead of sermons by rabbi and shochet, the service was followed by the speeches of the "moderns" – members of the Hibbat Zion, Lovers of Zion Society. Mordechai the teacher, who instilled into the children of liberal Jews such scraps of secular knowledge – Russian, German, and arithmetic – as their parents dared permit, was the main orator. My brother Chaim, chary of the moderns and their sudden ascent, formed the religious Zionist League, or Misrachi. Not to be outdone, I started the Zion Cubs and recruited my book-reading companions for the committee.

The Zionist heyday was short-lived. When the Jews saw that the Poles had substituted Polish scorpions for czarist *knouts* and Prussian whips without any respect for the Balfour Declaration, and that the Messiah was consequently as far off as ever, they turned their backs on the Zionist upstarts and their rods on the Zion Cubs.

Avremke and I were chastised by our parents, and although Motl and Reuben escaped punishment, the fall of two of their leaders had its effect on the rest of the cubs. We two were further rewarded for our good intentions by our erstwhile disciples, who named us "the flogged cubs".

The German Zwangsschule closed its doors soon after Schmalzgesicht's departure. The Gentiles, who were the first to rebel against the nuisance of primary education, reclaimed their offspring as soon as school ceased to be compulsory and sent them back to their labours in the fields, cowsheds and pigsties. The Jews followed suit on moral rather than practical grounds. The Holy

Law was reclaiming their children back to the fold, and the cheders reopened. The German teacher had beaten a retreat. Fräulein Zack had the grace to assemble the four forms – or what was left of them – and deliver a touching address; she begged us not to forget what we had learned and to keep up the civilised traditions that Germany had planted in us. But then Fräulein was always inclined toward melodrama. A few little girls, who had acted under her direction in the school plays, shed a tear; for the rest, the school was forgotten almost before it closed.

To return to Reb Lippe's jurisdiction after the comparative freedom of my grandfather's tutorship was hard to bear. The stolen hours on the Estate, spent in clandestine reading, had left their mark. I could not make my peace with such texts as, "He who walketh by the way and learneth and interrupteth his learning, saying, 'How beautiful is this tree! How beautiful this fallow field!' is regarded in the Holy Writ as if he had forfeited his life." Unlike the Holy Writ, Heine and Schiller, whom we had studied at the Zwangsschule, regarded the beauty of this world as good in itself; and if my mind remained unresolved, my heart sided with the poets against the rabbis. The return to fourteen hours' unrelieved Talmud study at cheder was the last straw. At the German school we had had our intervals between lessons, our games and gymnastics, our school plays and functions. The evenings with Zeide, too, had become less rigorous as the old man's watchfulness declined with his health, giving me the chance to play truant at the Estate. Now all that was gone.

After Schmalzgesicht sealed the cheder, I had been cited by many a parent as an example of how a good and clever Jewish boy should behave. But a clash on the first day of my return to Reb Lippe completely reversed this judgement.

Reinstated to authority over a score of pupils now less meek than before, Reb Lippe armed himself with a thin, pliable stick with which he proceeded to nudge us into submission. I sat before the large open volume of the Middle Tractate but did not hear him expound on who should be entitled to claim a garment lying on the public highway if two men came upon it simultaneously. My imagination was roaming elsewhere – on the Nuretz, making floats from water reeds, fifteen hundred years and twice as many miles away from the highway that the Babylonian rabbis had in mind.

Prodded out of my day-dreaming, I snapped back, "Let them have a trouser leg each."

I was sorry almost as soon as the words came out, but it was too late. The class was roaring with laughter, bent on increasing the teacher's wrath and my discomfort. When my neighbour hissed "flogged cub", I was driven so reckless by fury that I hit out at him with the holy Gemoreh – a tome over a foot wide and nearly two feet long and weighing as much as a half-bushel of grain. But it slipped from my grasp, overreached its mark, and came down upon the head of Reb Lippe's wife and thence into the slop bucket.

Reb Lippe struck my face viciously with his rod. The sight of blood stunned the cheder into sudden silence.

In the evening I was summoned before Rabbi Hannan, and a vow was elicited from me that I would henceforth be a good, God-fearing boy again. Realising the uselessness of open resistance, I decided that if I could not fight them, I would cheat them.

"Them" included a wide range of the powerful – Reb Lippe, Father, my brother Chaim, the rabbi, the whole town, and God. At evening prayers I stood dutifully before my father, swaying as piously as any worshipper, but my lips moved meaninglessly without uttering a word of the text. As the weeks of my secret sabotage of God and His commandments lengthened into months and no retribution came, my doubts matured into fully-fledged heresy.

# 27

# *The Doctors Were Wrong*

After the German evacuation we moved again, this time into upper New Street – a dozen houses further up from Diodie the oil presser's and, of course, Motl. My parents were loath to make this change because our new quarters, rented from a Polish craftsman named Tadeus Borowski, were a labourer's hut with an earthen floor and bare log walls. But smuggling had become unprofitable, owing to the wild currency devaluations and to the danger of travelling by road, and the hut had an acre of fruit trees.

Orchard renting was a common means of livelihood. A farmer who owned an acre or two of fruit trees or a landowner possessing anything up to thirty acres of orchard seldom bothered to tend his property himself or pick the fruit and sell it in the bigger towns. Furthermore, goyim were always in need of ready cash to see them through the summer until their harvest was threshed. By May they were ready to negotiate a rental with the professional renters, or *sadovniki*, who came to examine the trees in bloom and make their offers. In a good year, with no blight or late frost, the sadovnik could gather enough fruit to pay the rent and keep his family in clothes and food for the rest of the winter. But if the crop was poor, the renter's family had to subsist on fruit till the autumn and starve the rest of the year, unless a relative in America, importuned by heartrending letters, sent money to "bring in the Passover".

The Borowskis were a fine Polish family, outstandingly so in Botchki. Their boys never called "Zhid" after a Jew, and their girls often helped my ailing mother with household tasks. *Pani* – Mistress – Borowska, the mother, was "an angel in human disguise", Mother used to say. "Pity she's only a Gentile, or she would surely have a place in Paradise."

On a winter's day Pani Borowska brought us firewood and sometimes even a loaf of bread or a jar of butter. We could give but little in return except for some matzah at Passover. These the Borowski tribe consumed with as much relish as if it was manna from heaven, saying while munching, "Ah, Zhidzhi son dobri ludji" – The Jews are good people.

Old Pan Borowski was a source of constant wonder and admiration to me. The old man was a natural artist of rare talent. With scarcely a tool to aid him he built the most accurate of scales, sewed the finest boots, carved the prettiest friezes, and, with a piece of charcoal, drew uncannily accurate portraits. The children all inherited one or another of their father's gifts, and the eldest daughter, Helena – a tall, pretty, flaxen-haired girl of eighteen – was famed for leagues around as a seamstress and as the finest singer in the church. As she stood in the choir, her long mane cascading about her shoulders, the peasants whispered that she resembled the Madonna over the altar. On saints' days Helena strode majestically amid the garlanded statues of the saints and the black-and-silver banners of the procession.

Whenever I could escape the drudgery of the house and the tedium of Reb Lippe's cheder, I took refuge in Pan Borowski's workshop. There I found the warmth and freedom I craved. The old man taught me to work with chisel and plane and, on one occasion, made me a gift of a little model cottage. When my father saw it, he angrily threw it into the blazing oven: dutiful Jewish children must not divert their minds from study and prayer with such Gentile frivolities.

Sometimes the Borowskis teased their visitor, offering me slices of spiced ham or aromatic sausage. I recoiled in horror. Despite my free thinking, my aversion to pig's meat was stronger than reason. Everybody laughed, while Helena increased my confusion by hugging me. As soon as I could struggle free, I ran and hid in the stable or the thickest part of the orchard. Still, I soon returned: after the Borowskis, home was unbearable.

On the night of the great rainstorm, my father was out of town and I was doing guard duty in the orchard. I dared not desert my post in the lean-to, having been punished before for forgetting that fruit-thieves staged their worst raids in the worst weather. I lay benumbed and trembling in the water-logged straw. At the sound of approaching steps and in fear of dark threats, my heart raced. Then I heard Helena's whisper as she squatted by my side and chafed my hands and feet and held me close to warm me.

"Are you Shulamith of the Song of Songs?" I asked, disoriented by the sudden relief after my paralysing fear.

"My poor Davidku, you are feverish," she answered, and then, as she tried to disengage her hand from my icy fingers, added, "I must get help; if I don't, you'll be dead of pneumonia by morning."

"No, my Shulamith," I held on to her. "Don't leave me!"

"I'll be back with help," she called out as she rose to run to the house.

A few minutes later, her brother arrived to relieve me, and Pan Borowski carried me to his house. He put me down in front of the fire which Helena had hurriedly started, rubbed me to make me warm again and wrapped me in a bulky eiderdown, or *pereneh*. "Now, my dear boy," he called out with affection, "you must take a mouthful of this Zubrowka vodka to stop the shivers. It's a miraculous medicine against colds, our own Byeloviezh distillation. Look at the bison grass in the bottle."

And so I stayed the night with Pan Borowski and Panienka Helena – a night never to forget and one which made me like girls a lot more and hate goyim a lot less.

Late that summer, typhus, the last and worst of the war's scourges, descended upon sorely-tried Byelorussia. Villages were decimated without a doctor to attend them, or any medicines to save them. For three years the Germans had kept epidemics at bay by extending their rigorous discipline to delousing, vaccination, and isolation. Now, whole households were felled by the disease, the sick ministering to the dying. Lice, the heritage of generations of poverty, carried the disease from battlefield to homestead, from village to village, and waxed fat on the bodies of the sick. Townships like Botchki procured an occasional visit from the Byelsk or Byelostok doctor at outrageous fees.

Returning home from cheder one day, I knew that I was infected. Most of my schoolmates were down with it, several had died, and "Katherine" the grave-digger was so busy digging the graves that he no longer had time to heat the ritual baths on Fridays.

My head felt heavy as lead and dark rings floated before my eyes. To my friends I said almost proudly, "Mark you, I'll be down with the typhus tonight." My feet seemed reluctant to carry me further, but I continued obstinately on my way to Wolf the Atheist's house, which I had decided to visit before I went home.

I found that worthy philosopher sitting bareheaded on his porch.

"Please, Herr Wolf, I am going to be ill a very long time and will not be able to see you. May I have enough books to last me while I am sick?"

Wolf smiled and disappeared into the house. Later he came out carrying two fat volumes – the *Mysteries of Paris* and *Captain Grant*. By the time I reached home, I was almost crawling.

I remember someone forcing a thermometer between my lips; my teeth felt like stumps of wood and my limbs as if they did not belong to me. The next thing I remember, though that must have been days later, is jumping out of bed and making for the fire. Despite a temperature of $105°$, I was shaking violently with cold and trying to jump into the oven.

There was a doctor in the house, no, two doctors, gravely shaking their heads at each other, although I could not hear what they were saying, for the fever had made me deaf. And the rabbi was there. Tall, concerned and comforting.

I was carried back into bed and tied with towels to the bedposts. I still struggled. Rabbi Hannan bent down to soothe me, and as he stooped, I saw a yellow pencil in his waistcoat pocket. I wanted to ask for it but the words refused to come. A shudder ran down my spine, then a tremendous heat descended upon me and I was falling deeper and deeper into a blazing pit. Above me, around me, below me, yellow pencils were shooting like sheaves of arrows.

Father sold the horse and Mama pawned her fob watch to pay for a consultation with the Byelsk doctor. When he diagnosed meningitis and scolded my parents for wasting their last zlotys, Mama sold our garden to pay a specialist from Byelostok for a second opinion. The two doctors agreed I had not one chance in a thousand of recovering. Through the haze I felt wrapped in, I heard my father hissing at Mama: "And now we can all starve and freeze. There won't be any vegetables or potatoes to eat or the remnants of the timber yard to cook with. You are a bad woman!" He kicked out at her with his heavy boot and left, as she fell on to my bed and lay next to me through the night.

At some point in my crisis, I was measured for my grave, but only as a trick to cheat death. A beadle cut a length of rope corresponding to my height and proceeded to measure the distance between my bed and the spot where the next Jew to pass away would be buried. The pious geometer measured off over 3300 rope lengths, which was about right for the three miles separating me from my grave. Whether it was this ruse, the doctors' toils, or the intercession of our ancestors, may be debated; that a miracle happened is unquestionable.

After lying speechless and unconscious for four days and nights, I motioned to my mother to come near me and whispered, "I have come back and I'll be good a-g-a-i-n." Then I collapsed and slept a very long time.

Two weeks passed. One morning I awoke to find nobody at home. A gnawing hunger tore at my insides; I saw a crust of bread on the table at the far end of the room. Enveloping myself in the pereneh with which I was covered, I wobbled toward the crust and devoured it practically without chewing, as my jaws were too weak. I knew I had to make the journey back to bed quickly: the damp floor felt chilly beneath my feet, but try as I might I could not move one leg in front of the other. I pulled the pereneh tighter around me and lay down where I stood.

During my convalescence, I was unable to overcome the memory of my father's kick and my guilt for robbing the family of its food and fuel. I was sure that every time my face was turned, my father and my siblings were accusing me of taking the food out of their mouths. For me, the sale of the garden was a raw wound, an amputation. From the days when Father was a successful lumber merchant, the garden had held several triangular stacks of finished pine boards perhaps eight feet high, in which I found hiding places – to avoid my Father's wrath, to escape from unfriendly *shkotzim*, or to play truant from cheder. When I was about six, I played in the stacks with my friends and raced them up and down the sides; later, I used them as a clandestine reading room. I had great fun peeking through the boards, seeing but unseen, at boys sneaking through our garden and showing myself when they started pinching our carrots or radishes.

A special mortification to me was that Mama sold her garden to Old Tanne, the neighbour whom she had once caught stealing our vegetables at daybreak. The encounter had made her feel so terrible that she ran away from him, stumbling as she ran, as though she were the thief. "I suspect your mother of selling the garden cheap," Father kept scolding, "to compensate the thief for catching him. And who shall compensate us for going hungry and shivering? Just ask her!"

But for once God did not permit the evildoer to have it good and the righteous man to have it bad. Tanne developed *blinde kishke* – "blind bowel", or just plain appendicitis. Being a miser, he would not bring a doctor from the city and turned instead to Yanchuk the Knower for help. Yanchuk held that the best cure for twisted kishke was to untwist it in the roughest possible ride in the roughest available farm-wagon. "Get a plucky driver for the fastest horse and cart," he ordered Tanne's wife, "and have Tanne taken for a fast ride along the cobbles as far as your Jewish burial ground – three miles should do it."

Tanne's wife hired the wildest driver in Botchki, Abtchug's horse-thieving boy, and a mad-eyed horse and empty wagon, with only the bottom board and the two ladder-shaped sides left in place for the roping in of its patient, and ordered the boy to give the horse all the whip he could.

Abtchug's son went one better and supplemented the whip with a secret little bag of ground black pepper placed high under the horse's tail. The whole town turned out to watch. About five minutes from the start, the runaway beast threw the driver clean out, smashed the wagon to bits and broke several of the patient's ribs. However, the appendicitis did respond to the cure.

That I had no relapse, Mama attributed to her dead relatives and rabbinical ancestors who surely had intervened on my behalf before Him whose name one is not even worthy to mention. But despite my honestly meant promise to be good, I remained as far from God as ever.

# 28

## *Sixth Spoon Arrives*

For eleven years after bringing me into the world, Mama bore no children. It was she, therefore, who was the most surprised by the threat of another child growing within her, and, fearing my father's wrath, she kept her condition secret from him till it could no longer be hidden. Even then the news was not disclosed to us children, and all I knew was that the gloom hung more thickly over my home than ever before and that my father's morose silences deepened with each day. His impatience with us grew into exasperation, and his reproachful glances at Mama seemed to scowl, "A sixth spoon to fill from an already empty pot."

My mother continued with her tasks till the last moment, when she sank down upon the low wooden bed that I had helped her to fill with fresh straw the day before. We were alone in the house.

Calling me to her side, Mama put her arms round me and covered my face with her tears and kisses. Taken aback by such a show of affection, I held myself stiffly aloof, but could not account for it. When she begged me to run to Bobbe and tell her that "Mother is getting her pains," I realised the portent of her words. I felt a thrill that I was going to witness my little brother or sister arrive into the world. I hoped it would be a brother. Although I no longer believed that the soul took a material form such as a blue flame, I was still fascinated by birth and death.

But after I delivered my message, Bobbe made me stay at her house while she hurried to summon Meite the midwife, the very one who had predicted a miserable life for me the night she was summoned in a blizzard to help in my delivery.

On my return home the next morning, I was shown my new

little brother, puffy and scarlet, in the hollow of a cushion at Mama's side. I hoped to spend a little time with him, but I was hustled out of the house, though not before I caught a glimpse of my father sitting in the far corner of the room. His face was drawn with anxiety, yet it had softened and was almost kind.

My mother was very ill again: puerperal fever and the return of her rheumatism gave her little hope of recovery. As she lay prostrate and speechless, my father once more resorted to the old expedient: he sold his horse for the second time. The dealer led away the tall chestnut nag, but it seemed that no sooner would my father succeed in driving off poverty for a while than doctors' and chemists' fees brought it closer than before.

On the eighth day, Mama lay in one room, desperately struggling for her life, while in the other the *briss*, circumcision, was observed in a pathetic, almost funereal spirit. Anxious relatives prayed in hushed voices and congratulated my father in whispers as they tiptoed on the earthen floor, which Basheh had sprinkled with fresh yellow sand for the occasion.

Mama awoke from her coma when the congregation welcomed the prophet Elijah – invariably present wherever a Jewish boy is brought into the Covenant of Abraham: "Be welcome, Elijah . . . thou messenger of the Covenant! Lo! Thine is before thee. Do thou stand at my right hand and sustain me."

And the words, familiar and comforting, re-echoing as if from a great distance, gradually brought her back to consciousness. How full of promise were the words that rang through the partition: "Even so as the child hath been initiated into the Covenant, may he be initiated into the Law, into wedlock and into all good deeds."

When the guests, led by her husband and the rabbi, came into her room, they were astonished to find her wide awake and even faintly smiling. "Truly," they said, "a miracle has happened, for indeed we feared that in coming to wish the mother joy, we should not find her among the living."

It was then that Rabbi Hannan revealed that Mama's name had been changed by the family, with his consent, from Feigl to Chayeh-Feigl. This was an ancient way to prevent the Angel of Death from carrying out the verdict, for he dare not destroy a person whose name differed from that of the patient, especially since Chayeh comes from the word meaning life.

My father stood dazed and happy in the midst of it all. He had become reconciled to the baby and glad that the sixth "eater" had come to stay. The child was named Ber, after his own father, Reb Ber, "May his soul rest in peace."

Reduced from my position of Mama's spoiled youngest to that of mere third child, I had reason to resent the interloper, but I did not. My life, though, became more difficult. However severely my father had dealt with me, certain tasks and punishments had been spared me. Now life was one long sequence of beatings and drudgery. For the first time I was made the permanent all-night watchman of the orchard. Every time orchard thieves picked an apple tree clean of its fruit, I was beaten until I could cry no more. When Mama attempted to stand between father and son, my enraged father would make no distinction between us, and to see her thus manhandled infuriated me more than my own hurts. I vowed between clenched teeth to pay him back one day. As my resentment of my father hardened, so my love for my mother grew until it became an obsessional protectiveness.

The nights of terror in the orchard did have their compensations. After hours of anguish, the first hint of dawn with the accompaniment of birdsong followed by the rising sun brought cheer. Barefoot in the morning dew, I searched for the windfall of ripe apples brought down during the night for my breakfast. The rest I collected in large baskets to send away to market. Then I had time to read, and the straw in the tent afforded privacy for me and my books. When I exhausted Wolf's library, I derived as much pleasure from the second and third reading as I had from the first.

After the fruit had been picked that year, we moved again, once more through no fault of our own. Helena, without warning and out of wedlock, was going to have a child and her parents decided, for the sake of discretion, to give her our hut. We moved quietly into the Widow Reisele's "Doll's House", so-called because it was tiny and made of packing-case boards. By the time the fruit harvest was stored away in the loft, and with two beds and little Ber's wicker cradle fastened to a hook in the centre of the ceiling, our table and two stools threatened to fall into the street every time we opened the door. The only space left was on top of the oven. Apart from this, the doll's house was a permanent menace to the township, for it stood in the most crowded part of Market Square and

Israel and Feigl Zhager's wedding

Basheh (*back row, second from left*) and friends

Botchki's fire brigade – without helmets

The mikveh in Botchki and the Nuretz river (picture taken in 1989)

The wooden house of prayer

Portraits of author and his wife by Benn who also lived with the Meller family in Byelostok

The author and his wife, 1942

On top of a mountain in 1983

The author's ninetieth birthday, January 1998

showered sparks from its short chimney onto the thatched roofs of the neighbouring houses.

Reisele had rented out her house for the winter while she stayed with her daughter in Semiatitch, but Reisele was a quarrelsome woman who could not house with her in-laws. One fine afternoon, when Basheh, Mama and I were busy in the loft turning over and airing our store of apples, covering them with straw against the frost, we heard the tinkle of bells as a sledge drew up. Since Father was away in Byelostok with a load of fruit, we came down from the loft to see who had arrived. How great was our astonishment when we saw the sledge laden sky-high with bedsteads, bedding, boxes, pots and pans, on top of which sat Reisele, perched in the glacial majesty of a huge rabbit fur coat. Paying no heed to our stupefaction, she began to unload her belongings and to pile them neatly round little Ber's cradle. When the heap reached the ceiling, she sat down on one of the two stools, blew on her numbed hands, and said, "I have come back."

We had paid the whole winter's rent in advance and had nowhere else to go, so we did not budge. When Father returned, Botchki enjoyed a display of "fireworks", but Reisele out-shouted the lot and refused all appeals and threats.

Rabbi Hannan was summoned to exercise his authority, but when he was confronted with the not entirely passive resistance of Reisele and her admirably conceived invocations to her dead husband and ancestors, he waved his hand, half in despair, half in deprecation, and said, "O, well, let her be."

Henceforth Reisele occupied the top of the oven.

# 29

## *Cherries*

The summer of 1920 was the blackest in the town's history. The Botchkivites often said that if it were not "first for God and next for the *Jedeka*" – the American-Jewish Joint Distribution Committee – they would have succumbed "faster than flies in winter." Most Jews had nothing, not even the hope of a miserable potato harvest such as their peasant neighbours had. Trade was at a standstill, for the roads were infested with all manner of Polish, Byelorussian and other bands; some were guerrillas, some just bandits.

Creatures half human, half beast lurked in our forests, spreading terror over highways and villages. They were either deserters, escaped from the various campaigns, or Russian soldiers who still hid in the woodlands five years after they were cut off from the main body of the retreating army. From time to time they waylaid a passing cart to replenish their stock of food or, if they were desperate, banded together and raided the nearest village. Merchants and peasants, petrified by these grizzled apparitions, seldom offered resistance. The more timid among these forest dwellers refrained from even the casual contact with humans that robbery involved and kept to their subterranean lairs for years on end, living on forest grub, practically forgetting the human language and unaware that the war had ended and the regime had changed.

That summer was ushered in by the bleakest Passover since the Cossack scourge of 1648. Even the meagre supplies of flour, sugar and children's foods provided by the *Jedeka* failed to arrive. For the first time in Botchki's memory the Passover cakes were baked from coarse black rye and tasted like slate. The mead for the Four Goblets of the seder, the Passover supper, tasted of bitter ale.

The festival over, Father went in search of an orchard to rent for the summer, but he had little money and his competitors outbid him. Faced with missing the rental season, he pooled resources with two others as poor as he was – Havele the Usurer and Nisson the Repeater. Havele was a brisk little woman of about eighty who dressed all year round in layers of skirts and petticoats so stiff with grime that they gave off the gleam and sound of corrugated iron. She was perpetually mumbling, either prayers or curses at her own ill luck or at anyone who happened to be about. Her mouth functioned at all hours of the day as if on well-oiled hinges. She was nicknamed Usurer because she lent out her miserable few marks to those even poorer than herself. Her conditions were twenty per cent a month, take it or leave it, and many a poverty-stricken Jewess, waiting for dollars from America that never seemed to come, took it to get through the winter months.

Nisson, on the other hand, seldom prayed and never cursed; he had a yellow beard and a habit of repeating the tail end of his phrases several times over. Listening to conversations between Nisson and Havele, I often came upon priceless rhetoric.

"How many *pood* of fruit'll this cholera of an orchard yield this year, may a fire from heaven burn it?" asked Havele.

"The little orchard should, by a modest estimate, yield eight hundred pood, by a modest estimate it should, by a modest estimate, by a modest, by..." Nisson answered.

"Plague, really?"

"One never knows, though, one never, one. Does one? Hmph?"

Nisson's sentences were funnel-shaped. They started in a broad stately bass and rose in pitch until the rest of the mutilated phrase got lost in the upper regions of his whiskers.

The orchard that the three partners rented belonged to Pan Sendzinski and stood between his park and the village of Starosielo, four miles from Botchki. During the early season, when there was no fruit to sell and little to steal, my father used to send me to take his place. Nisson, who was a lonely widower, and Havele, who would not trust a saint with the money to buy a herring, moved to the orchard soon after the shedding of the blossom. When I went to keep watch over my father's property, I was given a loaf of bread, a little bag of salt and a prayer book, then packed off to Starosielo. In this way the household was rid of two eaters, for I had to fend for myself while the horse grazed in the orchard. When I arrived in Starosielo, I wished I had walked the four miles, since the horse's back was exceedingly lean. Later on, when the first apples ripened, my parents and the other children, including little Ber, followed me to the orchard.

Rumours of a new war came at the end of June. The Poles were losing ground to the Bolsheviks in the battle for Kiev; soon the first retreating Polish soldiers appeared in the village.

The supply of bread from home ceased. I was reduced to eating carrots, radishes, and new potatoes that Nisson and I "found" on our nocturnal expeditions to nearby gardens. On stormy nights kind-hearted *parobki*, serf-like labourers, gave us shelter and shared their scanty suppers of potatoes and curd. Fierce dogs barred all approaches to the prosperous, flower-girt manor of the landowner, Pan Sendzinski. The master had procured the dogs from Poznania; they were well trained and made straight for the intruder's throat. They were sufficient guard against attack, since the parobki, although desperate during the lean months before the harvest and encouraged by the advance of the Red Army, had as yet no firearms.

One evening the roll of guns over the marshes east of Starosielo was unmistakable. After each explosion the older peasants crossed themselves as they stood bent over their scythes in the hayfields, while the pan's family was gripped by fear and feverish activity. Nisson and Havele packed their sacks and, after reassuring me that nobody would hurt a little boy like me, made off for home.

I was left alone in the deserted orchard, in the path of the retreating soldiery.

A heavy rainstorm flooded the orchard up to my ankles. Lying on my bundle of straw, which squelched at my every movement, I was too chilled to feel terror at the dark, lonely night, and too numb to move, even if every tree were picked clean of its fruit. In the morning, as I struggled to build a fire from the wet brushwood, five Polish soldiers in bright blue caps with white eagles leapt over the hedge.

"Ha!" said one, "Who are you and what are you doing here?"

As he looked me up and down, his glance fell on the drenched prayer book, which floated in the corner of the tent.

"Oho, boys, he's a little Jew, the son of a whore. And what may you be reading in your devilish gibberish in this bloody book? Praying for the Bolsheviks, I shouldn't wonder," he added with a good-humoured grin. Turning to his buddies, who were tearing down the thatched tent, he said, "Let's string him up boys. A zhid less is always better than a zhid more. Well, little zhid, you might as well say your prayers before we hang you on this pretty little sugar-pear tree."

I stood, a miserable figure. The rain ran down my torn shirt and drenched shorts. For a while I remained paralysed, unable to bring out a word. Suddenly, however, I found both head and tongue: "If you don't hang me, pan, I know of a place where there are lots of cherries, big, black, ripe cherries."

The mention of ripe cherries piqued the others who, till then, had taken but a passive interest. They looked at one another. "Cherries, Jew? Real ripe cherries? Come on, let's get them."

Splashing their way across the orchard, the soldiers followed me to the cherry grove. The little purple orbs were dripping with rain, like eyes shedding tears. The fruit was too high to be reached even by the rifle butts.

"Climb up and pick a lot of cherries for us Polish soldiers. If you're quick, maybe we won't even hang you," the soldier added with a wink to his comrades.

I didn't wait to be told twice. I scrambled like a squirrel up the thin, swaying trunk. A shower of ripe cherries, some bursting from the rain, came down on the grass. I looked around for a footing to get down. A shot rang out directly under my feet, a bullet whizzed past my left ear and an angry bark reached me from the ground.

"You rotten Bolshevik, you wormy little Jew! So you're cheating a Polish trooper with rotten wormy fruit, are you?"

I looked into the gaping barrel as my executioner took aim again. Beneath me, perhaps fifteen paces to one side, was a hedge and near it a haystack. Without a thought I dived from the top of the cherry tree, arms stretched out before me, into the hay. I raced halfway across the meadow toward the safety of the rye field before they realised what had happened. Another shot sounded behind me, and another, but I was already beyond their reach, zig-zagging on all fours among the hairy, rain-heavy ears.

At home I was received without a blow or a word of reproach, to my surprise. I wondered why my parents looked at me as if they, and not I, were the offenders. With daybreak a fusillade broke over Botchki.

# 30

## Saint Takes Leave

Behind the bolted door we Zhagers lay low on the floor, not daring to breathe aloud. In the street, gun carriages rolled and hooves clattered, shaking the earth as artillery and cavalry thundered past. The Poles were now in headlong retreat. Twice Father climbed through the loft into the cowshed to shush our new cow, while Mother tried desperately to soothe Berele, who, tortured by dysentery, squealed feebly.

For myself, I was distressed by confusion about the Borowska girl, grateful for her goodness and resentful at her having exposed us to mortal danger. Had we stayed on in the hut, tucked away in the farmer's backyard and surrounded by goyim on all sides, we would have been safe even in these times of terror; living in the exposed trap of a packing case on the Jewish side of the market, we might part with our lives at any minute.

"That bellowing cow will be our undoing," my father grumbled, coming down from the loft, entangled in his prayer shawl and the straps of the tefillin. That morning, as throughout most of the troubled summer of 1920, few people went to synagogue to pray in congregation.

My father's prophecy was soon fulfilled: the door shook to the violent thumps of rifle butts. Mama, Berele in her arms, opened it. An officer and an orderly entered the hut.

"Any bread? No? Sure you are not hiding any? Any money, jewellery? You're too poor? You all say the same. We shall see for ourselves."

The officer kicked the bedding on to the floor, and the orderly turned the straw inside out.

"Any milk? We're thirsty," he continued. My father brought down an earthen jug from the loft and poured out the fresh milk into two glass pitchers.

"Oh, no, Jew," the officer said, "You drink first, and if it's poisoned it'll be the worse for you." He roared with laughter at his own forethought and subtle strategy. He was a good man and not uneducated. He sported a gold pince-nez and was polite. He even offered Father a cigarette.

Overwhelmed, Father effused gratitude. *"Ya ne koorashtchi,"* slipped the Byelorussian answer from his lips, "I don't smoke."

The officer's politeness melted away instantly. "Aha, you Jew, you think you are rid of us already. Speak Polish," and then he added, "And, by the way, if you have milk, you must have a cow."

My parents looked at each other in consternation. My father faltered. "Oh, no, the milk is from a neighbour."

Just at that moment a deep bellow shook the partition dividing the living room from the cowshed. The officer rose without a word and kicked the table and pitchers at my father, pinning him to the wall. The rest of us knelt before him, covering his hands and feet with our tears, as the orderly made ready to lead the cow away.

But our luck took a sudden turn. A captain passing by enquired the cause of the disturbance and motioned to his subordinate to leave us poor people alone. He advised us to seek better shelter than our wooden hut. As he was leaving, he whispered "Yehudi!" He too was a Jew.

By noon the Poles had evacuated Botchki. A few stragglers, fallen behind the rear guard, threw away their rifles and sought shelter in the nearest houses, where they changed into any civilian clothes they could lay their hands on.

For two hours Botchki was a no man's land; the advancing Reds proceeded cautiously through the wooded region, where ambuscades threatened at every step. The township was shelled and strafed by machine guns before the first scouts of the Red cavalry galloped down Byelsk Street into Market Square.

Acting on the captain's advice, we joined Zeide and Bobbe and found shelter with them in their potato pit, which ran under the house floor, and was the length of the oven. More than a dozen people, crammed shoulder to shoulder, stood in terror in the foul black pit, afraid a shell would bury us alive. At the sound of crashing doors, Zeide, in pious resignation, ordered us to chant after him, word for word, the prayer before meeting one's maker.

"We are to praise the Lord of all ... we bend the knee and offer worship and thanks before the Supreme King of Kings, the Holy One, blessed be He ... He is our God, there is none else: in truth He is our King, there is none beside Him ..."

We continued with the *Vidui* – the confession of the dying, then with the *Chotonu* – the Hebrew mea culpa – and the *Mi-Maamakim* – the de profundis. A sudden silence, louder than the shelling, descended on Market Square, and the firing stopped. We stayed in the pit till nightfall and offered our thanks to God for accepting our prayers

When we ventured out, we found that the gallanterie shop doors had been battered down and its shelves looted clean. What the retreating soldiers did not carry off they tossed on to the floor and trampled with their heels. Grandfather insisted that it was the will of God to take away our livelihood and spare our lives, but he retired to his bed with a bitter groan and did not cease groaning until the end – for he never rose from his bed again.

Zeide's departure from the Vale of Sorrows was, like his life therein, humble and contrite. The morning after the shelling, he timidly complained that his feet were cold. We placed hot bricks wrapped in old flannel at his soles and sent for the rabbi, since Reb Leibe would surely have portentous words for the community, and possibly even for all Jews, to impart before taking his leave. We brought him his quills to compose his *tzavoe*, but he was too weak to write his last will.

There were few worldly possessions – now fewer than ever – to dispose of. "This brick building, the wooden shed, and all that they contain I bequeath to my spouse and godly companion Soreh-Enie *bass* Reb Yitzhok, whose in all but form they indeed are," he dictated feebly in Hebrew to the scribe, Reb Mendl. Zeide filled most of the parchment with admonishments to the congregation to "pray and repent before the evil days which are still to come upon you". After Rabbi Hannan read the "crossing of the River Yabbock", Reb Leibe breathed his blessing to his children and grandchildren and closed his eyes as if in meditation. Half an hour later the death rattle, faint and brief, set in, and the feather placed under his nostrils did not move.

The tears, hitherto checked in deference to the departing, now burst their dams; I was summoned to the deathbed to join in the mourning. Most prostrated of all were Soreh-Enie and her still unmarried daughter Bashkeh. They rushed about from corner to corner, tearing their hair and sobbing disconsolately, "O, that our crown has been removed from our heads! That such a dear father, husband, and counsellor has gone from us! O, why has Thou done this unto us, Father in Heaven?" The others joined in their lament intermittently. Mother and I sat timidly at the far end of the room, weeping silently.

Not knowing what changes the new regime might bring the next day, the older people thought it best to proceed with the funeral quickly. Moreover, Reb Leibe had been the head of the *Chevrah Kaddishah*, the burial society, whose traditional tasks were to carry out the last offices, allot the burial plots according to the deserts of the dead, and impose the burial levy on the survivors. No levy was to be extracted from his family, and consequently none of the delays usually caused by bargaining relatives occurred. A rich Jew who had died that same week lay uninterred for four days, until his stingy son was brought to heel and paid out the sum of marks assessed.

Bobbe brought out a carefully locked, iron-bound chest in which she had stored for decades the *tachrichim* – the crude, seamless white linens for "after a hundred and twenty years". To resort to communal assistance for the shroud would have been the greatest conceivable disgrace, and Bobbe, a proud and independent housewife, had put away ell after ell of linen in the shroud chest with even greater assiduity than she had put by the fine linen for her daughters' trousseaux. The men from the *Chevrah Kaddishah* laid Reb Leibe on the cleansing board, washed his body, cut his nails, wrapped him in the shrouds, and placed him, feet toward the door, on the mortuary plank, ready for his last journey.

People, many a friendly Gentile among them, gathered in front of the house. Four of the elders of the congregation shouldered the *mittah* – the bier – and proceeded to carry it to the Old Synagogue, followed by the lamenting crowd of mourners. Despite the dangerous times, Reb Leibe was too beloved and esteemed to be interred without a funeral oration or to be conveyed straight to the cemetery by horse and cart. The respects shown him were those usually reserved for a practising rabbi. The elders carried the mittah into the synagogue itself, the cortege circled seven times round the bimeh, and finally the bier was placed on a high table before the open Ark. Rabbi Hannan paid his last tributes to Reb Leibe in an oration on the theme "For shortly before the evil, the righteous man is taken away..."

The evil was almost upon us.

# 31

## Shtoopl Forms a Militia

I woke up to the rumble of horse carts and the shuffling of feet and hoarse shouts. I could not identify them but I somehow associated them in my sleepy mind with the descent of the biblical locust. Even before I came down from the loft to read its meaning on the drawn, frightened faces of my family, I had heard the shouts "To Warsaw! To Warsaw!" in Russian.

The Bolsheviks were advancing through Botchki.

The gloom downstairs was eerie and frightening. Silently, we sat hour upon hour on the loam floor behind shuttered windows and barred doors, lit only by a flickering candle on an overturned bowl. Our silence had the throbbing quality of animal fear compounded by the softer but more powerful one of the *shiveh*, the mourning period. Only once did my father interrupt the ritual quiet. As he fingered the tear on his lapel – the sign of mourning – he mumbled to himself, "Father in Heaven, how can it get worse? And yet, and yet, the rabbi said that it would..." And only once did my mother interrupt her shiveh. Without stopping her flow of slow-rolling tears, she got up to inspect our depleted rations in the hiding places known to her alone. I heard no words, but her bent back said eloquently, "Oh, God, what am I going to feed them? The flesh of my breast?"

Yet there was protection in our very plight, and the thought of it, while it did not resolve the lump in my throat or lighten the gloom in the house, it offered some bittersweet relief. Even looting soldiers, even godless Bolsheviks, even Polish pogromists, would have to pause and retreat upon beholding our family, sitting in stockinged feet, on our low stools of mourning.

Well, the Bolsheviks did not pause or retreat from the shiveh, but neither did they loot the Zhagers, for we had nothing left to loot – neither food nor drink nor valuables nor, most important of all, boots. My father did have a pair of worn felt boots, but these were too small for the smallest of the Red troops. When the soldiers broke into the house – too impatient to wait for us to unbar the door – they reacted in different ways to the gloomy scene around the candle, some laughing, others spitting, and one even crossing himself. But they did not harm us and confined themselves to taking away the small cash savings hidden in a pot, disdaining the food scraps in the others.

In the short span of my memory I had already seen three regular armies and one or two "private" ones passing through Botchki. Nothing about the Red Army resembled either the czar's troops, especially the Cossacks, or the Germans, or even the Poles. There were no columns, no marching music, and no discipline. No two pieces of equipment looked alike, and none of the soldiers wore the same uniform. Almost the entire Bolshevik army was barefoot. The Bolsheviks did not loot but "confiscate", and they did not kill but "liquidate". The confiscations hurt the Jews badly, for what the Poles had not earlier discovered, buried in shallow ground in backyards or even bricked into false walls and chimneys, the Bolsheviks found as if led by divining rods. The liquidations did not touch us except in one instance – the innocent death of the leather merchant Yoshke for "hiding enemy troops". The Bolsheviks found two Polish soldiers in his barn and shot him even though it was obvious that Yoshke neither knew they were there nor could have figured out what to do if he had.

Botchki could not decide whether to feel relieved or frightened about this latest change of regime. True, "it couldn't be any worse" than it had been, but on the other hand – as Shaike the Lamenter kept repeating whether one listened or not – "couldn't it just?" Botchki, or at least its Jews who of course had no fields and no grain, was staring starvation straight in the eyes; there was no trade, no currency, no materials, and also no customers for anything except the one commodity that was completely absent – food. Moreover, the soul fared no better than the stomach: the cheders were closed, one synagogue was already sealed – "for a clubhouse" – someone said. "Perhaps for men and women together," it was whispered in shocked undertones. And I wondered, "together" for what?

Some people also pointed out that if the Poles returned, they might behave differently than when they retreated, but Botchki was too wise to its own history to put much trust in the vanity of hope. And there were those who pointed out that the Bolsheviks would have to let trade start again, and they would even have to stop interfering with religious activities because of world opinion. But Botchki put little hope in that one too, since we figured that our own fate was apart from that of the rest of mankind, and we were sure that we were too isolated to attract either attention or sympathy from outside.

And so the weeks of the Red regime in Botchki passed as if they had only been chapters of a tale rather than weeks out of our township's own living experience. In the village we never took anything to be real unless we had close contact with it: "I don't know you until I have consumed a pood of salt with you," the saying goes. When, at the end of that time, the Bolsheviks retreated even more motley than when they arrived and with hardly a horse cart for transportation, their withdrawal registered with Botchki, or with me, less as their departure than as the imminent return of the Poles. There was no sorrow to see the Bolsheviks go, nor relief – just stark terror of what the next day or night might bring.

The six weeks of Soviet rule had left marks on Botchki, but the village had a way of arching up its stubborn back against the tidal waves of history, absorbing their impact, and then rolling back to its normal state. This miraculous lasting power might be more readily credited to the community's weakness rather than its strength, for only the strong fall hard: Botchki's permanence could not be made insecure, because it was from time immemorial in a state of permanent insecurity. Botchki survived major upheavals, natural catastrophes and wars, but it was far from mindless of their significance. Each of them received a proper historical place – in the ancient cemetery headstones, in the synagogue annals or *pinkassim*, and in Botchki's lore and folk language. The Red interlude would stay in the minds of future generations both by way of the stone – Yoshke's epitaph – and by way of the spoken word – nicknaming the Soviet interlude "Shtoopl's *Memshole*", the regime of the cobbler Shtoopl. The village did not even attempt to evaluate the six-week regime while it lasted, for it was too be-wildering, but it was able to do so, and in leisurely fashion, once it was over. And despite the harder times that followed, its evaluation was clear and unequivocal: Law was law and Order was order, however hard they were when applied by a regime unfriendly to the Jews; nothing wild and unseemly, Botchki was sure, could last long. What kind of a law, then, and what sort of an order could permit a pock-scarred shoemaker – not a real shoemaker but a poor patcher at that, who had never rated anyone's good morning and was as friendless and unfriendly as a wild beast in the forest – to be invested with the emblems of law and order? Yet on the second morning of the Red regime, Shtoopl the shoemaker had started pacing up and down the marketplace with a red armlet on his patched sleeve and a rifle over his crooked shoulder – the Botchki "Peoples' Militia"!

Botchki decided then that the regime was "upside down" and would not last, but it took many months before the phrase "Shtoopl's Regime" was coined. By then the community had stumbled on to the fact that it must have been Shtoopl who had led the Red soldiers to the backyards and chimneys where its food and valuables lay hidden. However, by that time he had already met his end and Botchki never held a grudge against the dead. The idiom that immortalised him was meant less to be bitter than to be funny, less to describe him as evil than to pay a homespun tribute to the proprieties of social order and to affirm that the classless society which Shtoopl symbolised was neither good nor bad, just funny and impossible. I could not quite understand whether it was impossible because it was funny, or the other way around.

# 32

## *After the Miracle on the Vistula*

If the headlong retreat of the Red Army from the gates of Warsaw to the gates of Kiev, with the Poles in hot pursuit, was a miracle, who was to get the credit for it? The Madonna, of course, for she had been the special friend and protectress of Poland for centuries and, indeed, she appeared to the dug-in defenders of Warsaw on several nights of the siege in the summer of 1920.

And the French Army, of course, similarly a special friend and protector of the Poles, rushed to their rescue not for mere love, but to save Paris by saving Warsaw. If the Bolsheviks broke through the last Polish defence line – the Vistula – they would combine forces with the communists of defeated Germany and lay Western Europe wide open to Lenin's World Revolution. The French sent in the brilliant General Maxime Weygand to mount a counter-attack and powerful weapons to secure victory.

The pursuing Polish vanguard, trim and efficient in their smart new uniforms and French equipment, had hardly flashed through Botchki when tales of horror began to filter through. The retreating army had started a new and more frightful practice than anything the Jews had ever heard of – they were taking "hostages" from among the Jewish and Byelorussian communities on their return route. Botchki did not have to wait for the evidence that the hostages were taken less in an attempt to secure good behaviour than as revenge for the Russians' recent defeat.

From the loft of Reisele's hut, I watched a scene that brought to life the direst descriptions of Babylon's outrages over the Jewish captives in the Book of Jeremiah. Overnight Market Square beneath me had been transformed into one great bivouac. Crowded troops squatted shoulder to shoulder around their stacked rifles and smoking campfires. The picturesque scene offered by hundreds of small fires sending their lazy streaks of smoke into the sunshine of the late summer day was frequently and incongruously shattered by the screams of men and women from the houses around the square. After every such disturbance, I would see a band of soldiers coming out with a variety of plunder in their arms or tugging to straighten out their disarrayed trousers while blinking upon their sudden return into the sun.

The peasants who lived on the side streets fared better than the Jews of Market Square, but their squealing pigs, bellowing calves and catching fowl were being driven, dragged, or carried into Market Square from all directions.

At the centre of Market Square, between the fire barn and the water pump, six field kitchens were steaming in homely, reassuring, geometrical pattern. Around noon a shrill whistle tore through the bustling bivouac and an uncanny silence followed. Mess cans in hand, the soldiers stood where the whistle had found them, motionless. Then the gates of the great fire barn were thrown open and some fifty or sixty men were driven forward. They were made to line up in front of the field kitchens – for their dinner, I thought. Some of the men were bearded and clad in the long, black caftans of the Jewish dignitaries from the Chassidic townships across the Bug. Others wore the shirts and riding breeches affected by the *Revcom*, the Bolshevik revolutionary committees. All were held together in a rectangular column by chains, six abreast, and many tried to hold up their manacled hands to shield their eyes from the sun.

"Washing time!" roared a dapper young officer, holding up his sabre. "Wash the dirty curs and wash them well, the grimy Bolsheviks." A soldier walked over to the front of the column of prisoners and snapped out an order. The men, unmanacled but still encumbered by their connecting chains, reacted clumsily, but in a few minutes they all stood naked to the waist – the hairy chests of the older men clashing with the shy whiteness of the younger or weaker ones. The thick water pipes of the six black kitchens jutted out overhead like the arms of gibbets, and behind each kitchen stood a white-aproned army cook, hand poised on water lever.

When the dapper officer gave another blast on his whistle, six scalding jets shot from the six kitchens, directly onto the prisoners. Inhuman screams, groans, and sounds that strangely resembled laughter filled Market Square. Still the orders kept issuing from the dapper officer: "More! More!" and rifle butts continued to prod those prisoners who dodged the path of the scalding streams to get them in position. As each man fell writhing to the ground, he dragged his neighbour into position.

The nightmarish spectacle ceased, and I beheld the whole column of men lying on the wet ground, kicking, squirming, or biting their own hands in agony.

In the afternoon, the army struck camp, and the prisoners, who had been brought to Botchki on foot, left it in one large heap in a deep, canvas-covered truck. Through the Gentile grapevine, the story reached Botchki some days later that the entire column was disposed of in the forest. None of the men were ever seen again, and the more godly among them were mourned by their communities as martyrs, and buried with full rites in absentia.

As for Botchki, it considered itself lucky indeed, for it had escaped a pogrom such as Pinsk and other towns had suffered. Its only victim was Shtoopl. The cobbler was interred in an unmarked grave in the bog along the Byeloviezh Wilderness, but he would not have been given a resting space in hallowed ground anyway. In Botchki, heretics were buried "beyond the fence" and were not considered much of a loss.

Only days later a company from the dreaded Poznan Army of General Haller, intending to kill time rather than plunder seriously, chanced upon Rabbi Hannan as he sat before the open Gemoreh in full praying garb. The Hallerczyki yelled with delight: "Oh, lads, here's a real, life-size rabbi, as holy a Jew as we'll ever find. Oi, tattele, oi, mammele, oi, holy Moses, what a lovely, lovely beard!"

They heard the company bugle blow. Called away in mid-sport, the band had to content themselves with hacking off his long, curly beard with their bayonets.

Later that day, Rabbi Hannan, mutilated beard hidden in a towel, was again disturbed by a violent commotion at his front door. The Hallerczyki had come back. Dropping his prayer shawl and tefillin on the courtroom table and gathering up the skirts of his wide alpaca mantle, he made for the back door and ran through the gardens and hedges until he reached the only safe place he knew – the house of the priest, the ksiondz.

In ordinary times these two earthly representatives of competing gods never exchanged a greeting, smile or word. But the threat of death made Rabbi Hannan throw pride to the winds. When the bald, clean-shaven ksiondz saw the rabbi at his doorstep, he spat and closed the door in his face.

Not so Nasia. The ksiondz's plump, blue-eyed housekeeper – who had had several children without being married to anyone and whose children marvellously resembled her reverend master – took pity on the rabbi. She took hold of his sleeve and led him into her own quarters to hide him.

This act of biblical piety, like that of Ruth, earned the priest's mistress great respect. Mother, who had taught me from infancy that the Gentiles had souls but were merely misled from the right path – a rather courageous view for her to hold – admitted that she loved Nasia now as much as any Jewish woman of the township.

# 33

## A Mother's Heart Knows

The winter following the wars was unexpectedly lenient for us, even somewhat prosperous. By the time the late fruit was ready to be picked, the fury of the returning troops had exhausted itself, and my father, Chaim and I rode to Starosielo by cart and gathered what the soldiery had left on the upper branches. There were five cartloads of Anton, Crimean, and Rapp apples, as yet unripe, that would have to be stored for several months in straw before they could be eaten. Also, in settlement of a pre-war debt, farmer Piotr let my father dig up half an acre of potatoes from his field near the new cemetery.

Our cow gave birth to a strapping white-and-red male calf that was sold to the butcher on the eighth day for forty Polish marks and the return of the skin and the lung and liver, in accordance with custom. After Nitko had finished with the skin in his smelly abode on the forest edge, we had footwear made for the entire family. The lung and liver brought a long-forgotten air of prosperity to our Sabbath table and, as the price of winter apples rose, bread became a staple in our household.

The cheders had now reopened, but there was no rebbe in Botchki to pilot me any further on the Talmudic seas on which Zeide had launched me. Moishe-Aaron, the impoverished "merchant prince" of Botchki who had succeeeded my grandfather as the head of the *Chevrah Kaddishah*, agreed to give Avremke and me private tuition for a fee, but the old man's sight and memory were slowly failing. Rabbi Hannan soon had to send his son Avremke to the Byelostok rabbinical seminary, the *Tachkemoiny*, to receive not only the rabbinical training that would qualify him to sit in the judge's chair of the Botchki Beth Din "after a hundred and twenty years", but also a foundation of secular education. Left with me as his sole disciple, the reputedly pious Moishe-Aaron revealed himself to be almost as much of a free-thinker as Wolf the Atheist. He led me into long, disturbing discussions on predetermination, good and evil, Bible criticism, and the merits of certain agnostics of old, such as Rabbi Elishah ben Avuyah. At first I was all ears, but having plumbed the old man's depths and limits, I began taking the initiative.

Throughout the winter, we spent more time in pseudo-philosophical and exegetic debate than in the proper study of the Talmud. One early spring day, Reb Moishe-Aaron surprised me by closing the Gemoreh – in which we were just then involved in the intricacies of temple tithes – and saying, "You would be wiser to learn to read and write Polish and to study the science of fractions than to spend your time in mastering the arguments of the holy rabbis on the payment of tithes by Jews who have no fields to priests of a temple destroyed two thousand years ago."

With these words the former merchant unlocked his bookcase and took from behind the shelving several slim volumes, an inkpot and quills. That day I received my first Polish lesson and was unceremoniously plunged into the study of fractions and decimals.

Around Passover, Reb Moishe Aaron fell ill with asthmatic bronchitis and did not recover sufficiently to resume teaching me. Father now gave up hope of making something of me and took me into "the business". At eleven years of age I mastered the arts of packing a crate of apples, harnessing a horse, chaining in a cartload of crates, and even bargaining with the shrill stall-holders of the Byelostok market who were my father's customers.

I looked forward to our trips to the city. With loaded cart, my father and I would set out in the morning, travelling all day and night to reach Byelostok at daybreak. There we unchained and unloaded the crates, ripped off the jute-covered padding, and displayed our fruit before a shoving flock of female vendors. The art of selling lay in letting the women get so angry that they began to outbid each other. The best deals occurred when the women came to blows and tore off each other's wigs, provided the seller stayed out of the fracas, showing no apparent interest until an adequate bid had been reached. My value to Father grew as times became harder for the stall-keepers, for then I had to stay with them through most of the day, until they had sold enough to pay us for our crate of fruit. In the meantime my father carried out "commissions": making purchases from the city wholesalers for those Botchki shopkeepers who could not afford the trip to Byelostok themselves. In his newfound dignity as the commission agent, almost a wholesaler himself, Father was of course in competition with Shmuel, and this in turn complicated matters, raising strife in the councils of the synagogue. Shmuel, who secured dozens of commission packages to his already wide person, was more popular than my father.

Bylestok, with its impressive two- and three-storey buildings, its palace and park, its women even wearing hats instead of blanket-like kerchiefs, and most of all its boys and girls marching confidently in neat, brass-buttoned school uniforms and coloured caps with shiny peaks – all these spectacles filled me with a restless yearning for the city and a real school. If only I could persuade my father, the blue uniform of a "Gymnasist," with its shiny buttons and the silver eagle fixed to the cap, might be mine. And how terrific it would be to come home on holidays thus arrayed. I would be like a prince, especially in the heart of dark-eyed, dark-skinned little Hannah, whose father was a horse dealer, if not a horse thief, but whose older sister, Chaya, was nevertheless being courted by Victor – the son of Berl the apothecary – the only man in Botchki with a French name.

During our long nights on the road, travelling back at a trot between the high walls of the forest, I was often able to abstract myself from my physical surroundings. While my father slept fitfully in the straw among the empty crates at the bottom of the cart, with only the creaking of the wooden wheels making any sound in the great stillness, I let the horse amble at its own pace and gave my mind over to my musings. I was transported by my fantasies.

Like a traveller crossing the Equator, I felt I could almost touch the line separating Botchki from the world outside – a line I knew I had to cross if I were not to miss the world altogether. "And soon, by the time I'm bar mitzvah" I swore to myself. My oath came as I squatted bare-bottomed in the frozen snow of the back garden –

we didn't even have outdoor privies – and contemplated a three-quarter moon above me.

As the summer neared its end, my vague yearnings took shape. If my father would not let me go to a real school because that would make a goy of me, I would leave home.

I knew of an earthenware jug hidden under a loose brick far up on top of the oven. In it my mother kept the groschens and coppers she had saved up from her meagre budget against one of those catastrophes, which "please God should never happen", but which she knew would go on happening, irregularly perhaps, but for all that with fatalistic certainty.

Alone in the house one day, I climbed up and counted Mother's hardship fund: there were over fourteen marks in it, all in small coins. Four marks would pay my fare with one of the Hershes to Byelsk, and seven more would get me a rail ticket to the city.

Once I had devised my plan, I found it impossible to sleep at night. My resolution faltered: I was unable to make myself steal Mama's savings. Then, one night, my mind was suddenly made up and I dressed quietly – it was four o'clock.

I negotiated my passage across Basheh's straw sack on the floor, climbed up on the oven, and knotted the coins into my handkerchief. Still crouching on the oven, I made a tiny bundle with a square of linen of my new shoes, my two shirts, half a loaf of bread, and a chunk of cheese. I was confident that fate now favoured me, for if Reisele hadn't been away visiting a daughter in another village, I would not have escaped – since she slept lightly. I felt certain that my supplies and the fourteen marks would take me almost to the end of the world. I climbed up into the loft and let myself out through the shed door. Once in the open air, my last doubts left me, and I felt as though I was being carried away on the early morning breeze.

Barefoot, my bundle slung across a stick over my shoulder in true wayfarer's fashion, I sprinted up Byelsk Street and did not turn my head once until I was safely past the tollgate. The two Hershes were there with their horsecarts, but before they could pounce on me and fight over whose "right" I was, I swung myself with agility over the side of Hersh-Leib's vehicle and out of reach of Hersh-Loaf. I hoped against hope that Hersh-Loaf had not recognised me in the early dawn light and that Hersh-Leib would rather be in league with me than give me away.

I crouched at the bottom of the vehicle, between the two straw sacks that served as the passenger seats. Even after two other passengers mounted and took their places, shielding me further from sight with their voluminous garments and packages, I didn't look up, not even to see who these people were. Dawn was brightening, and still the carts did not move. Suddenly I heard fast, shuffling steps and then my mother's voice crying out in brief, harassed phrases as if short of breath, "Hersh-Leib! Wait, Hersh-Leib! Haven't you seen my child? My Dovid has run away!"

Mama's voice was close to me, almost at my ear, through the rungs of the cart, but before I could think how to get around the new situation, Hersh-Leib's powerful arm had grabbed me by the back of my coat and lifted me into the seat. "So you are running away, are you? So you are the son of Feigl Reb Israel's?" he continued as if he had only that minute identified me. "So you want a good hiding, do you?"

Having delivered himself of this short, playful speech, the giant carter raised his hand as if to make good his promise, but Mama took hold of his sleeve. "Oh, no, don't hurt him, Hersh-Leib! If he comes back home and his father finds out, he will beat him. You had better take him to Byelsk, buy him a ticket, and put him on the train, and with God's help, I'll pay you back, at so much a week, Hersh-Leib. The child has only a few marks. I have been saving them for him ever since I realised how keen he was to go into the wide world."

Mama took me in her arms. We remained silently embraced until Hersh-Leib separated us: "That'll do now. He's not going into the army, is he, so why the lamentations? It's time to go, or we will miss the train."

My mother pulled at her heavy kerchief, covering even more of her face, hunched her thin shoulders still higher, and disappeared swiftly down the hill and into the dissolving mist. As I reached for my handkerchief to wipe Mama's tears off my face I felt a large, heavy coin in my pocket. It was a ten-mark silver piece, like the one I had seen for the first time the day before in Father's money bag. I knew how dangerously my mother had come by it and what a struggle her honest soul must have experienced before she brought herself – for the first time in her life, as I well knew – to remove money from his bag, even to give it to his own son.

I remembered a scene from my early childhood, when I was about three years old. Mother was holding me in one arm and a parcel in the other and was pushing her way through the bushes and raw nettles behind a mud hut at the back of the hekdesh. When she got to the side window of the house of Yudl, the paralysed tailor, whose wife and children were said to be swollen with hunger, she looked around her several times. Then she carefully pushed the decayed window frame open, threw the parcel into the room, and ran into the shelter of the hedge, as if she had committed a crime.

I realised only now the meaning of that incident. "Like father, like daughter," I thought, remembering the rabbi's oration over Zeide's bier.

"I must become a great man, I really must. And when I do, it will be to make my mother proud of me," I said to myself as Hersh-Leib's cart sped me away from Botchki. "But not for my father. I don't love him and I'll never let him be anything more than a servant to my mother."

With these thoughts I fell asleep, as we drove through the awakening forest. The birds twittered merrily, the frogs croaked lustily, and in my sleepy mind I had a last articulate thought: that perhaps even the forest was not deaf that morning.

# 34

## The Soul Trappers

Within hours of my arrival in Byelostok, I found that the city could be cruel to penniless strangers and that my riches would hardly last me a week. Winter was approaching, and I had to secure food and a roof over my head. I went to the rabbinical seminary to find my only friend in the city, Avremke, and to seek his help.

As I wandered along the corridors I was astonished by the large, airy classrooms, the great blackboards on which the teachers had illustrated their lessons, and the high columns and arches of the synagogue hall, where some two hundred boys, thirteen to twenty in age, studied the Talmud texts, each one at his own pace. I saw the white-tiled kitchen and, after my long day without food, the smell of frying fish and boiling cocoa made my head swim.

After a while I located Avremke, who betrayed a shade of displeasure at my visit. I blushed at the thought that I must have appeared a very clumsy figure indeed in such surroundings, what with my country garb, my little linen bundle, and my diminutive size. Avremke merely told me how to find the director and then abruptly disappeared, mumbling that he was behind in his studies.

The director, whom I approached as one would approach the Seat of Heavenly Judgement, was a middle-aged rabbi with a fierce black beard that was contradicted by the mildest of eyes. He laughed good-naturedly at the sight of the tiny pilgrim who had come to seek entry to his temple of knowledge.

"How old are you, boy?"

"In ten months I shall be thirteen."

"And how much do you know?"

"The Three Tractates on Damages, with commentaries, the

Tractate on Betrothals, and more than half of Divorces." And without waiting for further questions, I added, "I have read Spinoza four times, Jules Verne and Victor Hugo once, and have done fractions right to the end of decimals."

Rabbi Pat suppressed a smile: "Your erudition appears to be a little mixed and uneven. It's certainly inadequate to admit you to our preparatory class. Nevertheless ... we might see ... some tutoring perhaps ... How much could your father pay to have you entered as a boarding scholar?"

I recoiled as from the blow of a cudgel. "My father," I said, groping for soft words in which to bring out the hard truth, "my father, well, my father cannot pay anything. He has no money and he does not wish me to have education."

Rabbi Pat was sympathetic but could not help me. He explained, as if I were a grown-up person whose opinion was of importance, that the aid he received for his school from America was diminishing while the expense of running it was increasing with every new enrolment. The college had to feed three hundred boys and retain the finest rabbis and professors as instructors *and* pay them in dollars! He offered to enroll me at half the regular fee, that is if by miracle I passed the entrance examinations, but that would still require my father to pay more than a hundred marks a month. With a sad smile into his fierce beard, Rabbi Pat terminated the interview.

I came out into the street, found a bench in the small triangle of park nearby, and sat down and cried. A stranger came and sat next to me. He was a very tall man with a slight stoop and chiselled features sharply framed by a trim little brown beard that gave him a half-rabbinical, half-aristocratic air. He kept flashing smiles at me, but each time that I tried to fix him with my own eyes, he would turn his face away with a furtive speed which aroused misgivings in me. At last the man spoke up, in a kind but somehow unreassuring voice, asking me where I was from, whether I knew anyone in Byelostok and whether I had been confirmed. To my own surprise, I replied to the stranger's questions without faltering.

"You must come along with me. I know of a place where they will give you a clean, warm bed, white bread even on weekdays, and all the education that your soul is thirsting for." Then, noting the utter disbelief on my face, the stranger explained, "You will learn neither Gemoreh nor commentaries. Instead of this we shall teach you many useful sciences and, of course, the Holy Bible – quite a lot of Holy Bible, to be sure, much more than you have had in Botchki."

My astonishment now gave way to outright suspicion and resentment. I knew full well that the Bible was one and the same everywhere, in Botchki, Byelsk, or in Byelostok, even in Warsaw itself. What exactly was this stranger offering and why? And what did he mean by a "lot of Bible"? Were there not exactly twenty-four books in the Bible? And didn't I know them all, virtually by heart – even the commentaries and the commentaries-upon-commentaries? How was it that neither I, nor Avremke, nor anyone else had ever heard of this marvellous place where they gave out room, food and education all for nothing? Surely there would be a thousand boys like me clamouring for entrance into such a school every day of the week!

The strange man gently took hold of my hand, but although he remained solicitous, he divulged no further details. He did not even say whether the place was a synagogue, a school or something different. "You just come along and have a look for yourself, and I am sure that you will like it, for you seem a most sensible boy for your age and not at all fanatical. Besides, you would not be afraid of another Jew, would you now?"

I followed the stranger through the wonderful gas-lit streets. Although he looked like a gentleman, the man insisted on carrying my parcel in his own delicate hand. When he stopped before a tall iron gate and pulled the bell-pull of a beautiful three-storey grey-stone building, I was once again overcome by fear. I would have bolted, while there was still a chance, but all my worldly belongings were in the little linen bundle to which the man now clung tenaciously. The gate was opened by a well-kempt, pink-faced matron who received me and my benefactor without a word and led the way through a maze of corridors. Two things were odd – she behaved as if we were both expected guests, and she was definitely Gentile!

They conducted me into a large, sumptuous, white room which was fitted with nickel taps and porcelain basins. They gave me a new suit, then advised me to bathe before changing into it. Once alone, I dared not breathe. I couldn't bring myself to turn on the bath tap or to put on the new suit. The coat was too long, and it had black buttons of the same cloth. The buttons! The explanation for the whole puzzle began to dawn on me – they were the same kind of buttons as I had seen on the surplice of the Botchki ksiondz! The stranger soon returned. Although he saw that I had not moved, he showed no surprise.

"Everything will be fine," he said, laying his delicate hand on my head and making me shiver. "You will soon get used to us. We mean only well by you, to help your body and to save your soul. Meanwhile come along and have some supper."

The reference to my soul, though made in clear ordinary Yiddish, was the strangest remark I had ever heard. In Botchki we never saved souls or spoke of saving them: we had our souls and we tried to keep them, but that was all.

I was hungry and, remembering the spikes on top of the gate outside, I also realised that it was probably impossible to run away now. The refectory was even more sumptuous than the bath chamber. Under the crystal chandeliers stood long tables covered with snow-white tablecloths, but the sole guests were two women and a man who looked more like vagrants than scholars. After a meal of fish, sweets, and hot chocolate I was led to a bedroom where my parcel was waiting for me.

I lay on the soft white feather cushions as if I were lying on a bed of thorns. Premonitions, all the more disturbing because they were vague, kept me awake. I waited for the lights to go out and for the people of this strange house to retire. At last, a little after the nearby railroad clock struck midnight, when everything became quiet, I stole through the dark corridors, then down the carpeted stairs until I reached the lofty room on the ground floor. In its centre stood a low platform. "This must be the synagogue hall," I hoped. Through the stained glass windows the moon shimmered in an eerie filter of colours and shapes. I mounted the platform by this strange light and looked at the volumes on the pulpit. What were they? I made out the larger print on the titles and found that they were in various languages. The Yiddish and Hebrew ones were entitled Luke and Mark – strange names! However, at the top of every frontispiece there were the same two words: "New Testament". When my eyes fell on the silver cross adorning the pulpit cover, I turned and fled back to my room. In haste I fastened my package to my belt, and climbed down the drainpipe, hand over hand, as I used to do in the orchards, until I reached the ground. With the ease born of years of tree-climbing, and fortified by stark fear, I negotiated the tall fence and its spike railings, jumped down to the street outside, spat out the ritual three times, and fled toward a poor Jewish section of the city.

I spent the rest of the night on the porch of a synagogue. I never mentioned my brief adventure in the greystone house to anyone.

In Botchki they called the missionaries the "soul trappers". Among all the religious institutions of both small parishes and large municipalities, the missionaries were the only ones able to do things on a large scale. The particular brand whose net I had so narrowly escaped were the Protestant missionaries, said to have benefitted chiefly from the wills of English spinsters. The Protestants had little success in a country that was predominantly Catholic and that had an excess of religious strife already, and they did least well among the Jews. In Botchki they had converted no Catholics, only two Orthodox Byelorussians, and the family of Jessiah the Bootmaker. Jessiah had had himself, his wife, and his children sprinkled with holy water after he was called up for the Portion of Curses, the meanest of all portions of the Scrolls, and was obliged to flee Botchki to escape the wrath of the horse dealers and horse thieves, the most zealous defenders of the Ten Commandments. After a few weeks of good and even luxurious care at the hands of his recruiters, Jessiah was left to fend for himself and lived in misery in the big city, in the warrens of Stevedores' Lane. As Jessiah had no relatives in Botchki, no one sat shiveh for him – the seven days of mourning that were as obligatory after a defection from the faith as they were after a death in the family.

# 35

## I Eat Days

On opening the prayerhouse at daybreak, the *shamess* or beadle found me sobbing and shivering and took me to his quarters in the back to revive me with some hot tea. His advice was that a penniless boy running away from home to look for a free school must seek entrance to either the Byelostok or Navaredok yeshivah. The first was like a hundred other yeshivahs – where *bocherim*, or young men, were prepared for *smicheh*, ordination – it was strictly observant but not fanatical. The other was a case to itself for there were few like it anywhere. It was a *mussar* institution, which meant that it was less concerned with training its disciples as future rabbis than with consecrating them to the selfless service of God. Worldly education did not penetrate either place, but homeless bocherim could sleep on the benches after studies and prayers were over, which was for a couple of hours between midnight and daybreak in the case of Navaredok. What was most important for a starved boy like myself, the beadle pointed out, was the students' privilege of "eating days". The Navaredokers' days were leaner and less regular, since their hosts felt duty-bound to discourage gluttony.

Eating days was the age-old way by which future rabbis managed to keep body and soul together in the long years of preparation. The principal of a yeshivah, or its treasurer, kept two lists, one of needy students and another of Jewish families willing to feed a student of God's law at their table. For every "day" offered to a yeshivah bachelor, the host and his family would earn a small portion of a plot in the Garden of Eden.

In bad times, the students often subsisted on alternate days, and the more devout made a virtue out of necessity, calling their off days elective fasts. The less devout ones analysed and discussed in minute detail the merits and demerits of each donor's "days".

A folk song that the girls of Botchki sang about the hardships of the rabbinical student went:

> What doth life signify,
> My life – what is the meaning of it?
> Eating days and drinking tears.
> And sleeping on a wooden bench.

I called first at the Byelostok yeshivah, but without success. The principal, Rabbi Jacob, judged me too young and altogether too weatherbeaten and clumsy to make a worthy candidate for an Orthodox "chair".

"Come back in two years' time, after which, if your soul still yearns for the Torah, we may accept you, boy," he ruled.

I was wholly unprepared for the scene I came upon in the study house of the yeshivah of Navaredok. Scores of men and boys, smooth-faced to long-bearded, in all manner of garb and headgear, sat, stood around or reclined over their volumes in every conceivable posture. Some swayed rapidly back and forth; others shouted as if tortured; some sang or chanted, gently or at the top of their voices; some contorted their faces and bodies in an ecstasy of pain, while others groaned or sighed resignedly, and some beat their breasts. This was not pandemonium, but proof that the students and devotees were the fervent disciples of the strict moralist Reb Joseph, the founder of Navaredok. They were praying, which they did several times each day and even during certain nights. Only a few hours were set aside for the study of the Talmud, normally the principal part of a yeshivah curriculum. Many of the Navaredokers were deeply involved in the Kabbalah, Jewish mysticism, and appeared unaware of reality.

I was uneasy at the prospect of joining them, but the thought of returning to Botchki forced me to assume the part of a novice as convincingly as I could.

The *Rosh Yeshivah* of Navaredok, the successor of the holy Reb Joseph himself, was a lean, fiery-eyed rabbi, younger than many of his students. The stray wisps of black hair on his beardless face accentuated rather than softened the impression of the zealot. Yet he was mild of speech and moved with an almost feminine grace. He asked me hardly any questions.

"Thank God that boys so young come from the forests of afar to worship Him and to magnify His name," he said, welcoming me. "Find a seat among the bachelors and take the *Beit Yosef*,* the *House of Joseph*, as your first text. Read and meditate on it. In the evening you will be taken to a decent house for supper." With these words, he turned back to his own volume, leaving me with mixed feelings of relief at being so easily accepted and shame at my imposture.

At the height of prayer, everyone gave themselves up to it, unaware of each other. I sought out a corner of a study table and took the *House of Joseph* down from the shelf to make its acquaintance, not forgetting to kiss the sacred book before opening and after closing it. On first glance, it was already clear to me that its theology was strange in language and method. The language was the usual mix of Hebrew and Aramaic, all right, but the logic and presentation were in no way those of the *Mishneh* (which embodies Jewish Oral Law) or *Gemoreh*. It reminded me in its strangeness of my experience at the missionaries the night before, a religion distinct from the Judaism I knew yet, if anything, more Jewish than mine. This time I was not repelled, of course, but rather ill at ease and a bit afraid. Everything in this world of *mussar* – fervency of devotion, atonement, expiation, penance, self-castigation, fasting, mortification of the flesh – the whole of the *House of Joseph* way – made the Navaredoker a total sacrifice to God, a *chatoss*. "But for whose sins?" I asked myself. Since they desired all Jews to follow their way, for whom would the *Baalei mussar* sacrifice themselves? Unlike the Christians, they cannot sacrifice their innocent souls for the sinful multitudes, since they are wholly dedicated to the redemption of their own sins. And

---

* By Joseph Caro (1488–1575), who also wrote the *Shulhan Arukh*, which has become the authoritative code of Jewish law for Orthodox Jewry. But this is an abridged version of his *magnum opus*, the *Beit Yosef*, in which Caro's aim was to investigate thoroughly every law, beginning with its source in the Talmud, investigating each stage of its development, bringing in every divergent view and thus finally arriving at the decisive ruling, at "one law and one Torah."

unlike conventional Jews, they concentrate exclusively on their duties to God, and hardly pay any heed to their duties to man. Indeed, all of a Navaredoker's ties are between God and himself.

After the shock received from my first reading in the *House of Joseph*, I was relieved and a little surprised to come across the *Chayeh Odom, Life of Man*, right near my corner of the study table. As I had never read it – Reb Lippe in Botchki had considered it too elementary for a senior Gemoreh boy – and as I was not especially keen on Talmud at the moment, I spent much of the afternoon on my first reading of the *Life of Man*. This text was pious enough for me, but fell far short of the *House of Joseph* and the Navaredokers' "way". Life in the *Life of Man* belonged to God, from daybreak to daybreak, but the God-fearing who followed this text faithfully earned the most *mitzvahs*, avoided the most sins, and obtained God's rewards in this life as well as in the world to come. The life of the *House of Joseph* belonged to God, too, but those who followed that text did not hope to amass good deeds and earn their reward in Eden, but only to atone for their sins and reduce their time in the fires of the *Gehennem*. The *Life of Man* orders a Jew to earn his family's bread and support Jewish works. The Jew of the *House of Joseph* must spend his life in penance and fasting in the isolation of the house of prayer and live on charity.

The *Life of Man* penned in the Orthodox Jew in regard to his thoughts as well as to his actions hour-by-hour, minute-by-minute, every day of the year, weekdays and Sabbaths, feast days and fast days, in regard to his person and his property. It was a fascinating book in its innocent reach for the total control of man's life from birth to death, but unlike Navaredok, it was still in the realm of sanity:

> Sleep is not for rest but to refresh a Jew's forces in the service of God. Intercourse is not obedience of the commandment to multiply but to put sons in the service of God.
>
> A Jew must put on his right shoe first, but not tie its laces before putting on his left shoe and tying it; only then may he tie his right shoe. Left-hand primacy is due to the left-side location of the teffilin arm.
>
> When a Jew washes his hands, he must transfer the jug from

his right hand to his left, pour the water on his right hand, transfer it again, to pour the water on his left hand.

On waking, says the *Life of Man*, a Jew may not lag. When naked in bed, he must put on his shirt while supine and not expose himself. He must keep a vessel of water by his bed for the ritual handwashing to drive off the evil spirits from his body, especially at night when these spirits exercise their rule.

The Torah may not be discussed in front of nakedness, nor before the uncovered hair of a married woman. If a Jew discusses Torah before his own nakedness while immersed in water to his chest, he must tie off his lower body by his shirt tails.

Jews must study the Torah and, if unable to, may hire a reader to replace them or contract him in exchange for sustenance.

The triple defences of a Jewish man consist of the *teffilin*, strapped to his left arm and between his eyes, the *tsitsis*, fringes woven into his *arbeh-kanfess* and *taless*, and the *mezzuzah* secured to his doors. The tsitsis are spun of sacred thread, while the teffilin and mezzuzah carry sacred texts inscribed on parchment.

Sacred objects may be exchanged or sold only for the acquisition of more sacred ones. A synagogue may be sold to buy a Torah, or a Torah sold to redeem a prisoner or educate an orphan or to marry off a penniless maiden.

A congregation of only ten adult males may prevent one of them from leaving for another congregation for the Days of Awe, unless he hires a replacement.

The Navaredokers expected more, though, than just scrupulous observance: they demanded total submission to God and total rejection of the world outside the study house. Only a man who could achieve this would in the afterlife sit among the righteous, the *tzaddikim*, to God's right.

By the time one of the junior Navaredokers touched me on the shoulder wordlessly to lead me to my "day", I had had nothing to eat or drink since my hot tea at daybreak.

My host must have been selected with an eye to the starved condition of the new boarder, for the supper was the best meal of my whole stay with the Baalei-Mussar. Reb Zekkele was a devoted follower of the *House of Joseph*, and a great one for atonement, he avowed, but never for an emaciated novice. After one look at me, his wife brought up from the cooling pit a chicken leg, rye bread, and a fishball with horseradish. My blessing over the washing of my hands I pronounced loud and clear, and did not sit down before the family, even the minors and women. Only after I tasted my *kozais* or first bite (size of an olive) did I look up to see the blushing daughter of the house put away the ewer and cloth. In front of my host with his foot-wide yellow beard and his foot-long side-locks and lesser growths sprouting from his nose and ears, his *sheitl*ed, or be-wigged, wife with her double chins, and their plump daughter whose features I cannot begin to recall, I felt nervous for this was my first charity meal. But I enjoyed it nevertheless.

I had decent meals almost every Friday night and Sabbath throughout my stay at Navaredok. but none as tasty as Reb Zekkele's. However, the meal I appreciated the most was donated by an unemployed yarn spinner who shared his sparse food with me. He was not even a disciple of Navaredok, but he yearned for his share of the good things in the world to come.

Some of the other days brought me to the kind of homes I had never seen before, rich men's homes with well-fed, well-dressed people. There were friendly families, and there were some who treated the "day-eater" like a house servant, giving him the most unpleasant chores to do. Yet even that had its fascination, for it took me to the private corners of city houses and showed me what I could never have seen in Botchki.

My residence at Navaredok lasted only a few weeks. My days were becoming irregular, but I was glad to forego them to visit and revisit Rabbi Pat at the Byelostok Tachkemoiny, and my persistence gradually wore him down. Whenever I was refused entry to his office, I waited for him in the corridors, in the synagogue, even on street corners. My chance came one day during the lunch hour, when he was helping a student with an algebraic problem on the blackboard – the factorisation of $a^3 - b^3$, where $a$ equalled 79 and $b$ equalled 11. Rabbi Pat was explaining how logical the correct method was and how much work it saved compared with the direct arithmetical one. "I don't think it saves any time," I piped up. "Seventy-nine cubed minus eleven cubed is 491,708."

The boys and the director looked at me incredulously and

somewhat sarcastically. Rabbi Pat's smile was even more benign than usual. "How on earth do you know the answer?"

"Because seventy-nine times seventy-nine times seventy-nine is 493,039 and eleven times eleven times eleven is 1,331. That is why the difference is 491,708."

Actually I had been multiplying the numbers feverishly in my head for a good ten minutes, while standing unobserved at the back of the scholars. But my interjection came at the right moment and achieved the feat of surprising Rabbi Pat, who had never had the opportunity to study secular subjects but who was passionately interested in mathematics. To learn more about the subject, he sat among the students during their algebra and geometry lectures.

Within the half hour I was a proud student of the Byelostok Tachkemoiny. Rabbi Pat had guaranteed my fees.

The net effect of my yeshivah experiences was to show me that there was no more sense in submitting to the gold chains of the promised rewards of the *Life of Man* than to the threat of the fiery chains of the *House of Joseph*. Either way I would forfeit my chances to act and think for myself. While no one could be sure that there is no God, we can be sure what kind of God we could not accept. If I ever do make peace with God, I thought, it will not be with the God whose forgiveness each Naveredoker seeks for himself; nor with the God of the soul trappers, who sacrificed Himself for the redemption of the sins of all; but with my familiar God, who is concerned with all His people.

I forgot my tribulations as soon as I was admitted to my secular heaven by the grace of Rabbi Pat.

# 36

## White Bread on Weekdays

Rabbi Pat's seminary was a world of marvels. Good food, and enough of it, was provided at the refectory by rich American Jews who appeared bent on civilising their unworldly brethren across the ocean. The building itself constituted a source of undiminished wonder to me and probably to most of my schoolmates, for the lofty, spacious halls and wide, well-polished stone staircases were full of eager students. It was a long time before this new and happy environment could claim me with the force of reality and months before the memory of the drab country cheder and the starvation and misery of my home began to recede – hesitantly – for I never fully believed that it was not all a dream.

After years of unrelenting paternal severity which had thwarted and frustrated me, the humane discipline of the Tachkemoiny lay lightly on me and brought relief to my spirit. The morning hours were still reminiscent of Botchki and the cheder, spent as they were in the synagogue hall studying the Talmud and its many commentaries, but even these were no longer oppressive, since I was surrounded by schoolmates who made no secret of their preference for secular learning and of their diminishing enthusiasm for the teachings of the rabbis.

The afternoons were paradise on earth. Instead of having to seek out the clandestine shelter of a hayloft or of some dank cellar, I was now actually challenged to immerse myself in what to me were still educational books instead of ordinary school texts. During the five afternoon class periods, a normal high-school curriculum was instilled, or rather pumped in great gushing bucketfuls, into Poland's future rabbis. To me and my fellow students, the "professors" – they were never addressed any other way or referred to as merely teachers or instructors, even in their absence – seemed to be great demigods enthroned on the heights of an educational Sinai, and the privilege of being near them and speaking to them, with their academic titles of "doctor" and "magister", continued to thrill me to the marrow even after the physical timidity of the first weeks had passed.

My hero and principal god was a weedy and physically insignificant little man named Doctor Boyarski, a chief engineer on the czar's railroads who had been reduced by the vagaries of the war to teaching mathematics and physical science in a provincial high school. Boyarski was blessed with eccentricities, not least among which was the ability to use both hands equally well, with a deliberate, puckish preference for doing the more complex things with his left hand. He used to stand erect before the blackboard, show the class a three-quarter profile like an emperor on a coin, and sail into the explanation of a new theorem while gesticulating staccato with his right hand and beating a fast rhythm of figures, symbols and diagrams across the blackboard with his left hand extended backwards. Boyarski's eyes held the class while his fascinating left hand did the writing behind his back!

Doctor Boyarski's gift elicited secret envy from his disciples, symbolising the incredible heights that the man must have attained, not only to master such intellectual sciences as algebra, geometry, physics, chemistry and "even trigonometry", but also to treat them off-handedly! As a result of his famous left hand's apparent independence from the rest of his small person, the students adoringly nicknamed Doctor Boyarski "The Tangent".

The great majority of the seminary students were the sons of provincial rabbis who were preparing to take over from their fathers in due course. Often gifted mathematicians, few of them, however, possessed an even average aptitude for any kind of manual skill such as drawing. For centuries, drawing was regarded with suspicion by Jews who took the commandment "Thou shalt not make thee *any* graven image" literally. In their anxiety to please their American benefactors with a full "worldly curriculum", the governors of the seminary had, after a great deal of hesitation, engaged a drawing master, and this person soon made known his view of the art. His mission, he stated modestly, was to bring symmetry into the inartistic ghetto souls – both forcibly and generously – on Thursday afternoons.

Rabbi Pat's apostle of symmetry, Professor Aaronberg, was a tall, loose-jointed and dishevelled Polonophile, an admirer of the fair race of symmetry-loving Poles, who was himself the extreme living challenge to the physical and æsthetic concept of symmetry. He was nevertheless in the habit of attributing all the troubles of his pupils, if not of all Jewry, to lack of symmetry: "Your drawing is all right," he would say of a passable representation of a candlestick, which the particular rabbinical son had meant to represent a lily, "but the symmetry is wrong. The symmetrical axis is in the wrong place, like many a Jewish spine. You have sinned woefully, for you have misplaced the axis. Take my word for it, young sirs, just watch your axis and you will be successful, not only in drawing but in everything."

Inevitably, we nicknamed him "Axis" and relished having a long series of entertaining Thursday afternoon periods. But Professor Aaronberg was dismissed just as he had begun to carry out his mission.

The natural sciences were taught by our grey-haired Professor Shocher. Although we could not fit him with a nickname, we spent many happy hours with him, especially when practical lessons took the class to meadows and ponds in search of plants and frogs to dissect.

Polish language and literature were the province of Dr Weitz, a magnetic personality from Galicia – "almost the same as Austria" – who wore a velvet riding hat, such as no other Jew before him had ever worn, with a green feather in it. In between the Polish classics and the grammatical exercises, he tried to sow the seeds of socialism among the young clerics. Subsequently he was arrested by the Ochrana, the Polish secret police, during my third year at the school, and was never seen again.

Modern Hebrew was taught by a short, corpulent, middle-aged member of the pre-war Byelostok intelligentsia, Professor Shuler. Under his guidance I wrote my first essays, which were, however, like all class work set by him, limited to one of the hundred or more aspects of his two exclusive subjects: "Zion" and "The True, the Good and the Beautiful."

The Talmud masters were of course a separate species altogether. Rabbi Solomon – "the Genius of Metchet", as he was known – reminded me of my grandfather. Unlike Reb Leibe, however, the Genius of Metchet was a highly-strung, fidgety personality given to chain-smoking. His discourses filled both the most advanced and the least devout scholars among us with wonder and sheer intellectual fascination. The masters of ancient Judea or Hellas could not have aroused greater adoration and attachment among their disciples than did Rabbi Solomon among his.

Rabbi Joseph was his antithesis and as meddlesome and petty as Rabbi Solomon was dignified and intellectually generous. He devoted a part of every discourse to denouncing secular education, and he painted terrifying pictures of heavenly revenge against those who might be tempted into the paths of doubt by such knowledge. The more spirited boys jeered and drew caricatures of him and even denounced him to Rabbi Pat as a slanderer of the secular faculty.

A most important figure at the new Tachkemoiny was the Supervisor of Studies. The duties of this worthy follower of the ancient rabbinical calling of *mashgiah* combined a multitude of chores – tutoring, acting as beadle and porter, waking the sleepy, prodding the lazy or those of wandering mind, and being a general trouble-maker. This one was a goateed ex-rabbi, whose village had been burned. He was given food and shelter by the governors in return for his somewhat dubious services.

The mashgiah had known hunger in the years between jobs and probably even while on his village's rabbinical chair. At every meal in the refectory, he showed up to supervise the crowd of students, gliding along between the trestle tables, leaning over them in his long alpaca surplice as he pretended to admonish some wayward boy while greedily shoving into his large pockets and under his shirt as much from the bread baskets as he thought safe. Whereas he was severe and vociferous when he entered the refectory, shouting at the students to cease their loud talk or over-spirited hymn-singing, his demeanour would cave in when his surplice bulged out, and he would depart in guilty docility each time. He was dubbed "Rabbi Pincher", but we knew he had a large hungry family at home.

During Talmud instruction, he prowled, searching out miscreants or laggards and administering low-grade, cheder-type correction – tweaking ears and smacking faces – in defiance of the governors' rules. Often he did not come out in the open but peeped through curtains or from the latticed walls of the women's gallery, seeing but unseen, perhaps searching for onanite sinners. Woe betide the boy he spied with an algebra book between the great folio leaves of the Gemoreh or scribbling verses in the holy book's spacious margins. "Rabbi Pincher" dragged the offender by the ear to Rabbi Pat, who reprimanded the boy more out of regard for the ex-rabbi than out of censure of the impropriety itself.

I was his frequent victim. I had much to catch up on in my secular subjects but little cause to fear falling behind in the Talmud class. Whenever Rabbi Pincher brought me before Rabbi Pat, I would stand shaking in the presence of my benefactor. Often, after the mashgiah left, Rabbi Pat would ask me to stay behind and, with a barely suppressed smile, demand details of my latest offence.

On one occasion, he admitted that he did not share the mashgiah's inquisitional bias and that he particularly disliked him slapping students. However, he could not undermine the mashgiah's authority too much and asked me to promise to stop rebelling against him.

"I can promise. I can even keep my promise," I said respectfully. "But I cannot do it with conviction. Our mashgiah opposes secular education and fights against the Tachkemoiny itself, but he has not got the charity of Judaism either."

"Well, Dovid" – for once he addressed me by my name – "I understand. I even agree. But the mashgiah is a troubled man, so we can be a little charitable ourselves. Just try to be as kind to him as you can."

My battles with the supervisor so endeared me to my peers that I came to be treated as the class mascot. Avremke, to my chagrin, was not among my admirers. He was a senior, and the snobbery of the higher classes at the seminary had effectively separated us two village friends.

No picture of the Tachkemoiny is complete without "Cookie", a woman whose real name was Rebeccah and whose husband had hanged himself after being beaten up by the police for a matter of no consequence. Rebeccah was an expert at her job, for with only one assistant she managed to provide wholesome meals for more than two hundred hungry stomachs. They were tasty meals, though they were prepared in great cauldrons. For the first couple of weeks, Rebeccah had seen to it that I tucked in to double helpings of everything, and soon the diet of white bread on weekdays wiped the signs of starvation from my face.

# 37

## *Chaim the Ape*

Because the governors of Rabbi Pat's seminary subscribed to new-fangled notions of school hygiene, the students were not permitted to sleep on the benches of the synagogue hall and so I had to find lodgings for myself.

The ten marks left from Mama's farewell gift bought me a bed for two months, actually a corner on top of the oven at Griske the baker's. Its heat and fumes reminded me of the descriptions of Gehennem in Mama's "Women's Reader for the Sabbath". No sun had ever penetrated Griske's abode. His crippled stepson ruled over the twilit, netherworld of the bakery cellar. The cripple had shrivelled legs, an inflated belly, a weedy neck incongruously resembling a young gentlewoman's, and a watermelon head as bald and shiny as the bakery's copper kettle. He was an outcast within his own family which avoided physical contact with him, yet with the uncanny force of the helpless, the cripple dominated the cellar by his mere presence, thickening the pall of physical and spiritual misery. I couldn't decide whether his malevolence caused his rejection, or the reverse. It was I, hale and healthy, who was afraid of him, the helpless one, banned from human companionship.

In all seasons, the cripple went out to beg for alms, propelling himself through the narrow lanes of the synagogue quarter on a little wooden board mounted on tiny iron wheels that grated and bumped on the cobblestones. At night, whatever the weather, he always shivered with cold – large, irregular shakes. He sought the warmth of my body, since we shared the same side of the oven top and I, recoiling, was obliged to draw away further and further, leaving my blanket to him as the spoils of the petty undeclared war that existed between us, which he always won. The cripple's most effective weapon were his eyes, and whenever he fixed me with their large, lifeless orbits, I felt paralysed. But I stayed at Griske's, for it was shelter, until my money ran out.

One evening, I trudged home through a blizzard to find my bundle of clothes and books on the bakery steps: Griske would no longer shelter me without being paid. As I walked away from the bakery, I saw the cripple's saucer eyes peering through the spider-webbed pane and heard his falsetto laughter cursing me on my way.

I wandered through the snowdrifts that the blizzard had milled to sharp needle points. Down Suraz Street, my companions were a homeless cur, a Christian beggar laden with wooden rosaries, and two Jewish lunatics. One was beating – as he had for twenty years – on a battered enamel bowl with a stick and calling on the Jews to revolt against the chief rabbi who had usurped his rights. In the cadence of a haunting dirge he chanted, "Take heed ye men of Byelo-Sodom-and-Gomorrah-stok, when on the holy Sabbath the chief rabbi set fire to the city, the wrath of God was gre-e-e-e-at, gre-e-e-e-eat." The other was a quiet, dignified madman who thought he was the Messiah. He wandered throughout the city, blowing a tin trumpet that, he insisted, was the original, long-hidden horn of the Messiah and he gently urged the people to pack their worldly belongings and make ready for the *Gilgul Mechilloth*, the great subterranean pilgrimage of the rising dead.

The howling of starved dogs and the cacophony of the city's two star madmen escorted me as I searched for shelter. I did not know where to turn. Although I knew that Rabbi Pat would not fail to come to my rescue, I resolved not to burden the generous man again, even if I were to die in the snow. Then I thought of my only other contact in the city, Benyomin the fruit commissioner, the agent for the region's fruit suppliers and the city's market women, and I walked toward the Sand Market. When at last I found Benyomin's house, it was dark and, not daring to wake him up, I stood shivering in the scanty shelter of the porch. A kerchiefed, stooping figure hurried past me under the weak lights of the snow-driven square. Much later, a tall, hunched-up young woman halted her incongruously mincing steps in front of me and whispered hoarsely through thin, rouged lips, "Why don't you go to bed? This weather will be the death of you if you don't."

I pointed out the bundle beside me and mumbled an explanation through chattering teeth. She seemed to argue with herself, "That is tough ... Of course, I could make you a bed on my table ... I have no customers tonight and not likely to have 'em in this dogs' weather ... But then ... you are only a child and a student of the Holy Torah, and I am a whore and not worthy to stand near you ... On the other hand, you will die if I leave you here, and be my greatest sin. You'd better come along, now ... In the morning I shall speak to Benyomin."

I followed her to her attic. She did not strike a light, and we hardly spoke. She helped me on to the rickety table, covered me with the big shawl from her shoulders and slunk away. For a long time I heard her groan and toss on the creaking boards of her squalid bed, and then I fell asleep.

At daybreak, she took me over to the fruit commissioner and declared that she would not move from the door until Benyomin promised to find lodgings for the "holy boy". In daylight, her haggard face looked waxen, and her lips blue.

"If your softhearted, even-tempered father hears where you slept the night, he'll twist your scrawny neck," the fruit commissioner said sarcastically. He had been at loggerheads with my father for years on account of my father's temper, and he seldom missed a chance to take him down a peg. "I heard you were lodging at Griske's, so why did you wander out into the freezing night? If Griske threw you out, I'll have Chaim the Ape knock his head off, the *mamzer*."

"He did throw me out, but then he hadn't received any payment from me in a long time."

Benyomin changed his tone to reassure me. "Let me talk to Chaim and see if he'll take you in. Maybe you can offer to teach his daughter to read and write. But whatever happens, I won't let you spend another night freezing in the street – or forget this girl's help either."

Before it was time for me to go to school, I had, through Benyomin's intercession, become the lodger of the giant curly-headed market porter, Chaim the Ape.

Chaim shook his great head in vigorous consent to Benyomin's

proposition. He could not bring out any sound, as he was munching a winter apple, which he had committed to his vast mouth in
its entirety. After he had swallowed most of it, he picked me up by
my coat collar with two fingers, as if he were taking a delicate
pinch of snuff, and set me on the bench.

"If I be paid four marks month – is cheap. Cheap. Then you
teach daughter writing. She ginger ... red-head ... more brains
than Chaim. She's young man America. She must writing."
Chaim's speech was still in its infancy.

I feared being turned out into the street once again and
explained to my new benefactor that I had no money at all, not
even four marks, and that my father would haul me back to
Botchki if money should ever be demanded of him. The Ape roared
with mirth:

"Your father? Little Srolke? No fear! Srolke pay Chaim, pay
quick, no trouble. Chaim the Ape strongest man ... Me pick all up
– little horse, little cart, little Srolke's apples, little Srolke too,
altogether. Chaim make kashe out of him; Srolke behave good."

With that reassuring but brain-taxing speech, the giant porter
put me back on the floor as if I were the full stop to the sentence he
had just uttered. The impact made me fold up on the ground.

Chaim grinned apologetically. "Must never touch boy again.
Delicate. Jus' brain. Chaim the Ape only big meat. Shake hands, be
frien's." I backed away from the proffered paw with mixed fear
and reverence.

Up to that time I had not seen my father. I had in fact avoided
the Sand Market to which he still hauled his weekly loads of fruit.
Despite Mama's tearful intercessions, my father angrily refused to
visit me or to help me in any way, even with a few pieces of fruit.
But things changed once Chaim the Ape took matters into his big
hands. Chaim must have convinced my father of his intent to "pick
up little horse, little cart, little Srolke altogether", for not only did
Father start to pay my rent, but he also visited me at school and
brought me small hampers of fruit.

Deeply beholden for the slightest kindness, I applied myself
diligently to teaching Chaim's daughter. But ginger-headed Zelde
had no more brains than her doting father. It took six months to
teach her how to sign her name without interspersing a few upside-
down or mirror letters into it. Zelde always stuck out her tongue

and propelled it in the same circles and curlicues as the letters that she laboriously fashioned with her pen. Chaim stood there by the hour, watching his daughter's "lessons" with huge affection and many exclamations of pride.

He inhabited two rooms in a wobbling three-storey apartment house in Butcher Street – widely known as the Street of Zamenhof, the ghetto Jew who created Esperanto. Chaim's home was only two buildings away from the ancient timbered house in which Zamenhof was born and which bore his commemorative plaque. Every year, on the birthday of the great man, crowds of foreigners, some in horseless carriages, descended on Butcher Street in a procession, and made speeches in strange tongues in front of the house.

Chaim's furniture consisted of three oak stools, designed by him to cope with his great size, a limping but sturdy table and two great benches. These coffin-shaped boxes opened at night to serve as beds. The mattresses were bundles of straw, changed with great regularity, and the bedding consisted of huge red ticking quilts and pillows. And then there was the chair, on which no one was ever permitted to sit except me, and then only during the solemn hour of teaching Zelde to write.

For a Jewish stevedore, Chaim was well off. He had bread every day and meat every Sabbath. This was the direct result of his phenomenal, almost legendary strength. He could carry two cases of fruit roped together on his great shoulders while other porters groaned and stumbled with only one. Even the badge-wearing Polish porters from the railway station, who considered themselves part of an official and therefore Jew-free body, knew to look the other way whenever Chaim solicited one of their customers.

Later that winter, Father was summoned before the governors of the seminary and told that he had to contribute to my boarding, if not to my tuition. Rabbi Pat explained that the seminary was going through a serious crisis and that they would be forced to send me home, despite the great hopes the school had for my future. Due to the inflation that had hit the country, whatever fees they collected at the beginning of each month were worth ninety per cent less by the month's end, and *Jedeka* (the American Joint Distribution Commitee) funds had begun to diminish as well.

My father, himself nearly ruined by the inflation, groaned helplessly. But the presence of so many famous rabbis and professors, and above all the praise that they lavished on his son, made it inconceivable for him to refuse. He promised to pay what he could and tearfully begged Rabbi Pat not to send me away. "I shall pay you all the money I get for my merchandise, as long as I have any to sell. And when I have no more, I will come and ask you to put it down as a debt, which, with God's help, I shall repay one day."

The governors looked at one another and at the frail, ill-clad villager who stood before them in his bulky felt boots, and Rabbi Pat pronounced their decision: "Go home, Reb Yisroel, and remember that we shall be satisfied if you pay in a quarter of your takings. Keep the rest for the needs of your household."

Father retired with profuse thanks, walking out of the room backwards, and marvelling at the goodness of these great men and even more at the change that had taken place within himself.

# 38

## Cold Pogrom

For some months Father contributed to the school fees regularly.
And when his merchandise failed, I was able to step in and make
good.

I earned my first million – in devalued marks – at fourteen by
coaching some of my more backward schoolmates in the Talmud.
My first pupil was Solomon the Ox, a fat, bulgy-eyed boy who
paid me in paper money. An original five-mark note, it had been
repeatedly overstamped – due to the shortage of paper or, as they
quipped in those days, because the paper was more valuable as
wallpaper than as money – until it had become a million marks.
With it I paid a fortnight's school fees. But by the next month a
pound of butter cost five million. People lost count of their money
and spoke with indifference and ignorance in terms of millions,
hundreds of millions, and billions. When at last the zloty replaced
the mark, the Jewish traders found themselves with bags stuffed
with billions – and penniless.

In the first elections of the new Poland, held in 1922, the Jews
joined forces with other minorities, chiefly the Byelorussians, and
elected forty deputies to Parliament, the Sejm, a big enough voice,
they thought, to be heard abroad and to ensure their rights inside
the country. The authorities responded by introducing a policy
which we called the "cold pogrom": electoral intimidation, denial
of trading permits, *numerus clausus* at the universities, exclusion
from public jobs, and confiscatory taxation which wiped out our
means of livelihood. I recall our indignation when we heard that
the Government had denied the Polish Jews permission to drain the
Pripet Marshes for farmland at their own expense – all while

reviling them as a race of parasites. After a year or two of the cold pogrom, Byelostok's famed textile industry collapsed. Thousands of spinners and weavers were out of work, and the great chimneys stood smokeless.

For a brief moment, Jewish hope revived when the Polish liberal, Gabriel Narutowicz, was elected president, but he was assassinated in December of the same year on the way to his swearing-in. The victorious reactionaries did not even pretend to condemn his murder and the government's poets wrote hymns glorifying the assassin. All of which did not prevent the director of secular studies of our seminary, Dr Tilson, from addressing his students at the graduation of the senior class with the following words:

"Remember your responsibilities. You are going out into the great world destined to become the leaders of your communities in the towns and villages of eastern Poland. From your midst, Jewry will elect its deputies to the Sejm of this country. Be ever loyal to your own people and good citizens of your homeland at the same time."

The prospect of becoming a member of parliament thrilled me, although I was still years away from graduation. Perhaps I would one day be elected as deputy for Podlasie; then I would award a rye field, a potato patch and an orchard to every one of my Jewish constituents, and in exchange I would give the Jewish shops to the Poles who claimed that the Jewish shopkeepers were sucking the marrow out of the land. And I would build schools where Jewish children could get a secular education and learn trades, so that within one generation they could all become respected citizens and leave the Poles nothing to complain about and no one to hate.

In those days of acute distress, the seminary was the only oasis amid the bleak desperation of Byelostok's Jewish community. The governors placed their faith in the charity and riches of their American brethren and expected that they would rescue not only the Tachkemoiny but the whole of Poland's Jewry. And Rabbi Pat refused to admit the word "despair" to the vocabulary of his school.

The seminary, like its founder, was liberal and conciliatory and committed to the synthesis between Torah and enlightenment. It aimed at merging the values of traditional Judaism and the eternal appeal of Zion, despite the frequent denunciations of the Zionists by their foes, the ultra-orthodox Agudists. Religious texts were read in ancient Hebrew and Aramaic; mathematics and the sciences taught in modern Hebrew; geography, history and European literature in Polish. But despite its scrupulous loyalty to the State, the seminary had never been able to obtain a government subsidy, not even a fraction of what it was entitled to under state laws. Since it failed equally to get the support of either the Agudists or the Zionists, the seminary depended on America. But the American Jews, beset by outstretched hands from virtually every Jewish community in the world, had to reduce their contribution. The school had to manage on the fees of its pauperised students, and early in my third year Rabbi Pat was obliged to send home all who could not pay.

My return to Botchki was less dramatic than my departure had been. I went to the Sand Market with my bundle, climbed into my father's cart and, after a long night during which we exchanged few words but frequent sighs, arrived in Botchki the next afternoon. Mother cried for a while and then settled down to her usual state of resigned melancholy. Instead of the fattened calf, there were only potatoes for my homecoming meal, unrelieved as so often by even a drop of fat. Bread had again become a rarity to be partaken of on Sabbath only. Father's orchard-keeping and his wholesale commissions earned him an ever-shrinking income out of which he was paying for two separate trading licences, a turnover tax, an income tax, a variety of municipal and district taxes, a road tax, a horse tax, a cart tax and so on. Like a million other Polish Jews, we Zhagers sucked so little of the marrow of Poland that we became badly undernourished.

At first, I shared the family yoke with the two breadwinners, Father and Chaim. I helped in the orchard and house, harnessed the horse and took it at nights to the village common for clandestine grazing, and drove with Father on his weekly trips to the city. Soon, however, we all realised that our small business didn't require my contribution, and Father gave me leave to fend for my own livelihood. The suggestion as to what that livelihood might be came from an unexpected source.

Bobbe's home, which had always been my sanctuary from the grimness of my own family life, and on which I now depended more than ever for warmth and peace, had been transformed during my absence by a miracle. A suitor had been brought over all the way from Melnik on the "Polish" bank of the Bug to the "Litvishe" side, met Bashke der Bobbe's, been attracted to her, and married her after a mere couple of months of courtship. Bobbe transferred the gallanterie to her new son-in-law, Shieh, and didn't regret it. He was reliable and steady, yet imaginative, and he provided her with a grandson after ten months. "Noo, what can we say? *Alte moid, alte moid*, but caught the best fish in the river," said Bobbe. And her tic, the outward manifestation of her dissatisfaction with the world, vanished for good.

In the crowded space of the one-room dwelling, Shieh found me place for an occasional Friday night meal and for belated instructions in the things a father and an older brother should have taught me. It was only with his arrival that I learned how to shave, and not with Chaim's depilatory powder, either; how to trim a tie; how to speak to a girl; even how to write a love letter. And it was at his suggestion that I became Botchki's first English teacher.

I had Rabbi Pat to thank for my ability, however modest, to earn my bread in this manner. A year earlier, when the foundations of the seminary had begun to totter, the wise and prescient man had made a parting gift to his beloved students. Summoning the three senior classes, he explained to us that anti-Semitism was growing and would soon drive many of us from Poland.

"If you emigrate, very little of what you have learned here will be of much use to you unless you know the language of the new land. I have engaged a professor of English for you. Study well."

The professor turned out to be a tailor who had recently returned from Canada, and whose vocabulary, spelling and pronunciation wrought havoc with the tongue of Shakespeare and Dickens. But it was the best that was to be had. And it was to change the rest of my life in, and eventually provide my ticket out of, Botchki.

# 39

## *Little Wolf Crosses My Path*

During my years away, Botchki had undergone a new kind of division, between the hopeful and the less hopeful. The former had relatives abroad, usually in America, and lived with the dream of emigrating, and the latter left no stone unturned in the search for such relatives. Once it became known that I was qualified and willing to teach English, I was beleaguered by would-be pupils of both sexes and all ages.

But, however thin I sliced my daily doses from the first half of the *Berlitz Reader* – the extent of my own mastery of the textbook – the course could not be stretched beyond one *zman*, or semester. My fees, the exorbitant sum of one American dollar a month for an hour a day, or about four cents an hour, outraged the whole village. In any case, by the middle of the semester, I was so hoarse and run down that I had to be sent away to recuperate in the poor man's "resort" of Dubno, a pine forest two hours' walk from Botchki.

There I stayed with a Byelorussian peasant named Petko, who had eyes the colour of forget-me-nots, a beard like flax and a voice like a rolling barrel. As with the other Dubnovites whose best land was sand and whose worst was marshes, Petko was even poorer than a Botchki Jew. His broad-shouldered daughter Yevdosia and wife Katia had never tasted white bread or the other good things of life, and bore in their large grey eyes the piercing look which to the initiated told of years of hunger. Unlike the Botchkivites, the Dubnovites did not even know what good food looked like. They accepted the starvation of their bodies and the misery of their souls like mute beasts of burden.

My kosher food was sent to me from Botchki and, since I paid for it from my own earnings, it included bread, an occasional egg and a little meat. I was embarrassed whenever I had to eat in Petko's presence. Dubno was even more depressing than Botchki – that is, until I met Welfke.

Welfke, or Little Wolf, cut across my path in the sand dunes one day, as sudden an apparition as the Protestant missionary I had encountered in Byelostok.

"*Acheinu, bruderke*", Hi, little brother, he sang out, imitating a synagogue chant. "You are casting your shadow on my freckles. Do I know you? Yes, I do. You are Diodie the English teacher of Botchki, aren't you? Sholem aleichem, chaver!"

This chanted monologue came pouring out from the girlish mouth of a short but muscular lad of my age or a bit older. He seemed a bundle of contrasts too great to take in at first sight. He was a Jew with challenging blue eyes, but his long blond locks were those of a *shikse*. Though poor enough to have to convalesce in Dubno, he wore a puffy-sleeved, somewhat poetic, magenta blouse hanging over his trousers and looked like a wealthy city boy playing the aristocratic anarchist.

He seemed to fill up all the space around him. An aspiring artist and full of himself, I decided: a boy of much feeling but little sense. I was fascinated, though I did not quite trust him. The tough pose seemed to cover uncertainty and fragility, and his jolly sallies skated over a barely veiled melancholy.

Welfke was in Dubno as a suspected case of tuberculosis, but he was only there for a week, as his father could not afford a longer stay. When I asked him what he did to help financially, he spoke in a style that was both sad and humorous at the same time. His father had had many failures despite his excess of talents, and had come down in the world. Once the major domo of Jewish manufacturers, he had been forced to change jobs as rapidly as the government taxed his employers out of existence. "*Abroch tzoom Polack ganeff mitn kaltn pogrom*" – Let breakbone fever smite the Polish thief with his cold pogrom!

Currently he was self-employed in a branch of "commerce" over which the tax assessors had no control. In fact, he worked in two such branches: as a *shadchan*, or marriage broker, and as a salesman for a dental technician. "But despite all that it goes badly for my father because everybody, every Jewish body anyway, is broke. A marriage broker can bring off his matches if he can match the parties who fit each other. That, Tatte can accomplish." With a grin, he added, "His victims love to sacrifice themselves on the altar of love. But with the depression reaching rock bottom and inflation hitting the ceiling, brides have laundry baskets of devalued marks for dowries and look for husbands who can feed their wives, not the other way."

"The dental trade is just as hopeless," he went on. "It all started when Tatte found a dental technician in Byelostok to make dentures for his mother, my Kishinev Bobbe, and it turned into a job when he began selling artificial teeth for him. Tatte finds the gums easily enough, but the trouble is, they belong to old men who have no money, and his technician won't even start on a denture or a bridge unless the patient furnishes the gold. So, how does he manage? That we eat at all is thanks to the occasional widow who has an old wedding ring or the gold of a departed spouse's bridge to bring to the technician."

Welfke's father suffered from heart disease. "But he never fusses. I admire the old man: there's no one like him. We're more like chums than like father and son."

"I envy you," I said. "Mine is always complaining about indigestion: and he's a pious *mentchenfresser*, though I admit he's got his reasons. The worst is, he takes God too seriously. I wish I lived in Byelostok, in a big city like you do, with culture and art. But how did you pay for your silk shirt?"

Welfke interrupted me, "I'm from Byelsk, which isn't much more cultural than Botchki. I do have good friends in Byelostok, and they always keep the door open for me. Girlfriends give me these blouses – some give the silk, some sew the shirt, and there's one who does both. I have talented *chavertes*."

"I wish I had," I said. "But I don't have your looks."

"Or my TB either, my good friend. A man must have something that's special about him, no? He should swim, not float like a log."

"Life is the log," I said.

"A philosopher, eh? Where did you study?"

"Tachkemoiny, but they just closed the door on me this winter."

"Why are you so gloomy? In my family, we laugh all the time, even at ourselves, even at our Kishinev Bobbe because every day for the past forty years she has made the same eggplant *mamellige* which, by the way, is the best in Moldavia. You should sing, maybe write your own songs, like I do."

I had never heard such ideas before, or known anyone like him, and I was intrigued. We agreed to meet again in the forest, and spent the next few days in intense conversation, sharing our fantasies and visions of the future. We parted with assurances of friendship and promises that whoever got "there" first would stretch out his arm to bring the other one up.

To me Welfke was a messenger from the wide world I yearned for since my escape from Botchki, a person who made light of rules and regulations from any source, a Jewish *Wandervogel*. He spurned cheder, prayerhouse, dietary prohibitions as well as the rules of the Gentiles. I envied him his freedom, and I certainly envied him his father who, instead of rebuking him for fighting against the established regime, actually taught him how to sidestep punishment and survive. But I resented his discarding everything which made me feel that I was a Jew.

Was there a contradiction in my so minding Welfke's rejection of Jewish ways, while at the same time so disapproving of the scrupulous adherence to the Law displayed by my brother and his like? Should I have been ashamed of my dual loyalties, of my roles of both worshipper and dissenter, of my questioning the existence of God while gripped by the God-intoxicated Days of Awe, of seeing one and the same object, the arbeh kanfess, both as a symbol of reverence and as a straitjacket? In any case, I was not ashamed, and did not feel that I lacked decisiveness or loyalty; I even felt proud of being both emotionally bound to Orthodox Judaism and rationally iconoclastic of many of its practices. My whole life had been shaped by the struggle between my feelings and my views. It sometimes seemed to me that I was two people in one, Jacob and Esau in Rebeccah's womb, wrestling for their right to be me. I could not accept all the limitations of our religion, but I could not give up our traditions without losing my Jewishness, my self. My association with Welfke made me even more conscious of the conflict within me. But it also served as my guide to the world outside.

When my health had improved enough, I returned to Botchki and my teaching. By the end of the zman I had saved up a small fortune – thirty-two American dollars which my father, in one of his great recurring financial reverses, was obliged to appropriate as a "loan". I also had to face an approaching crisis. My stock of English would soon be exhausted, so how was I to force an unsmiling world to make room for me?

In Byelostok, I had attended meetings of the Socialist Zionists, who appeared to me the most practical and yet the most idealistic of all the Jewish parties on "the Jewish street." I learned about their pioneers' movement, the *Halutz*, and its training farms which claimed to be transforming weedy Jewish youths into brawny farmers for Palestine.

As my brief career as an English teacher was fizzling out, I got my sister Basheh and my friends interested in the junior branch of the organisation, the Young Halutz. To qualify for the British government certificates to settle in Palestine, we had to form a *kvutzeh* or farm where we could train ourselves in agriculture and get used to communal life. To do this, we would have to defy the whole town and live and eat together, boys and girls. Botchki was sure we were going to lead immoral lives and put the village to shame.

I was not really confident that I could defy the family and go through with the project, but my problem was taken out of my hands when my father caught me writing a poem on the Sabbath, beat me, and drove me out of the house. I was on my own again.

Some twenty young Botchkivites, the sons and daughters of impoverished Jewish shopkeepers and tradesmen, formed a local Halutz Youth group. We pooled our zlotys and groschens and in the summer rented a little farm, establishing ourselves as a kvutzeh, in accordance with the mandate of the central Zionist headquarters in Warsaw.

As our group had no money, after paying the year's rent, to secure implements, livestock, or food, we hired ourselves out as lumberjacks for the winter in order to save enough cash to run our farm the next summer. The Byeloviezh sawmills paid two zlotys a day to every male and put two huts at the disposal of the Botchki Halutzim, one for the boys and one for the girls. While the boys worked in the forest felling trees, loading the trunks on to sledges, and attending to the saws, the girls prepared the food, washed and mended, and looked after the young calves who bore the optimistic names of Pioneer, Ziona and Hope and with which we planned to stock our farm in the spring.

The winter passed. We did not go home for Passover, since most of us had been ostracised by our families. Botchki had stormed and shouted and even threatened violence to the immoral and godless rebels who had gone to live like pagans in the forest, ate God knows what unkosher food, maybe even worked on the Sabbath, and anticipated the Messiah's return to Zion as if the Lord did not know best when it was time for our suffering to come to an end!

With the first spring thaw, I and my *chaverim* started the real work on the farm. Soon the fame of the little settlement and of the "heroic" winter that its members had weathered in the Byeloviezh Wilderness had spread so far that the Jewish newspapers began to take notice of us. Every week brought a new pilgrim or two from some village – a penniless boy or girl who had run away from home and arrived with a miserable bundle of clothing and perhaps a pitchfork, flail, or scythe, a burning appetite to go to Palestine some day and to have a bite of food immediately. Though uninvited, they were never turned back.

The farm soon became too small to support its numbers. Our winter savings were running out and our inexperience showed in our mounting deficits. Finally, we were obliged to forego renewal of our lease and instead observed, in festive manner, the first anniversary and the end of our pioneering venture simultaneously. We were anything but a failure, though, since the Central Zionist Organisation, which disposed of the coveted certificates that meant immediate emigration to Palestine, allotted our tiny kvutzeh four places, a far higher ratio than the big Halutz organisations of Byelostok or even Warsaw received. The certificates were drawn by lot, but I drew a blank.

# 40

## *Out of the Frying Pan*

I was nowhere and saw no way out, except possibly to try the Byelostok Meller family of unemployed weavers, whose hospitality Welfke had promised to share with me whenever we got to the city. True, Welfke's run-away optimism had failed to get him anywhere himself and would very likely not do any better for me, but the Meller's offer of shelter was my only chance of being in a city, of having stimulating company, of finding pupils of elementary English or perhaps even a regular job.

Arrival at the Mellers' was more like a homecoming than the intrusion of a penniless stranger, and their way of life was even more fascinating than Welfke's account of it had been.

"First things first," announced Papa Meller. "You two must be starved. We'll warm up some boiled potatoes and you can dip into the barrel for a dill pickle to go with it."

The Meller parents were self-sacrificing, warm-hearted and un-critical hosts to all who needed a corner to sleep in, a bit of food, shelter from arrest by the Ochrana, or escape from angry parents. Even during the Revolution of 1905 and its attendant pogroms, their house had given sanctuary to "politicals" on the run.

Papa Meller was now in his fifties, a sickly unemployed master weaver who had worked in Byelostok's great textile mills along with thousands of Jewish spinners and weavers, most of whom, like himself, had been out of work since the Poles had taken over the city. Starving and spitting up their wasted lungs, they provided ideal hunting ground for Bundist and "illegal" recruiters.

On the "Jewish Street," there were two socialist camps: the Bundists and the Linke, or Left. The Bundists were the legals, while the left consisted of several revolutionary, even terrorist, parties: Bolsheviks, Mensheviks, Social Revolutionaries, and Anarchists. Because belonging to one of the illegal parties could lead to deadly consequences, all of these groupings hid behind the common name of Linke.

Though worn with hunger and worry for his family, Papa Meller retained his good humour and generosity from better times and never let poverty or persecution interfere with his hospitality. Mama Meller, still a beautiful blonde at fifty, spent her days scrounging for firewood and scraps of food, mostly half-spoiled potatoes or cucumbers that she pickled in dill throughout the autumn.

Their pride was their only child, buxom, good-natured Luba. She was an activist, an overworked salesgirl by day and a devoted distributor of illegal "literature" by night.

Mama Meller served equal portions to everybody, even recent acquaintances, without regard to their claim on her hospitality or their affiliations. She admired all of her guests equally: Welfke, who admired only himself; me, who admired the Meller parents more than my own; Benn, who was so gifted an artist that the Byelostok municipality gave him a scholarship to study with the great painters in Paris; and Niome, a vociferous critic of everybody and everything, who admired only three people – Luba, Israel Furie and Comrade Stalin. Israel Furie, whom Niome called his "only real revolutionary", crossed the Soviet border once or twice a month guiding Comintern messengers.

According to Niome, Furie once told him that he knew his luck was running out and that a Polish bullet in the back was not far away. But he did not expect that the bullet would come on his very next border crossing, or that it was going to be fired by an agent of his own Comrade Stalin.

When Furie disappeared, it was Welfke, of all the Meller crowd, who offered to solve the puzzle. "We have to find out what happened to Izzy," he announced, "and it's up to me to do it."

Luba dressed him up in a Polish Gymnasium girl's uniform and used contacts to provide the papers for "her" visit to "her hometown" on the Soviet border, near Furie's usual crossing point.

"*Noo, sei mir gesunt oon shtark*," said Mama Meller, holding back tears. "God knows how you can find out about poor Izzy. But please watch out for yourself and come back to us, dear boy."

"Now don't you get any sad ideas," Welfke said. "I'll be back in four days, and by that time I'll need a good meal – sweet herring with potatoes would be just fine ... Don't worry, it's not my first excursion to a closed border, you know."

As promised, he came back on the fourth day, with an account of Furie's execution on reaching the Soviet side. There were no challenges, no talk, just the muffled sound of a bullet from a silencer. We listened dumbstruck. No one mentioned, or even hinted at betrayal but the word was in the air, like a rock suspended over our heads.

What was strangest to me, the outsider, was to hear Niome, who had been Furie's closest and most trusted friend, break in on Welfke's shattering account: "No way to tell what happened in the dark or who fired. Could have been a Polish border guard, or a smuggler afraid of discovery. If he was shot by a comrade, it would shock me, but might also warn us not to be too trusting, not even of our closest friends. I always trusted Izzy, but never a hundred per cent, and now you can see that maybe I was right."

Niome's little speech stunned us with its cynicism.

"I prefer to trust Furie than his untrusting friends," I said, cutting in on him. "His liquidation may have been the penalty for his total trust in his own comrades." And I would not count out Niome himself as the informer, I thought.

When I brought up the subject later with Welfke, he looked baffled, but didn't say a word. Watching Papa and Mama Meller's shocked, frozen expressions, I was sure that the same idea had occurred to them, too. When things get bad enough, I concluded in my own mind, each of us is on his own.

That winter the Meller "club" was raided by the Ochrana four times, and each time the guests escaped over the tumbling roofs of the Piaski quarter. The most zealously hidden escape hatch, through the false back of a wardrobe, had once been reserved for Israel Furie. During the raids, Papa, Mama and Luba Meller always stayed behind, often amid clear evidence of guests who had just escaped, and the Ochrana paid them for their silence each time by savage beatings and days, even weeks, of solitary confinement.

I had tried to get pupils for my beginners' English, but in

Byelostok even my former English teacher could not find paying clients. Unlike Welfke, I didn't have admiring chavertes to call on or poetry to protect me against materialist contamination, so that that winter I never stopped scrounging for jobs, however menial or brief or badly paid. I don't think I worked more than two or three months in all during my stay with the Mellers. Two of these jobs were particularly memorable, though neither lasted more than a week or two – the first one was at the Modern Stationery of Mr Gershuni and the other at Tsaref's the ironmonger's, both on the main avenue across from City Hall.

Gershuni's store was the fanciest stationery store in the city and had as its clients rich "gymnasists", doctors, engineers, and even the burgomaster. Gershuni sold such luxury goods as Waterman pens and pink writing-paper with embossed roses. He did not need an assistant to his saleswoman, Ronni, but took me in because he was on the governors' committee of the Tachkemoiny and had known me as a pupil.

Ronni was a short-legged, frizzy-haired girl in her early twenties who was hard-faced and never addressed me until the afternoon the Gershunis had to attend a funeral. As soon as they left, Ronni bolted the front door, motioned to me to follow her through the narrow back exit to a backyard full of empty crates and cartons, ordered me to sit down where we could see without being seen from neighbouring shops, and without the least preparation hissed out: "We want you to join our party – the Communist Party of Poland, shop assistants' cell. And don't ask any questions, because I won't know the answers, and wouldn't tell you if I did."

I was dumbfounded at her suggestion, which was delivered like a command, and I was afraid. Was she a reckless recruiter or an informer? I pleaded that I did not know anything about revolutionary ideas and didn't want to find out. Ronni snapped at me not to play the innocent: "I know that you live with the Mellers, up to your neck in leftist connections. So think about it. The working class expects every intelligent person seeking justice for the oppressed to do his bit. In the meantime, just remember that I never talked to you." With that she jumped off her crate and ran back to the shop without giving me a look, then or ever again, until she was taken away.

Several days later, my employer dismissed me, hinting that he was surprised at the kind of people I lived with. Before long I heard from Luba that Ronni had been tortured by the Ochrana and then had disappeared without trace.

I got the Tsaref job after knocking at the doors of dozens of businesses. My employer was over six feet tall with a powerful frame, but used me to move, cut, bundle and deliver to the waiting wheelbarrow lengths of iron rail twice my own weight.

On the third or fourth day, Mr Tsaref looked at the wounds on my hands and face, and the bumps on my head, shook his head angrily, and said he was sorry and that he would take me off the heavy work in the mornings and send me to his house to rest up a bit while helping his wife with the housekeeping.

Mrs Tsaref was delicate, pretty and very lazy. My first "rest-up" job was to prepare the oak floor of her dining room by sanding, varnishing, waxing and polishing it on my hands and knees, until mid-afternoon. Finally I became so hungry as to ask whether I could have something to eat. "No," she said, "you get food with your wages." I replied that I had not been paid yet, ran out of the house and back to the Mellers.

But man, even Dovid from Botchki and Welfke from Byelsk, cannot live indefinitely on dill pickles or on the charity and self-lessness of his hosts. It was time for us to leave. Welfke shelved his poetic mission to help his ailing father, and began spending his days in the workshop of the dental technician, "just to stay out of the cold", he claimed. But soon he was able to fashion himself all the dentures his father could sell – a talent which did not surprise his father or me, but was a shock to the technician whom he displaced. Welfke went back to Byelsk to produce prostheses for his father.

In the six winter months I had spent in the stricken city, I was never at peace. No day was like another; no friend or acquaintance like another. The hardships made life in Botchki look safe and comfortable by comparison – but I cannot think of that winter without some pride at having learned to survive.

At my parting from the Mellers, who provided sanctuary to godless revolutionaries, I was struck by the strange thought that in their selflessness they much resembled my sainted grandfather, Reb Leibe. The time I had spent with them left me with a greater belief in the heights to which man can reach, but with little faith in my own future. Now that I was leaving them, I again did not know where to turn. "I will lift up mine eyes unto the hills: from whence cometh my help," but there were no hills in Podlasie and there was no reply.

# 41

## *A Goat Named Elijah*

I thought my best chance of finding food and shelter while continuing to look for English students or other work was with my Uncle Marim-Yosl, my father's twin brother who lived in Zheludek, a shtetl near Vilno. He was a *karabelnik*, an itinerant buyer of peasant products, like my father but more successful.

The trouble with this uncle was that, as he was deeply observant, he couldn't give me shelter, although he had several rooms in his house and he and his wife were childless. I could not stay with them on account of *Yihud*, the Talmudic prohibition against the unchaperoned presence of any Jewess, even for a minute, under a roof with any male over thirteen who was not her son or grandson. Aunt Shifreh was a stick-shaped woman of fifty and almost as hirsute as my uncle, and I was only eighteen, but she was a woman and the Law made no exceptions.

Nor could I share the apartment of my sick cousin, Levi Podolski, the son of my father's late sister, Blume. Levi was an intellectual in his mid-twenties, and the least provincial person I had ever met. In our talks I felt like the disciple of a dying master. Without formal schooling, without teachers, and without friends with whom to share his thoughts, he had attained a level of learning equal to that of my most admired teachers at the Tachkemoiny.

During the many hours we spent talking together, Levi would make me sit at the farthest end of the room because he was in the last and most infectious stage of tuberculosis. He occupied the best room of Yeruchem the turner's house – the front room – to get as much sun as possible and to watch people walk by as they went to the market place. It was in that bright room that I found out about free love. Levi's childhood friend, Lily, had nursed him throughout his illness and had moved in with him after he had become bedridden.

My visits meant a great deal to both of them – "a messenger from the outside world" they called me. During our conversations, Lily was mostly the listener, but a very sensitive one. Neither of them would permit me to come near their bed or his bloodstained towels. Lily told me that they lived "as husband and wife," and that he was a passionate lover. She said that she was determined to keep him alive as long as she could, in as much comfort as possible, and with all the joy they could derive in whatever time was left to them. I never saw her waver in her cheerful devotion, even happiness, in her role as the giver of life and love.

My cousin carried on such a rageful quarrel with God as to make the Berditchever Rebbe, who after every major calamity took God to task for His unfair treatment of His people, look meek. The worse his condition grew, the louder his protests became, until he came to give God as good as he got. And yet he loved life as unconditionally as he loved Lily.

Zheludek's behaviour towards them was astonishing. The Orthodox, who zealously condemned all offences against the Law, deliberately overlooked Levi and Lily's most sinful and defiant cohabitation, perhaps recognising it as worthy of exemption from the laws of God and man. Not one of them wanted to sit in judgement on them, and for once humanity prevailed over God.

Could this have happened in Botchki? Zheludek was in many ways different from Botchki. Its Jews, less persecuted by the Byelorussian goyim than we were by the Poles, were still old-world in their ways and resisted newfangled notions like culture, Zionism, or socialism.

Unfortunately, Zheludek had few Jews who wanted to emigrate and there was little call for an English teacher, so Uncle Marim-Yosl drove me in his karabelnik's wagon to nearby Rozhanke, where I was employed to teach two hours of evening classes. The Rozhanke school was fervently Zionist and had looked askance at my preference for Yiddish over Hebrew. I was engaged temporarily as a Hebrew, and not an English, teacher.

I commuted to Zheludek for the weekends and holy days since

Uncle never failed to get home then. My aunt and uncle were a joyless couple who exchanged not a word during meals and few words even on business matters.

I had arrived at Uncle Marim-Yosl's on the eve of Passover and received a stinging tongue lashing for asking Aunt Shifreh for a matzah with goosefat. My uncle led me by the ear to his own copy of the *Chayeh Odom* and made me read out the *din*, the law, concerning tasting of matzah prematurely:

"An adult tasting matzah before the *Seder* is like a man who forces himself on his bride before the Seven Wedding Blessings are spoken, for he partakes of the matzah before the Seven Passover blessings are spoken."

Fortunately, my mute, oppressive relatives observed the Passover meal, the Seder, at the house of my other Zheludek uncle, Uncle Shneyer, and the event turned into a great success. Uncle Shneyer believed so literally in the Seder visit of the Prophet Elijah that he set out the best armchair and the biggest beaker of Passover wine for him and, as is the custom, always left the door ajar for the ritual chant of invitation, the *Boruch ha-boh*.

This time, a visitor answered his welcome – a billy-goat of venerable age and sharp odour that happened to be roaming in the neighbourhood and was driven in by some scamps. Uncle Shneyer continued with the chant and seemed even to lend an ear to the hints of the ungodly gawking from the doorway that the guest was indeed the Prophet Elijah in disguise. In his enormous Chassidic enthusiasm, Uncle Shneyer got all of us, even the urchins who had staged the goat's visit, to join in the lusty singing of the ancient Aramaic tale of "The kid that Father bought for two *zoozim*," the *Chad Gadia*. It is the story of the little kid that was devoured by the cat, the cat devoured by the dog, and so on through all the stages of the strong devouring the weak and in their turn being devoured by those still stronger, stage by stage, until God, blessed be He, slaughtered the Angel of Death.

I had to leave Zheludek soon after this great event because I could not get enough students to provide for my board and lodging. Another escape route tried and failed, I went back home to Botchki to find it sinking further into dissolution.

My family was now installed in the narrower half of Berl the Apothecary's house – one of the better residences in town, with a glassed-in porch looking on to Market Square. It was not that they had grown less impecunious, but dwellings had become plentiful and cheap to rent as the cold pogrom thinned out the Jewish population and Jews emigrated or were reduced to beggary by confiscatory taxes. Berl, Botchki's most privileged Jew, had been squeezed so dry by the tax committee that he was forced to partition his house into two long, very narrow halves, and to rent out one of them.

Berl the Apothecary was not a qualified pharmacist, for even in czarist times the universities granted only provisional pharmacy licences to Jewish graduates. The provisors, as these pharmacists were called, were allowed to sell only milder prescription drugs. For the more potent medicines, Botchkivites had to go to the Polish pharmacist Pan Poznanski.

Mama received me with a flood of joyful tears, and my father, though offering me no word of welcome, was visibly affected by the prodigal's return. They still dreaded abandonment by their children, who were bent on escape by any means, by any route, and to any destination, but they dreaded even more our failure to escape. My sister Basheh, now of marriageable age, spent hours each day on her knees, waxing her narrow strip of "salon" parquet in the vain hope that our fancy new quarters might secure her a husband even if she had no dowry. If she failed to entice one, Father had agreed to let her join a Halutz training farm and qualify for a certificate to Palestine.

Chaim was away in Brest-Litovsk preparing for ordination in the multiple offices of *mohel*, shochet, kosher meat inspector, and reader of the Torah. He was already assured of his fare and an appointment by the Orthodox congregation of Buenos Aires, once he was certified by the High Rabbinate of Brest.

My parents knew that I too meant to get out of Poland and that only my seven-year-old brother Berele, who was an average scholar at the cheder, would remain at home. I was worried about him, for he had inherited none of Father's vigour and too much of Mama's diffidence for the kind of world he was to face. I was also saddened to see my father offer no opposition to any of our very different ways of quitting the family. The fight had gone out of him, and I felt for him in his defeat as though it were my own.

The mood in the brightest quarters which we had occupied since our house was destroyed in the War was black. With the break-up of the family in the offing, we already saw one another as shadows and heard one another as echoes.

# 42

## New Life

One vocation I had not tried while in the city was that of a writer, for I had been unable to work up my self-confidence to the point of submitting my "first fruits" to professional judgment. Now, back in Botchki, I decided to write a series of prose portraits describing the villagers and to take them to the redoubtable editor of the Byelo-stok's *Dos Naye Lebn*, or *New Life*.

This Jewish daily alternated in name between *Life* and *New Life* as frequently as the censors ordered its suppression for such offences as blaming the government for pogroms or alluding too pointedly to corruption in high places. *Life* would have run out of names had it not been for an oversight in the censorship law that forgot to stipulate that the name of a banned publication could not be used again. Most Jewish newspapers had a lead block made of the word "New", which they added or subtracted from the mast-head each time they were ordered to close, so that they could go to press without loss of time, prestige, or money. The censorship law was one of those all-too-rare instances in which the last laugh was on the oppressor.

With pockets bulging with the manuscripts on which I had spent as much time in calligraphy as in composition and thought, I tried to see the editor of the *New Life*, but he was a busy man who had to act as his own feature writer, news agency and proof-reader in addition to his primary duties as editor. Indeed, when finances were especially low, which was most of the time, he also had to help out with the typesetting. His single employee, honoured by the title chief of staff, was a young singing teacher who practised his profession part-time and otherwise fulfilled the functions of city reporter and errand boy for *Life* or *New Life*. Irritated, he advised me to wait until they put the paper to bed, late in the evening, and then seek out the editor at his home instead of the office.

"At this moment the boss is on the telephone to Marshal Pilsudski. We are expecting a call from the Prime Minister of England any minute now. I am busy, too, with somewhat smaller fry, having a half dozen ambassadors and the minister of railroads to dispose of between now and going to press. I see that you have a pocketful of masterpieces. I know that they are masterpieces even without reading them. Recently we have been flooded with masterpieces. In fact I have worked it out statistically; there are nine point two literary geniuses per thousand Jews in this part of Poland. Around here we are more ignorant than any other people in the world, but the gifted ones among us are far more gifted than anywhere else. What I mean is ... O, may all the devils take the entire profession. We already have more contributors than readers, believe me!"

He wound up his histrionics by throwing up both hands above his head: "Yet who am I, a mere mortal, to stand between you and posterity, maybe even immortality! For all I know I may be talking to a future Tolstoy. The editor, if I may make so bold, young sir, is best seen and most approachable at supper."

"And," he added with a flourish of his hat, which he had kept on throughout the interview, "that's all. I wish you a very good day and fine sleighing."

Despite his ridicule, I knocked on the door of the editor's home the same evening with a diffidence that alternated wildly between hope and apprehension.

The object of my worshipful pilgrimage was a small white-haired, clean-shaven, professional-looking man who sat with incredible dignity over a wooden bowl full of steaming potatoes. He ate heartily with a kitchen-sized wooden spoon – a potato and a slice of salt-herring at a bite. The editor manoeuvered his scalding potatoes with his tongue, shifting them from one side of his mouth to the other, while reaching for the jug of cool curds. The part of the table where he supped was covered with a starched white cloth; the rest was littered with books, manuscripts and great piles of newspaper clippings. The homely scene and the editor's wise, twinkling eyes set me at ease. Unable to smile because of the troublesome hot potato, he beamed at me over his spectacles and at long last brought forth a monosyllable, "Well?"

I spoke swiftly, determined to get in my piece before the editor had a chance to proffer the same kind of reception as his chief of staff.

"Please, sir, I would like to show you some short stories, or rather some portraits in prose. They are sketches of village characters. I know that lots of people are writing stories these days and that most of them write badly; but I want your opinion of my work. Will I ever be able to write, or am I devoid of talent?"

The editor looked at me squarely. He stopped manoeuvering his potatoes to reply, "Uh! This is a new one. Without exception they all first ask to be published. My critical opinion, they do mostly ask for it, but only as a formality or, even worse, as a calculated sop to my vanity, because they are always convinced of their own talent. You sure you don't think the same, young fellow?"

"I really don't know. Although I believe my stories have something to them, I cannot be my own critic."

"Good. Fire at will, then! Let's hear one," said the editor abruptly, between a hot potato and a gulp of curds.

Warming to my task, I read in an even voice; but as I read on, page after page, and the editor remained absorbed in his potatoes and curds, my confidence withered. Turning over a page, I looked at my judge and found him pondering the ceiling in apparent abstraction. The wooden spoon in his hand was suspended midway between the wooden bowl and the editorial mouth, like a question mark.

The two portraits he picked for immediate publication were "The Brothers Harkavi" and "The Jew-eater". The former was a rather unkind portrait of poor twin brothers who, lacking curlers, used to wave their long hair with wooden rolling pins. Payment reached me swiftly – on a street corner by the newspaper office – in a well-deserved but perhaps overdone beating of the author by the brothers themselves, their friends and, shock of shocks, my own best friends, including Avremke.

My "Village Portraits" began appearing weekly in *Dos Naye Lebn* – without honorarium. The recognition of its famous editor, Pessach Kaplan, was reward enough.

I hardly imagined that my first venture into Yiddish writing would be overtaken so soon by my meeting with the poet Rachel Korn. "Meeting" is not the right word, though, for it was far less, yet far more than a meeting.

# 43

## Rachel Korn

I fell in love with Rachel Korn in an act of double recognition: her photograph in the *Literarische Bletter* was that of the beloved face I had composed in my imagination over the years of my boyhood; and in the poems below the portrait was the soul with which I had endowed her over those years.

I do not know whether it was the beauty of the face that made me fall in love with the poems or the beauty of the poems that made me fall in love with the face. "Three Sketches of Village Misery" were the works of a poet of extraordinary talent and rare compassion. Would such a woman acknowledge the admiration of an uncouth young worshipper? I had to find out.

My letter to the goddess described me as an unimpressive, small-grown boy from a forsaken Podlasic village, choking on an excess of fresh air and lacking human companionship, unworthy of her attention, but longing to know more about her, all she could tell me. I overdid the frog self-portrait a little to call up the magic fairy in her that would turn me into a prince.

Rachel Korn proved as generous in her reply as in her poetry, writing that my letter had touched her. She would not yet tell me about herself, she said, except to admit that she too was unhappy – "No poet is happy, for if she were happy she would not be a poet." I simply would have to discover her for myself. But she did want to know everything about me: What were my hopes and longings? My realised dreams and disillusions? My future plans? Was I, too, a poet, a painter? She also wanted a photo of me, "even an old one, since the eyes don't change."

My phantom love had become a reality, accepting my worship and even demanding tribute. With her friendship my life would no longer be dreary. My faltering talents would burst into creative bloom. I would make her proud of me, gain her admiration and – everything becoming magically possible – win her love. But then my mood reversed itself, from elation to dejection. I berated myself knowing that my knock at her door was likelier to lead to rejection than to paradise.

I would have to submit to inspection both my soul and, by photograph, my body – an inspection I couldn't pass. My spiritual possessions were pathetically meagre, and my physical attributes equally inadequate. Terrified of losing her before I had even found her, I tried to characterise myself as a suffering villager of small achievement but great promise and thus arouse both her compassion and admiration. The photograph I sent, which showed an unfashionably attired village boy with a dreamy "poetic" look over a dreamy "poetic" bow tie, carried a similar message. In my answers to her questions, too, I exaggerated my weak points as well as my strong ones. I spoke of my traumatic past, my physical and spiritual hunger, my strong dislike of pretension, boundaries and regulations; of my hope that I would not remain standing with a vainly outstretched hand in search of an answering hand; of my longing to tell in poems what I could not say in prose; of my disillusion in those around me but faith in those close to me; and of my determination to move ever upward, both for the attraction of the peaks and for the exhilaration of the climb. Was I a poet? A painter? Certainly not the latter; and for the former I would need help, inspiration and love.

Her reply was prompt and volcanic:

You ask what I am, but the cost of my answers will be heavy. I am a human being whose feelings for others are intense, whose youth is as self-renewing as the ever-renewing earth. I find it terribly hard to write this letter. And why? Because facing my ever-young, vital humanity stand, like telegraph poles, my nine-and-twenty years.

My hands, too, find it very difficult to be the messengers of this kind of disappointment. They have done much harm, these hands of mine. With their small script, as though by a stranger's will, they have wrought misery on a number of human beings and maybe destroyed one.

She then told the story of her innocent romance at sixteen with a teacher whose passion soon bored her and whose sentimental letters she began to leave unanswered. His final letter, threatening suicide and ostensibly written by a friend, she had regarded as tasteless.

A few days later he was found lying in the fields strangled by his own tie, her photo and letters beside him.

And who eight years ago forced me to marry a man other than the one I loved? her letter went on – a shock to me since I had repressed the knowledge that she was married, a truth which the declension of her name, Kornova, would have made obvious if I had been willing to see it.

I seem to bring unhappiness to all who are close to me. It is hard to lose a friend, a tender heart, but I must tell you: escape from me Dovid Zhager, dear Dovid, while there is still time; it could one day become too late. Your heart stands open, your heart is rich like a granary in years of famine. I am sure that many take from its riches. I myself am taking from it.

Your photo is very different from what I imagined you to look like. It does not have the simplicity I expected, but your beautiful eyes and noble forehead and even your childlike, pouting lips have not disenchanted me.

I never did and probably never would try to sort out the hurt from the happier reactions upon crossing Rachel Korn's star. I lost the love of a tragic woman I had never met and was consoled by the radiance she had let shine upon me. The hand behind the scalpel that touched me was the hand of a healing friend, not of a femme fatale.

# 44

## Yankl's Suicide

At the age of nineteen, as my mother grew more and more anxious and dejected, I became more withdrawn and less rebellious. I wandered about the fringes of the great Byeloviezh forest seeking its stillness. The evenings were the worst, whether I walked along the unlit village lanes in aimless discussions with my unhappy chaver Yankl, Areh the Hebrew teacher's son, or punted our flat-bottomed skiff among the reeds of the Nuretz. We both felt trapped by the same darkness which seemed to envelop us in a solitude like a shroud.

Yankl and his father were of the unhappy species of deep-thinking, deep-feeling Jews who lack the will or the force to fight for survival. Areh was the most erudite modern Hebrew teacher in the village, but his bread was as scarce as his students. Yankl was both a better Talmudist and a more principled agnostic than I was, but did not have the push to fight his way. He accepted the place that was readily offered him in the Navaredoker Yeshivah, but the compromise of his beliefs soon drove him back to Botchki. There he wandered about the streets in despair, day and night, in rain or sunshine, seen but unseeing. His chosen haunts were the attic of the old shul and the bridges of the Nuretz. On moonlit nights Yankl, who had once studied forbidden agnostic books with Avremke and me, would commit his desolation to haunted char-coal sketches whose trees wept and reeds knelt in numb despair, and whose moonlight cast a deathly pall over all.

Yankl and I and all our friends had been driven into varying depths of despair. A wave of suicide, unequalled since the Cossack persecutions three centuries back, swept the Jewish communities of Poland, and Yankl hanged himself in the attic of the Old Synagogue.

As in the battle for his soul, the same conflicting forces seemed to have competed for his body. From the sacred texts' burial room in the shul attic came the pull of his origins, the demand that he mingle with the remains of the parchments and disintegrate with them. From the river came the offer of liberation from life's shackles, of a return to origins older than those of his people, the void older than the world. Yankl had chosen the death of a Jew over the death of a man.

My bond to Botchki was cut at the same moment that we took him down from the centre beam of the synagogue attic. Areh followed his only son a few days later, in the same place and manner. I knew that unless I found a way out of the village, my end would be the same.

Yankl had not been a talker, but in our last conversation, the evening before he died, he was more excited and talkative than I had ever seen him. We talked of our existence and felt a powerful identification in the very disparity of our views.

"What does your existence mean, Dovid?" Yankl started in a rushing whisper, as he continued to work on a sketch of a nearby willow, while I held the skiff level.

"Meaning?" I asked.

"I mean," he said, "why are you here, do you actually exist or are you a sketch by a cruel Artist, what is your aim and will you be satisfied if you reach it?"

"That's several questions in one," I retorted. "I have given up searching for the answers to stillborn questions. I want to understand and above all conquer my obsession with transience, the idea that being dead tomorrow means being dead already. I've been obsessed with the moment of the crossing-over since our days in cheder when I secretly sacrificed a cat to watch its soul departing."

"It wasn't secret enough, Diodie," he almost smiled as he corrected me. "I saw you working on it in the alley. It was Gruneh's tomcat. But," he hurled a hard missile at me, "if there is nothing left to want, isn't it better to be dead?"

"No, there is no point rushing. Tomorrow's death is as good as today's, and you can get in a night's dreams. In the short run, I can be satisfied with the short-term gifts of a short-term life. If you don't keep looking in its teeth, life can be quite good."

The moon was growing paler and Yankl's energy seemed to pale too. His excitement died away as he spoke: "The only thing I've ever wanted is to know, to be certain. To me, the word agnostic is a curse. How can I live if I don't know?"

"But, isn't uncertainty the very element that gives you freedom of thought and freedom of will? If you knew, you'd either have to obey God or float at random in the void."

I could now barely hear him. "No," he answered, "I will not live in a mute universe. If I cannot know, I cannot be!" He turned away his face and I thought I heard him weep silently.

Yankl did not remember that, even if in doubt, you must say Kaddish. If he had, he would perhaps have said Kaddish for the approaching death of both himself and his father.

# 45

## *A Family Learns English*

When Yankl hanged himself, I felt my umbilical link to the shtetl loosen, and I thought that if I did not find a way out of Botchki, my end would be the same as his. And then the road out opened, and hope appeared in the shape of Sophie from the neighbouring town of Bransk.

Her family brought me over to Bransk to teach them English. They were in a hurry, with only a few months left before they joined their father, a carpenter who had emigrated to South Africa. They wanted daily lessons, they didn't bargain, and they paid in sterling for seven half-day sessions a week. This family tutorial was bigger than any class I had ever taught, taking in sixteen-year-old Sophie, her four younger sisters and three younger brothers, her mother, and three of her grandparents, all forming one beginner's English class.

I was taken aback to come across Welfke on my very first day in Bransk. I saw him in one of the town's main streets, and greeted him in our usual spoofing style, "Sholem aleichem, *bocher*. Are you following me about? What are you doing for food? And who's made this gorgeous blouse of yours?"

A year had passed since we had seen each other, but within minutes we were reminiscing about our days at the Mellers as though we had never parted. Welfke had returned to Byelsk to fashion prostheses and to eat more of the Kishinev Bobbe's "tastiest mamellige in Moldavia." Welfke had many skills, and many uses for them, but had never succeeded in making them pay until he took up dentures.

"What about the gold?" I asked. "Can you take me along next time you go to your mine?"

"No money again, Diodke?" he teased. "Do you have to be hungry to travel to Bransk?"

He told me that he had acquired a tiny supply of gold from the "diamond of a chaverte". After using it up on dentures for Tatte himself and a few clients, he had found a job – against his principles – with a Dostoyevskian character: a middle-aged, pale, dyspeptic but most self-respecting lady dentist, a semi-illegal Russian refugee who now lived in Bransk. She engaged him as her technician, gave him a corner of her small dental surgery for a lab, and paid him as much as she could afford, which was not much. "But it keeps my ancestors in bread to put between their dentures and leaves something for me."

"With your seductive blouses and your healthy looks, surely you aren't tubercular any longer?" I asked. "I've just arrived in Bransk, and this morning I started instilling the great English language into a family of twelve – from a toothless baby to an equally toothless grandpa of eighty-three. I'll introduce you to my oldest pupil if you swear to keep away from the ones who eat with their own teeth."

"Any '*lialkes*' in the lot, professor?" he asked. "A woman is the only way out of this Gehennem. You know I can cross any border, but even I can't go across the ocean without money or affidavits. And that's where my lialke comes in."

"Is your dream city still New York?"

"Right you are!" he exclaimed, throwing back his locks defiantly. "Think I'm going to go on sculpting dentures for ever? I'm still Wolf the poet. I had a poem printed in New York two months ago and I want you to see it."

"As soon as you wish. And in New York!" I said. "Now, back to your lialke. What mermaid gets the privilege of carrying you over to New York?"

"Oh, it's a girl named Menke. Pretty in a dumpy way and dumb in a pretty way. Her papa is in New York in some line of business – probably a small-time gangster, but I'll have to risk it."

While we were in Bransk, Welfke and I spent many of our evenings together and visited each other's lialkes. My days there were unusually peaceful. My class went along well and everyone was enthusiastic and studious.

As in the fable, the class swan, pike and crab were harnessed into the same cart. Sophie was the swan of the team, outsoaring not only her classmates but threatening to overtake her tutor's store of the language. She was top in all lessons but reached her elocutionary peak with her recital of the "Fred" poem, modesty of subject and arbitrary pronunciation notwithstanding:

> And so at dinner Fred began:
> "Papa, you think you see
> Two apples on the dish,
> Now I'll prove them three.
> For this is one, and that is two,
> And one and two make three!"
> "If this is so," replied Papa,
> And if what you say is true,
> I'll have one, Mama'll have one
> And the third we'll leave for you!"

At the triumphant crescendo of "Yo-o-ou-u!" Sophie would throw back her chestnut mane with delight. Her mother cast looks of pride at her eldest while Sophie's grandparents exchanged looks of wonderment accompanied by tears of joy, or maybe dread at their forthcoming voyage. Only the deaf maternal grandfather looked on dully with his watery eyes. All that he had learned after three months was to render good morning and goodnight, which came out something like "wut mogin" and "wut nayie", without distinguishing between which time of day he meant. However, as Sophie's mother rightly pointed out, since the lessons were paid for, why shouldn't everybody benefit?

In the many hours that we were alone, I poured out my predicament and confided the full extent of my fears to my softhearted star pupil. To her mother, our long conversations and frequent walks together meant only one thing: courtship. She was delicate about it, alluding to a match as "it" and leaving the initiative to God: "It will prosper, God willing." But there was no doubt that a claim was in the making.

Not so Sophie. In the way she looked at me I discerned the message: I know better, Dovid. I know you're not in love with me – possibly because it was the message I hoped for. I thought I wasn't really in love and, indeed, had no idea what I would feel if I were.

Among the girls in the kvutzeh there had been slim, dark-eyed Hannah, the daughter of Izzy the horsetrader. Unlike her brothers, who stole horses at night and sold them by day, Hannah came to be so respected for her honesty and intelligence that she was elected kvutzeh treasurer. Most of the male Halutzim had imagined themselves in love with her, to the chagrin of the other chavertes, but she seemed to favour me. Whenever Hannah was alone with me, she'd lead the talk to love, which meant "up to kissing".

Once or twice I had also joined the other boys in peeping around the river bend at the bathing women some hundred yards away, but otherwise the closest I had come to a sex adventure was the episode at the bay island.

One hot summer afternoon, while I was punting my flat-bottomed skiff around the hay island in the middle of the Nuretz tributary, I was hailed from the shore by a straw-haired peasant girl. She asked me to take her across to the island to retrieve her scythe. She was about the same age as me, and she wore only a brief calico smock. She stood in the stern, her body exposed through the flimsy wet smock, and started laughing when I blushed. As the skiff slid up against the low meadow of the island, she came up hard against me as she disembarked. She seemed in no rush to get her scythe. We sat down on the bank, feet in the water, and looked for words to start a conversation. I stroked her hair lightly, tentatively. The girl giggled, threw her saucy arms around me, gave me a smacking kiss on the mouth and ran off.

My relationship with Sophie began to take shape through our long evenings talking together. I had come to admire her, and I grew more and more impressed by her insight, for she understood everyone around us more deeply than I did.

She had never taken to Welfke. One evening, shortly after he migrated, Sophie confided her distaste for Welfke and her conviction that he was trouble.

"What makes you say that?" I asked her. "He has his good points."

"That's true. And he has his bad points. Except that his bad points are worse than his good ones. I can't admire anything about him, because he admires himself so much." Then she added, "He's trouble because he plays Welfke instead of being it."

Welfke had used his lialke as a ticket to his coveted New York, but he soon came to fear that her father – a bootlegger, it turned out – might "rub him out" if he didn't marry his daughter. In his first letter from America, Welfke wrote to me how he had escaped by stowing away on a banana boat to Costa Rica.

Sophie's words about Welfke found their target. I could not stop dwelling on him and most searchingly on our disturbing relationship. For three years our bantering dialogues had not only hidden each from the other, but had also started to turn us into caricatures of ourselves. They had made me begin doubting my own reality – the truth of my own feelings and views.

As for Sophie, with each day my admiration for her grew, and our friendship deepened, but whatever equilibrium her company had restored to me was shattered by my imprisonment.

# 46

## Disaster . . .

Far from opening the road to a better life, my breakthrough as a writer with the "Village Portraits" almost cost me my life. My honorarium for *"Der Yidnfresser"* or "The Jew-Eater" brought me the dire vengeance of its subject – Pan Lukas, the village burgomaster.

I had been very careful to render him unrecognisable. I had substituted "the village of N. near Grodno" for Botchki, made the subject a tax assessor – the nemesis of Jewish shtetl small-traders everywhere – instead of a burgomaster, and altered his physiognomy in every detail but one: I could not resist dubbing him the "one-eyed knave" – and Pan Lukas had lost an eye in a duck-shooting accident.

Like his model, my fictional tax assessor had fed "his" Jews to the authorities so faithfully and so profitably that he was kept in office by every regime in turn – czarist, Prussian and Polish alike.

Jews who did not grease his palm or who did so inadequately were denounced – this one for not reporting income, that one for cheating on one of the numerous other taxes, a third for trading on Sundays through the back door of his store, and yet another for maiming his own hand to avoid the draft. Like his model, too, my assessor was a discerning cannibal who didn't devour his own: like many patriotic Poles, he sought out the Jews, who were the enemies of Christ and the Christian nation, and natural victims to boot.

Jewish Botchki read *"Der Yidnfresser"* in the only copy of the *Dos Naye Lebn* that reached the village. They chuckled at the lampooning of their foe, and hoped that Pan Lukas would not hear about it.

Since all of the Jews disliked the burgomaster and none of the goyim could read Yiddish, he probably heard the news from his friends in the Ochrana, which obtained daily translations of all Yiddish publications, for a week after the story appeared, and with no warning, Pan Lukas struck.

It was a winter morning. The windowpanes were frosted over and the snow was deep. I was leading the family English class at pronouncing the 'th' sound, if not correctly, then at least *somewhere* between the 's' and 't' sounds, when the door was kicked in and two policemen in sheepskin greatcoats barged in with rifles and put handcuffs on my wrists.

Sophie and her mother went on their knees to beg for mercy, hinting that a gift would be forthcoming if the police took me to the burgomaster of Botchki, Pan Lukas, before marching me directly to Byelsk so that my family might help me. Sophie's mother held out a ten-zloty note. The senior of the pair took it readily enough and said that sending me to Pan Lukas was the very last thing they should ask for. "He's in a raging fury against this Zhid. It's on his charge of arson that we have to take him to Byelsk for trial before higher authority. So don't ask us to bring the chicken to the fox's lair."

The ten-zloty note nevertheless saved my life. I was allowed to wait for all the winter clothes the family could gather together, including the father's felt overboots, which he had left behind since they were useless in Africa. The family stuffed them with rags to make them fit me. As she crouched to help me with the overboots, Sophie whispered, "I'll get you out. I know I will."

"And here, Zhidek," teased the junior policeman, "is how we keep you real warm. Just stretch your arms forward." He put his rifle across my forearms after marching me out on to the icebound Byelsk Road. As my arms sagged from exhaustion, the rifle slid lower and lower and squeezed the handcuffs into my flesh. When I slipped and fell on my face, the policemen at first cursed and kicked me but soon decided that punishment would slow our march so much that we might not reach Byelsk by daylight, and so risk a wolfpack attack after nightfall. They took the rifle off my arms and the handcuffs off my wrists. "You aren't running away, not into the woods and in this weather, and anyway, you'd just get your Zhid arse full of lead if you tried." We got to the lockup as night fell. They summoned the watchman, and then threw me on to a straw pile in the muddy, windowless cell. No one said a word about food, water or anything else.

In a few minutes, just enough time to gather from their uncouth noises and smells that my two cellmates were drunks, I was fast asleep. I woke up several times during the night, numb with the chill but feeling little bodily pain and no mental distress. I knew that I was in mortal danger, but this awareness left me emotionally indifferent. I should have been terrorised by the arrest, the forced march and now the company of two criminals in a pitch black cell. There was no explanation for my calm, though I thought I saw a parallel to the calamitous events years back, when the soldiers had taken potshots at me in the cherry tree. Then, too, I had been unable to feel panic or dread.

Daylight was creeping through the bottom of the door when I woke to the guffaws of my companions as they went through my pockets. I was surprised to find myself grinning back at them as I handed over my change and one small banknote. This instinctive gesture earned me a friendly slap on the back and the compliment of *dobri Zhidek, jak Boga kocham* – "You're a real nice Jewboy, as I love God."

The friendly louts were farmhands who had been jailed the day before with the loot of a small-time robbery still on them. They had been so drunk that they couldn't rightly recall how badly they had hurt the victim. If he was dead – and they rather feared he might be – it was the noose. *"Hospodi pomiluy!"* May the Lord have mercy! said one, switching into Byelorussian. The other made the sign of the cross.

There was only one way out of the reach of the rope, they confided, and that was through a hole that they planned to dig that night using their bare hands and some chunks of flint lying about. The prison where they were sure to be transferred to next would have brick walls and cement floors and armed guards at the door. They had no idea where they would run once they got out, but out they meant to get. I was welcome to join them unless I expected a pat on the back as the penalty for arson. If I survived the interrogations and the beatings by cellmates over the months to come, I'd be lucky to get off with ten years. I really should go with them.

I said nothing and went back to sleep. There was no cell check or food delivery that day, and I slept almost right through it, experiencing little discomfort and no hunger or thirst. The Byelorussians spent the evening conversing in whispers. It was near midnight when I fell asleep again.

A sudden blast of icy air blowing in through the hole the two men had dug during the night woke me up. I felt a calloused hand pressing on my face and heard the older farmhand whisper, "Run or stay behind, Zhidek friend, but make no sound and tell no tales until our escape is discovered. If I thought you not trustworthy, I'd strangle you right here and now, like this." He pressed my throat in his huge hand, but only lightly, and with a little laugh.

"Don't worry, you two," I answered. "I never saw or heard a thing except that you took my money, called me Zhid, and gave me quite a few whacks. Good luck. But I won't join you because I wouldn't last another day in this weather. I don't know what time you made your break because I slept right through until the alarm was given. Right?"

They slid through the hole on their bellies and into the blizzard. I covered myself with the now abundant supply of straw and pretended to sleep. Of all crazy irrelevancies to occupy me during the empty hours in the cell was the *Chayeh Odom*, especially the two among the thousands of *dinim* or laws dealing with prison. One says: "As a Jew comes out of prison, he must recite the prayer for miracles, before no fewer than ten men, two of whom must be Torah scholars."

"Why should I bless His Name for getting me out," I thought, "since I'm not allowed to curse Him for getting me in here?" The other piece of helpful rabbinical jurisprudence, in the midst of the laws of the Sabbath, stipulates that a man may wear on the Sabbath certain objects of clothing and jewellery on his person, but not carry them, for that constitutes labour. The rabbis generously allow the Jewish inmate to wear his chains on the Sabbath and even walk in them.

When the police came to fetch me, I was marched to the district chief of police's office by a single policeman. The other stayed behind to organise the chase after the two Byelorussians. In an anteroom I was given a dish of hot kasha. The chief seemed to accept my protestations of ignorance about the jail break, nor did he regard my alleged fire-setting crimes as being of any great consequence.

"Listen, Zhidku. I don't like you Jews any better than your 'one-eyed knave'," he gave me a little smile. "But I don't like to watch that leech, who makes such a deal about Jews sucking Polish blood, gorge himself on other people's blood, even Jews' blood. He sends you to me charged with arson but does not mention times and places. He ties you to a 'Red cell' – or to a mysterious Jewish kabal. Yet I wasn't about to let you off just like that without some proof that you're innocent. Your staying in your cell after the jail break provides us with all the proof we need. Now keep your big nose clean and get back to Botchki before we change our minds," he concluded with a wink. "If you keep to yourself what you heard here, even from your parents, we'll do what we can. One last bit of advice, Panie Zhid: your one-eyed knave will get you in the end unless you get yourself to Africa as, we're told, you wish to do. And so, I won't say *do widzenia* but goodbye."

Only in Poland could you meet perfectly decent human beings who *pretended* to be anti-Semites.

# 47

## . . . and Deliverance

During the short time I was in prison, the Jews of Botchki and quite a few goyim had resorted to truly heroic measures to save me. They stormed both the sacred and profane seats of power.

My mother led the women of "half the town" into the men's domain during the Sabbath eve service, defying, as did their grand-mothers before them in times of great calamity, the unwritten interdiction against female trespass in the synagogue proper or approach to its Holy Ark, wherein dwelt the *Shechine*, the presence of God. My mother rushed to the portals of the Ark before she could be stopped. The women opened the gold-and-blue velvet *parocheth*, stuck their heads into the innermost depths of the holy-of-holies, and sobbed out their challenge to their Father in Heaven to intercede on behalf of Dovid *ben* Reb Yisroel.

Earlier in the day a big crowd had also invaded the village hall to petition Pan Lukas to intercede with the authorities. The arson charge against their innocent Dovid was an outrage and they thought it their burgomaster's duty to fling it back into the accusers' faces. Pan Lukas sat in his official armchair, strangely ill at ease, twirling his wax moustache and mumbling something about arrogant Jews bringing about their own downfall. He said he would see what could be done. Never suspecting that it was he and he alone who was the perpetrator of the outrage, the petition-ers withdrew.

When I returned from my incarceration and told the villagers of the police chief's warning, they took it seriously. The arson charges against me had not been refuted, other charges could be trumped up at any moment and I would return to prison, this time perhaps for good. I had to be rescued.

In the end deliverance came from a most unexpected quarter: young Dr Schleifman who had just settled in Botchki as the shtetl's first doctor and as his first post. Both sides had been rather disappointed. As the only assimilated Jew in the village – a goy to the Orthodox Jews and a Jew to the goyim of his class – he felt like neither and was very lonely. He and his wife befriended me, a callow youth, and often invited me to share the earphones of their crystal radio and to talk about the unsatisfactory conditions of our lives.

Schleifman's classmate at the Warsaw medical school was Dr Kuniarski who, since he was Christian and a Pole, obtained the position of surgeon to the Byelsk military district as his first posting, which meant few official duties, good pay, and fringe benefits, including getting bribes for certifying young men as medically ineligible for the draft. As a Jew, Schleifman was lucky to get a practice at all, even one in the wilderness, and it was Kuniarski's influence – they had been, after all, classmates for six years – that had got him there. Dr Schleifman returned the favour by referring any draft-shy young man who could pay for an exemption to his friend. Most of these clients were Jews who wanted to avoid the *treyf* or non-kosher army diet at all costs or who dreaded three years of bullying by Christian officers and enlisted men.

Dr Schleifman meanwhile protected me from Pan Lukas and the danger of new charges he might invent by making it known that I had entered his service as a volunteer assistant. Right in the eye of the storm raging around me, an opportunity for me to make a favourable impression on Dr Kuniarski had arisen when the Botchki policeman shot himself in the forest. This was the first officially serious case for Dr Schleifman and he became involved in the county level investigation.

He took me with him to the forest as witness to his examination of the head wound and the position of the gun in relation to it, and as his messenger to give the alarm to Byelsk – for he was obliged to stay with the dying man until the relevant officials arrived. Pan Lukas was now unlikely to go after me, for a while at least.

Although Dr Schleifman had the head of a goy – hatless, beardless and free-thinking – his heart was compassionately Jewish and outraged by injustice. He was determined to help me and enlisted the help of Dr Kuniarski who, in turn, went to work on his friend the district police chief. The solution they devised called for thirty American dollars to be slipped into the palm of Pan Lukas by no less a personage than the police chief, in exchange for withdrawing the charges and speeding me on my way out of the country. The burgomaster was to change my date of birth in the official register, making me two years younger and thus entitling me to an emigration visa. Another thirty dollars would then be transmitted through Schleifman to Kuniarski to back up the job done by Pan Lukas: Dr Kuniarski, through the special procedure of "age estimation" by the district draft board based on his professional medical examination, guaranteed the applicant an external passport.

Upon the smooth conclusion of the matter, Dr Kuniarski would "lose" forty dollars to his friend the police chief in a friendly card game – for making the miracle of my deliverance possible. The only player in this musical chairs' bribery game who never gained a groschen was the Jew with the goy head.

Sophie, meanwhile, warned her father that unless he rushed the affidavit for my admittance to South Africa, it might be too late. The affidavit arrived in the same week as my passport. Sophie, the dear, faithful friend who gave so much and took so little, came to visit me in Botchki to hurry me on my way.

We kissed for the first time and she told me that all she wanted was that I should save myself. She smiled through her tears. Was this love?

By February I had a passport and a ticket from Danzig to London by ship. My ransom had been paid by contributions from Botchki's Jews, and I signed notes promising to reimburse – from my first earnings overseas – all who had contributed to my hundred-dollar ransom. I hoped to get the payment for my passage to South Africa from an uncle I had in London, Nahum Zhager.

The "draft" Uncle Marim-Yosl wrote out for me to take to Uncle Nahum was more an appeal than a legal demand. It was for the equivalent of the hundred roubles Marim-Yosl had lent Nahum some forty years earlier to help him move to England. If Nahum honoured it, I would be able to buy my ticket to Cape Town and not have to importune Sophie's father, for the future depended more on him than on us. He was used to having things his own way and wouldn't put up with our plan to postpone settling down until I got a university degree.

The "draft" would reduce my obligation to him, and it would also help me repay my ransom. It read as follows:

With the help of God, Lord of Abraham, Isaac and Jacob, greetings to our famed and Godly brother Nahum, in the far land of Anglia:

DRAFT.

Whereas I, thy younger and less worthy brother, advanced thee the sum of one hundred roubles upon thy departure to far shores in the year 5648 of the Creation.

Whereas, not having heard from thee in several sevens of years, I trust that thou hast indeed, with the help of the Almighty, prospered.

Now, then, the bearer of this DRAFT, Dovid, son of our brother Israel, as much thy nephew as mine, flesh of thy flesh and blood of thy blood, having by miracle escaped imprisonment and possibly death at the hands of the new Hammans, is seeking thy aid and succour to speed him on his way from Anglia to safety and prosperity in the most distant land of South Africa.

In mercy and brotherly justice, though not literally in the letter of the Law of the Rabbis, this DRAFT shall entitle him – by God's charity and thine own pious conscience – to the amount of thy debt to me, with or without lawful increase, which thou pay to him according to thy prosperity.

And may there be peace on Israel.

Thy younger brother who shall ever honour and bless thee,

*Ha-katan* Marim-Yosl ben Berl Zhager.

Given on the sixth day of Nissan in the

Year of the Creation of the World 5688.

# 48

## I Discover My Father

On the last Sabbath before my departure from Botchki, I went to shul to be called up for the *maftir* – the last and most honorific portion of the week's reading of the Torah. After years fighting God and his earthly emissaries, I was happy to be welcomed back. My imprisonment and the town's intercession and ransom on my behalf had brought me once again into the Botchki I had repeatedly, but never fully, rejected.

At the summons of *Yaimeid* ("Let him stand up"), I mounted the bimeh. I intoned the Blessing of the Torah, my voice rising as if greeting a re-discovered friend, and the reader began chanting the portion. As I listened, I felt a dissociation between the present and the past. The reader's voice faded and was displaced by the voices of the distressed, in the frantic stormings of the Holy Ark demanding God's intervention in such calamities as the Great Fire of 1917; and by the rare voices of jubilation, in the thanksgiving Hallel on happy events such as the Balfour Declaration or the welcoming of Rabbi Hannan.

I also recalled the moments of anguish in our synagogue – Reuben's haemorrhage as his father, Reb Gershon-Ber, chanted the Kol Nidrei; Yankl's suicide; Zeide's funeral; and my insane friend Motl's desecration of the Sabbath prayers by an outburst of blasphemy.

When I lifted my eyes from the Scroll, I saw my father sobbing under his talless and many of the people who had parted with their savings for my ransom moist-eyed. Why was I discovering only now, as I was about to leave them forever, how much they meant to me? Why had I so often under-rated them? Was I not to be pitied more than the poorest among them? Should I not have known in all the years of my antagonistic symbiosis with them that their compassion was greater than mine?

I descended from the bimeh after reciting the closing blessing, with voice quavering and throat choked up.

In that moment of witnessing my father's sobbing self-abasement, I stumbled on to his secret. There are two ways in which men in my father's predicament weep – in the hope for forgiveness and in accepting their own damnation. There was no mistaking in which way my father wept. In my early teens, I had begun to wonder whether his rage against Mama and me might not be directed more at himself than at us, and whether it could have stemmed from an unforgivable real or imagined sin demanding punishment. Could it have been his rushing to the forest fire on the Sabbath, his subsequent trial, and the exoneration that did not convince him? The man, once doting – still doting – on his son and wife, who now lived with a zealous God's sword over his head, may have done what he had to do to provide for them, at the cost of losing both worlds.

Could not this have started Father's decline into a reclusive, hostile stranger in his own home? The more we suffered, the angrier he became. The more we cringed, the more despairing he grew. Only the sudden turn of events with my imprisonment showed us a glimpse of what could have been, and of a life he had perhaps sold for nothing.

Father's tragic life may have originated not so much from his zeal as from darker corners of himself. What a shame to have been deprived of a father's love while having a father, and to recover it only in parting from him! Knowing that he would rather die than speak of it, or even lend his ear to a son so far from God, I said nothing.

After I left the lectern, we sat in silence, but not in peace. Only in my thoughts did I say, "Peace be with you, Tatte." I wanted to believe that in his mind he answered, "and unto you be peace, my child."

I knew that the impact of my last maftir would be short-lived. Even in the heart of my surrender to the prayers' power, I caught myself demanding an account from the Creator.

On the faces of my neighbours, I saw no resentment that I was the one to go free. Their forlorn dreams of better times had, for a magic moment, turned to hope again – the hope that their fellow countryman Dovid might yet intercede for them in another land.

On our way back from shul to Bobbe's, I confided in Uncle Shieh. He was obviously overcome, but kept silent for a while before reacting: "How do you feel now about leaving the family, Diodie?"

"Too agitated to be certain," I answered. "I feel as though I have just found my father, but that I still cannot forgive him for the misery he brought upon us, especially on Mama. And I'm still worried about the future."

"I wish I could help in some way," he said, "but how?"

"Keep a protective eye on Mama, Uncle Shieh, when I have gone, and see that Father makes it easier for her. I also beg you to watch over little Berele. Our house will not be much of a home for my timid little brother."

"That I will, I swear," Uncle Shieh assured me tearfully, "with all my strength, Diodie."

My last Sabbath was chock-full. Just about half of Botchki, not just close friends or relatives, tried to entice me for a parting drink, for tea and cake, or just to *gezegenen* – to say goodbye and maybe offer a little memento of them. By evening, my pockets were bulging with forget-me-not enamel stickpins from the girls, amulets against evil spirits and dangerous beasts from the old people, and some practical objects such as a safety razor or a tie from chaverim. There was a good bit of crying by some of the girls and a whispered regret from Hannah for failing to take our friendship "beyond kissing".

# 49

## *Escape*

In one terrifying moment everything changed. Surrounded by the family, Father was just "seeing off the Sabbath" in the chant separating the sacred day from weekdays when Dr Schleifman entered without knocking and signalled silence with his finger on his lips. In a whisper, he warned us that Pan Lukas had made new charges against me and that the police chief would not be able to hold him off. I had a few hours at most to get away.

I blew out the *Havdolleh*, the Sabbath candle, and in the dark I warned: "Don't look worried, and just say that Dr Schleifman came by to examine me and ordered me to stay in bed." On my way out, I grabbed my wicker valise to hide it in the cowshed and, knee-deep in the snowdrifts, pushed on through the back lanes until I got to Izzy, the horse-dealer's house. Hannah, who only a few hours earlier had regretted our thwarted romance, blanched when she saw me, but tried bravely to spoof: "Come to collect already, Diodie?"

"No, Hanneleh, just to get my life saved," I quipped back. "It seems that Pan Lukas accepted our bribe just to trick me, and never meant to let me get away. Now you have to help. No one knows I'm here."

Hannah took me up to see her father and three brothers in the "trading room". Thanks to the weather, all of them were home.

Hannah suggested how I might be smuggled out "past the mamzer's nose" that very night in one of father's padded fruit crates, loaded on to Noah's Ark.

"Father," she explained, "will get a sudden attack of appendicitis and will have to be urgently moved in the mail van to a hospital, with me as his nurse." Hersh-Loaf would be dissuaded from driving them through a blizzard and asked to lend his sleigh to Izzy's sons, who would promise to return it to him in time for his regular morning trip to Byelsk, weather permitting. "We will only pretend to be going to Byelsk in the Ark but stop in Dziecian, where Tatte's light sleigh is already awaiting us, and transfer Diodie to it."

Yoshke went off to deal with Hersh-Loaf and Bentzi, Hannah's second brother, took a hand-sled to fetch the crate and my valise. I asked Bentzi to hang around our cowshed till my mother came for the evening milking, and tell her gently from me to walk slowly along the road by the water pump at exactly an hour before midnight.

When the crate arrived, Hannah fetched a mirror. "I must let you look at yourself," she cried and laughed at the same time, "in your brother Chaim's black-satin made-over suit and the 'commissar' leather jacket much too big for you! Do you still love me, my Diodele? Before we crate you up, let me just try to give some of my life to you with a last kiss." She half threw herself into the crate after me in a flood of tears. I could hardly let go of her hand to fasten the cover over me. Through the breathing holes, I could only see her knees.

At eleven, Izzy and Hannah were installed inside the sleigh on a mountain of pillows over my crate. One of the brothers was in the driver's seat with the other two riding their own horses and leading the reserve animals by the bridle.

I began to feel disoriented. Mama was coming to help me in my escape, but which escape? When I ran away from home before? "As soon as I see Mama, I must thank her for the silver piece she took from Father's pocket," I mumbled. "I must also ask her pardon for not saying goodbye properly and for not being able to look at each other one last time."

We neared the spot where, I had heard them say, "Feigl will be waiting." Feigl? Who was Feigl? I knew only Mama. Who will cry for Feigl *bass* Reb Leibe watching the sleigh which was taking me away from her a second time? Inarticulate, timorous, stricken, how could she cope when I was gone? Would she even want to cope? The monstrous thought struck me that if she did, I would feel abandoned.

The sleigh stopped but the rage of the snowstorm made it impossible for Mama and me to hear or see each other. I could dimly make out a dark, sagging figure of despair, straining to see me through the white-out. I must have imagined her lips forming my name. She could not have heard me call out to her, for my voice would be less than a whisper in this furious white hell.

Yoshke tugged on the reins and we moved on, Hannah and I holding fingers through the peephole. We cleared the village without discovery or pursuit and soon reached Dziecian about a mile away. Yoshke had cut the telephone wire overhead, in case Lukas should get suspicious and try to call Byelsk.

The brothers carried the crate into the barn where Izzy's sleigh was parked. Hannah pulled me up, relieved that I was only numb, and gave me a sip of vodka. Yoshke was to drive her and Izzy back and return the Ark, explaining that they had turned around when Izzy suddenly recovered before they had got half-way to Byelsk.

Bentzi and the youngest brother, Peiske, meanwhile harnessed two of the horses to Izzy's sleigh and tethered the other two to the sides for some protection from the storm. "Hannah told us to take you to the Czeremcha rail junction," said Bentzi, "on the direct line to Warsaw, hand you over to a friendly railway worker who owes us a favour and asks no questions, to take you as far as Warsaw and put you on the night train to Gdansk. You will be safe."

The ten miles from Dziecian to Czeremcha took the rest of the night, and the only clue to the road were the occasional glimpses of telegraph poles. The harnessed horses sank once into a snowed-over pit and had to be pulled up by the spare horses. But the steel-shod sleigh held steady and seemed to float over the drifts. When the horses reared on an open stretch of road, we knew that we were being followed by wolves, and Peiske dipped pine torches into the bucket of pitch and lit one for each of us.

How much had changed in these few hours! Now I was no longer leaving my country, I was being spat out by it. Yet, how sorry I felt to leave behind the good Jewesses who had followed my mother in the storming of the Holy Ark and the good Jews who had pawned their rings and watches for my ransom! And how I regretted parting from the good goyim who had befriended and protected me – the Stolkowskis, Helena, Marcinova!

Had the midwife's prophecy, boding trouble for the newborn

when he arrived in the cataclysmic storm of 1908, caught up with me as I was leaving in the storm of 1927? Or was it still the same storm? In my trance-like state, I saw Zeide hanging up amulets to fend off the Evil Eye and the chair of Elijah on which I was pledged to the congregation of God's Chosen. Was the battle against the designs of Pan Lukas – waged by Mama, Schleifman, Sophie, Hannah, and most wondrously, by Botchki's tender-hearted horse thieves – the sequel to Zeide's battle against the original fiend?

At daybreak, we reached the cottage of the Czeremcha railwayman. While we thawed out, Bentzi told me about his meeting with my mother in the cowshed: "I listened to the milk spurting into the bucket and to her sobs and I was shaken up."

"Did you by any chance hear my mother say 'Let the harm coming to him fall on my head'?"

Bentzi was incredulous: "How did you know?"

So we did say goodbye, Mama and I, after all, through a messenger who was tongue-tied but heard the sounds of milking and sobbing merge into a single voice – the voice of my mother.

From the train window I looked down the platform at the brothers, my last link to my mother and my village, and I intoned inwardly:

> Let my right hand forget her cunning
> If I forget you, Mother,
> If I forget you, Botchki.

# Epilogue

## VEGA ZAGIER ROBERTS

My father's Uncle Nahum in London did not honour the forty-year-old debt, and the fare to South Africa was provided by Sophie's father. As soon as Dovid arrived in Capetown, Sophie's father insisted that he marry Sophie immediately and enter the family business, rather than postponing the marriage until he finished university. But the dream of getting an education was not one he was prepared to give up; after a tearful midnight farewell with the ever-understanding Sophie, Dovid left the home of the only people he knew in this new land to make his own way.

For the next few years, he scraped a living from a variety of jobs. Besides writing for the Yiddish monthly *Dorem Afrike* (*South Africa*), he worked as a shop assistant in the colliery town of Witbank, a bus conductor, a rice seller, a carbon-paper salesman, and even for a few weeks helped to collect penguin eggs on Dassen Island. He attended night-school to learn English and was then admitted to Capetown University where he earned a B.A. and a master's degree in Biblical Exegesis. Always a rebel against convention, he had a long relationship with an Indian woman, Zarini, who introduced him to leaders of the South African India Congress, to the Gandhi family, and to many others who brought him into the centre of political events. He was outspoken against racial prejudice, published an impassioned poem "Johannesburg", about the black miners, and made a speech against discrimination before the South African India Congress which drew much attention and was widely quoted in the press. Increasingly, he was able to make a living as a journalist, including getting a contract with the official Polish government news service PAT as its correspondent for Southern Africa. He arranged for the modest stipend for this work to be paid directly to his family in Botchki.

Seven years after arriving in Capetown, his growing reputation as a journalist and the friendship of a liberal minister procured him a British passport: within a fortnight, he was on his way to London. In 1936, he became the chief European correspondent for *Africopa*, a news agency for the South African liberal press with its headquarters in Paris. His assignments included a long stint at the League of Nations in Geneva, reporting from countries threatened by Hitler or Mussolini, and covering the Spanish Civil War in Catalonia. His articles were collected into a book, *Seven Days Among the Loyalists*, which was later accepted for publication in London in 1939 (though in the event not published because of the outbreak of war), but which led to his expulsion from Spain by Franco. It was during this period that he managed a brief assignment in Warsaw, which enabled him to make a visit to Botchki. His family was living in relative comfort, not only because of the money he had been providing, but because receiving money from a Polish government agency meant that they were treated as "government employees". His brother Chaim had long since emigrated to Argentina, and his sister Basheh to Palestine, but Berel, "sixth spoon", was still living in Botchki, married and with one child. Bobbe was still alive, old and bedridden but still lucid, and very proud to see her grandson arrive in a droshki.

By the summer of 1939, with the threat of imminent war, *Africopa* closed its Paris office and my father returned to London. When his attempt to join the war effort in Britain was turned down, he booked a passage to the United States on the *Athenia*, but sold his ticket when Reuters contracted to fly him into Poland as their battlefront correspondent. Fortunately for him, this plan had to be abandoned when the Germans closed all access to Poland from the West. He was doubly fortunate, in that the *Athenia* was sunk by a German submarine just hours after Britain declared war on Hitler. He had to wait fifteen months before he was able to get on a British convoy ship to New York, and it was during this long wait that he wrote the first draft of *Botchki*.

In New York, he enrolled at the Columbia School of Journalism.

Contacts there helped obtain him work assignments on various newspapers, and his career soon flourished again. He married my mother in 1942, having fallen in love with her at first sight, a deep love that lasted the rest of his life. During this period, besides starting a doctorate for the third time, this time on anti-Semitism in the United States, he had his own news analysis radio programme, but both these ventures were interrupted when he was drafted into the US Army in late 1942. For two years he wrote a weekly newspaper column, *Diary of a Jewish Soldier*, for the Yiddish daily *Der Tog*, but then his journalistic experience of both Europe and Africa, his many languages, and his special gift for analysing information led to his being recruited into OSS (Office of Strategic Services, the war-time American intelligence service and precursor to the CIA) counter-espionage. At one point, he expected to be parachuted into Poland, but this plan was abandoned at the last minute.

In 1946, he was commended by his chief of section, James Murphy, for "work that was important to the winning of the war". He continued intelligence work in the fledgling CIA where, despite prejudice against foreigners and Jews, he was repeatedly promoted, reaching the highest levels. He was stationed in Germany where he was intelligence advisor to the head of the Carusi world refugee service, which concentrated on the flood of refugees from the Soviet side to the zones of Germany under the Western occupying powers, and later in Japan where he was responsible for inspecting operations in China. Here his outspokenness again led him into trouble when he uncovered a high-level scam based on sending false intelligence reports to Washington. Once again, he made powerful enemies.

In 1954 he was abruptly recalled to Washington "for consultation." Instead of the official praise he expected for the work he had been doing in the Far East, he was seized, his passport was confiscated, and he was subjected to a virtual inquisition, including two weeks' continuous polygraph testing, the ransacking of his belongings and breaking into his private bank-vault. This was the period of the McCarthy "witch-hunts". He was charged with being a Soviet "mole", his pre-war years of contact with anti-Fascist individuals and groups being cited as evidence. He later learned that his boyhood friend Welfke, who was an illegal immigrant in

New York, had been threatened with expulsion to Poland unless he signed a denunciation of my father as a communist stooge or sympathiser. Eventually he was totally exonerated, receiving a life-long pension, but was forbidden to mention his story to anyone or to undertake any press employment, and his passport was withheld for several years until his knowledge of the CIA was considered obsolete. These embargoes, with the consequent unexplainable gap in his CV, together with the national paranoia of the 1950s and the shattering personal impact of this pogrom-like experience, left him without a career and even without permanent employment for several years. His faith in his adopted country, for which he had been ready to give his life, never recovered.

He moved with his family from one state to another until, in California in 1959, a new friend, Irving Goleman, arranged for him to be employed at a local university teaching journalism, creative writing and political science. This was the beginning of a new career. His disenchantment with the United States continued, however, and as soon as we, his children, finished high school, he moved the family to Europe, settling in Switzerland where he continued as a college professor, later becoming Dean and then Vice-President of an American college. While the challenges were relatively small compared to those of the world arena in which he had spent so many years, he met them with his usual imagination and energy, turning a small institution on the verge of bankruptcy into an academic and financial success.

Retirement was initially unbearable, but when my mother retired three years later, they began the final major chapter of his life. For the next twenty years, Dovid of Botchki travelled the world, revisiting Africa and exploring many of the places he had dreamed of as a boy when he swore to himself to visit all the one hundred and twenty-seven provinces ruled over by Ahasuerus. He undoubtedly eventually saw most of them, meeting peasants and landowners, artists and chieftains, his journalist's eye and immense curiosity about life as sharp as they had been in his youth. It was only in his late eighties that he had to give way to age and give up long-distance travelling, though he continued to keep his finger on the pulse of world events. To the last, he read the news every day, commenting on it sometimes angrily, often sadly, always with at least a hint of irony and humour.

He was still writing after his ninetieth birthday, which he celebrated with his family around him. He died peacefully in Switzerland just weeks after completing a summary of his life with these words:

> With the disasters of my long years listed on one side and my wonderful experiences on the other, what do I have to say about my life? Would I want it to have been different, calmer? The miseries that peppered my existence were the salt of it. My seven escapes from Death – from the bullets whistling around me when I was at the top of the cherry tree, through Pan Lukas' determination to kill me, my Reuters' assignment to Poland at the outbreak of the Second World War, the last-minute discovery by a passerby that the milk bottles at my door were still full and my being rushed to an emergency operation at a London hospital, the sinking of the *Athenia*, and the cancellation of my assignment to Italy because of my flat feet – are balanced by having turned distant foreign lands into my back-yard and by my family's success and support. We have just celebrated our special birthdays as in the Yiddish folksong (though with ten years added to the ages):

> *Der Zeide oon die Bobbe*
> *zenen kurtz oon klain*
> *oon beide tantzn moley Khein,*
> *weil 90 er oon 80 sie.*

*   *   *

As to what became of the other people in Botchki, my father had few contacts with anyone after he left. Sophie had already married an assistant of her father's before my father left South Africa, and the entire family prospered. One of my father's first world-trips included a visit to South Africa where he learned that Sophie had died in 1959 of cancer. He met some of her children and grandchildren, and Sophie's youngest sister stayed in contact with him thereafter. Rachel Korn escaped to the Soviet Union where she lived for many years, continuing to write. Eventually she emigrated to Canada where she had children and grandchildren. She died in Israel at the age of 86. Benn, the gifted painter he had known as a guest in the Meller household, who had gone to Paris to study, was hidden by friends during the Nazi occupation. My father had been in contact with him while working in Paris in the 1930s, and renewed the friendship when he returned to Europe after the war, when Benn painted both my parents' portraits. Welfke, who had a talent for finding ways to cross borders which were closed to others, eventually emigrated illegally to New York, still earning a scant livelihood as an itinerant dental technician. He stayed in touch with my father, often writing or visiting to borrow money. On one occasion when this was refused, he became very angry, making threats against my father which fate led him to carry out.

Wellie Farber has not figured by name in this book, but was one of Dovid's English students in the late 1920s. He and one companion jumped off the transport train on the way to Treblinka and hid in the forests for the remainder of the war, after which he obtained a visa for Venezuela, together with a brief transit visa for the United States. While there, he managed to locate my father in Washington and told him the fate of the Botchki Jews. All had been transported to Treblinka on 2 November 1943. So far as he knew, all had gone immediately to the gas chambers. There were no other survivors.

My father was haunted by the Holocaust all his life. Because of his CIA connections, he was warned not to visit Poland on an American passport, since this declared his Polish origins. In 1987, having acquired Swiss citizenship, he made a *Kaddish* trip to Botchki, where he found virtually no trace of his shtetl though the *mikveh* still stood near the river. Stones from the graveyard and synagogue foundations had been used for paving, and all the sacred places had been made into parks. Although it was what he had expected, he was deeply disturbed by seeing the old places and way of life obliterated, so utterly forgotten, and the trip strengthened his determination to finish re-writing the story he had first drafted in 1939.

He himself never forgot.

LONDON
*November 1999*

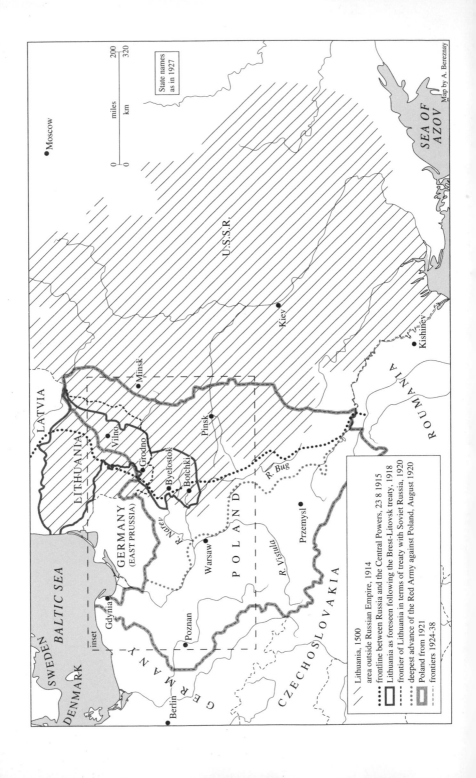

Map by A. Bereznay

State names
as in 1927

miles
km

0        200
0        320

SWEDEN

DENMARK

BALTIC SEA

Moscow

LATVIA

LITHUANIA

Vilno

Grodno

Byelostok

Botchki

Minsk

Pinsk

Kiev

U.S.S.R.

SEA OF
AZOV

Kishinev

ROUMANIA

R. Bug

GERMANY
(EAST PRUSSIA)

Gdynia

inset

R. Niemen

R. Narev

Warsaw

POLAND

Przemysl

R. Vistula

Poznan

GERMANY

Berlin

CZECHOSLOVAKIA

Lithuania, 1500
area outside Russian Empire, 1914
frontline between Russia and the Central Powers, 23 8 1915
Lithuania as foreseen following the Brest-Litovsk treaty, 1918
frontier of Lithuania in terms of treaty with Soviet Russia, 1920
deepest advance of the Red Army against Poland, August 1920
Poland from 1921
frontiers 1924-38